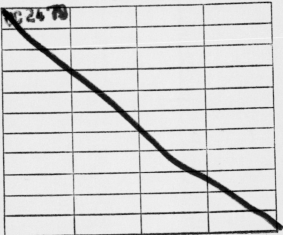

CIANO'S
HIDDEN DIARY
1937-1938

E·P·DUTTON & CO. INC
1852 1953
CREATIVE·101 YEARS·PUBLISHING

CIANO'S
HIDDEN DIARY
1937-1938

Translation and notes by
ANDREAS MAYOR
With an introduction by
MALCOLM MUGGERIDGE

New York
E. P. DUTTON & CO., INC.
1953

LIBRARY OF CONGRESS CATALOG CARD NUMBER: 53-6079

CONTENTS

CIANO'S FOREWORD

Written on the page of the diary for August 22, 1937

My writer's vanity makes me beg that, if one day publicity is given to these notes, it will be remembered that they were thrown on to the paper by me, in bits and pieces, between an interview and a telephone call. I was obliged, though not against my will, to wring the neck of literature, and I confined myself to brief memoranda of the events of which I was, by turn, actor, author or spectator. The interest will spring from the facts, not from the hurried reporting.

EDDA CIANO'S FOREWORD TO THE ITALIAN EDITION

The present volume of the diaries of my husband is, like that already published, absolutely authentic and reproduced in its entirety. Nothing has been omitted or altered. It was my wish that this should be done, in order that, once the whole truth had been told, for good and for evil, the notes left by my husband might help to reconstruct five of the most interesting years in the history of Italy and of the world.

INTRODUCTION

The already published portion of Ciano's Diary started on January 1, 1939, and ended with his final, and very pitiable, apologia written in a cell in Verona Gaol on December 23, 1943, when he was waiting to be executed. He, however, became Italian Foreign Minister in 1936. Thus, with the publication of the present volume, covering the period from August 23, 1937, when he began the Diary, to December 31, 1938, the record is nearly complete. His Diplomatic Papers, which have also been published in an English translation, are often referred to in the Diary, and provide the official counterpart of his private observations and reflections.

It will be noted that in this earlier portion of the Diary there are occasional missing entries (indicated in Mr. Mayor's notes) whose disappearance has never been explained, though it has been suggested that they were removed because they incriminated living persons. Professor Salvemini and others have argued with some plausibility that the text may here and there have been tampered with, but base this proposition on conjecture rather than evidence. The original manuscript of the Diary is extant, written in Ciano's unmistakable hand; and the style is throughout characteristically his—an odd blend of literary and journalistic mannerisms, of banality and liveliness, which would be difficult to reproduce. No one has seriously questioned its value as an outstanding historical document of our time.

Its very survival was remarkable enough. Ciano (who, as readers of the Diary soon come to realize, remained in some respects exceedingly naïve) hoped to use it as a bargaining counter to save his own skin in the final débâcle. Goebbels indicates that matters were carried to the point of supplies of Spanish currency being considered. In Ciano's favour there was the circumstance, also remarked on by Goebbels with some acerbity, that Mussolini was reluctant to have his son-in-law liquidated, despite his treachery at the famous meeting of the Fascist Grand Council at which Mussolini was deposed. By this time, the Duce (who had given up wearing uniform, and reverted to the old-style bowler hat which he favoured before the March on Rome) seems to have become sick even of vengeance. All the fire had gone out of him; like Macbeth in a not altogether dissimilar case, he had begun to be aweary of the sun. Another factor which may have played some part in the situation, was that Edda Ciano, according to an obscure reference of Goebbels's, was in a position to blackmail her father—though one would have thought that the Duce's vulnerability to blackmail was so enormous as to make him immune.

What purports to be an authentic account of Ciano's curious transactions with the Sicherheitsdienst regarding his Diary is given in
Die Geheime Front, published in Vienna in 1950. The relevant extracts
appeared in the September 10, 1950, issue of *L'Illustrazione Italiana*.
According to the author of this work (who uses the pseudonym Walter
Hagen), a written contract was drawn up between Ciano and Kalten-
brunner whereby, in return for being released from prison, Ciano was
to hand over his Diary. To give the Germans an idea of the value
of what they were getting, he arranged for the first section to be fetched
from Rome, where he had hidden the whole. A female secretary of the
S.D. Officer with whom the negotiations were conducted acted as
intermediary. She went to Rome on Ciano's behalf, and duly returned
with the portion of the Diary published in this volume, which somehow
escaped when, on Hitler's orders, the archives of the Reichssicherheits-
Hauptampt were destroyed at the end of April, 1945. According to
another account, the first part of the Diary was left behind by Edda
Ciano in a Parma clinic when she fled in disguise to Switzerland, taking
the rest of the manuscript Diary with her, in 1944. It was then handed
over to the Gestapo by the clinic doctor under threat of death, but
subsequently recovered and published in Italy in 1948. There can be
no possible doubt that it is genuine—the beginning of the fascinating
journal in which Ciano recorded all his thoughts and impressions of
people and events during his years of office, and from which he would
occasionally read extracts to the Duce and his more eminent visitors.
One of these was Mr. Sumner Welles, who has described in his *The
Time for Decision* how Ciano, in the course of a conversation on
February 26, 1940, 'took out of a safe his famous red Diary in which he
recorded in his own handwriting his daily activities'.

In any case, we may be grateful that accident, curiosity and cupidity
should thus have conspired to ensure the preservation of the Diary in
its entirety. It is an incomparable document, which provides a detailed
and vivid picture of Italian Fascism in its last phases, and conveys in a
quite unique way the climate of these curious times, as well as the whole
character of the Fascist regime—the strange mixture of bombast, lies,
cynicism and sincerity which furnished its mystique, the bizarre
personalities and lurid atmosphere it generated. Above all, there
emerges in his true lineaments the fabulous being round whom the
regime revolved—Mussolini, who, until right at the end, Ciano deeply
revered, whose manner and very appearance he aped, and whose
words he faithfully echoed however inconsequential or preposterous
they might be.

When the Diary opens, Ciano was at the beginning of his career as
Foreign Minister. The responsibilities and eminence which his sudden
translation from relative obscurity entailed were still fresh; the

essential pattern of Italian foreign policy, whose ultimate consequences were to be, for him personally and for Italy, so catastrophic, was already set, but there still remained room for manœuvre. No irrevocable decisions had been taken. If relations with Berlin were growing ever closer, London continued to present a possible line of retreat. The Spanish Civil War seemed as far as ever from being ended in Franco's favour; the conquest of Albania was no more than a remote, though increasingly attractive, project; Austria continued to enjoy a precarious independence, and Ribbentrop had not yet become a frequent and abhorred visitor. Racial laws, the introduction of the goose-step or passo Romano, and other unsuitable enterprises whereby Mussolini tried to give the Italian temperament a Nordic flavour, were still only under consideration.

As the Diary proceeds, we see the Gadarene rush appreciably accelerated. Ciano himself, in the preparation of this catastrophe, was no more than an instrument. If he was not wholly devoid of understanding, he lacked the qualities of character which would have enabled him to use it to advantage. He was hustled along by events which he could neither shape nor understand. Though from time to time he adopts, in the circumstances, an infinitely absurd high moral tone, he was in fact wholly devoid of morality in his judgements, or for that matter behaviour. Like most of those who have been washed up into eminence since the Century of the Common Man began its dreadful course, he proves on closer examination to have been, not so much unprincipled, as unaware that principles ever have played, or could play, any part in human affairs. He records, for instance, with grave appreciation Mussolini's remark about the French suffering from the mortal disease of lying, but fails to relate it to the bland references to his own and the Duce's lies in which the Diary abounds. In the same way, Harry Hopkins (in the American context, a comparable figure) found nothing incompatible between a passionate belief in democratic institutions and practices and an equally passionate admiration for the Soviet regime in which they were notably lacking.

G. K. Chesterton once remarked that, contrary to the popular supposition, when men cease to believe in God they do not then believe in nothing, but in anything. In the same way, when men cease to govern their conduct by principles, however derived, they do not then become more rational, but less. As with Mussolini and Ciano, there is no pattern whatsoever to be observed in their behaviour and their judgements; no consistency discernible at all from day to day, or even from moment to moment. Indeed, it is interesting to note that Mussolini, far from being as was commonly believed resolute and decisive, lived in a constant state of fluctuating purpose. He made up his mind with difficulty, and changed it frequently. No maturing of judgement or ripening of intellectual powers is discernible in him. The only change was in his temper—a rage boiling up in him and directed equally against associates and opponents; Victor Emmanuel and Hitler and Mr. Eden and General Franco alike its targets. He was enraged by Hitler's strength and Neville Chamberlain's feebleness and Roosevelt's banalities. He was enraged by everything and everyone, and, being so, tended to revert to his original anarchism, lunging out wildly in the days of his glory at the bourgeoisie, the King, the Vatican, with the same ferocity as in his seedy revolutionary days. His pursuit of power, the only consistent purpose in his life, as so often happens, led him back to where he began.

All this Ciano reveals without being fully aware of the extent of the revelation. Like Boswell, he is an incomparable chronicler because largely a fool. His inordinate vanity (again like Boswell) gives his Diary a piquancy, and even a kind of verisimilitude, which it would otherwise lack. His very deceptions are so preposterous that they defeat their object and disclose the truth they are intended to obscure. Blake says that the fool who persists in his folly becomes wise. Ciano certainly persisted in his folly, and to that extent may be credited with wisdom. A word of caution should, however, be added against accepting his testimony at its face value. In every encounter, Ciano saw himself as holding the centre of the stage. All his arguments, in his own estimation, were unanswerable; he was invariably dominant. This was, in fact, far from being always the case. If Lord Perth, and his successor as British Ambassador in Rome, Sir Percy Loraine, had given their accounts of their transactions with Ciano, they would doubtless differ materially from Ciano's. Even in the privacy of his Diary he could not afford to give others the credit for standing up to him (in reality, no very difficult feat), nor for puncturing his inexhaustible self-esteem. Self-dramatists like Ciano are always in the right. It is to be so that they indulge in self-dramatisation.

This first portion of the Diary is of particular interest to English readers if only because one of the chief preoccupations throughout is Anglo-Italian relations. It is easy now to ridicule the efforts made by the hapless Chamberlain Government to bring about a rapprochement with Fascist Italy. The policy, as such, was sound enough—to prevent the consolidation of the Axis by seeking to persuade Mussolini to hold back from finally committing himself to a German alliance. It was the means adopted rather than the end to which they were directed which were at fault. Like all power-addicts, Mussolini was impressed only by strength. Every effort at conciliation seemed to him a manifestation of weakness, and so only served to confirm, in his eyes, the advantages of persisting in an alignment with Hitler for aggressive ends. Ciano's Diary show this melancholy process at work. What London intended to be a sedative invariably acted as a stimulant; each new dose further inflamed the complaint it was intended to cure.

Yet, looking back now, and in possession of all, or at any rate most of, the facts, it is tragically clear that a different treatment could have produced different results. Mussolini, and still more Ciano, had moments of grave doubt and indecision about their Axis policy, especially after the Nazi conquest of Austria—about which, to their great chagrin, they were not even given advance information. By an unhappy fatality, however, a renewed effort of appeasement invariably came from London just when a show of strength and resolution was most required. They were pushed into Hitler's arms by the very eagerness of Chamberlain to embrace them on any terms. In the unlikely event of some functionary in the Kremlin having kept a journal during the post-war years, it would be surprising if it did not likewise record a comparable strengthening of aggressive tendencies by the well-meant efforts of those who sought, through conciliatory gestures, to abate them. 'The fundamental ideas in our Note', Ciano wrote on October 14, 1937, 'have been accepted in London and Paris. I am surprised. After the threats of the last few days this withdrawal is enough to make one speculate about the decline of the French and British peoples.' It was not the obduracy, but the feebleness, of the British and French Governments which drove Mussolini on, against his better judgement, to throw in his lot irretrievably with Hitler. If they had given way less he would have hesitated longer, and perhaps at last have decided against a course which was in many ways personally distasteful to him, and of whose possibly ruinous consequences he was well aware. In the event, as in a Greek tragedy, everyone—well-intentioned and ill-intentioned alike—consciously or unconsciously ministered towards producing the catastrophe of September 3, 1939, with all that flowed from it in terms of individual and collective desolation.

The march of events in our time has been so fast and so furious that the past, like the wake of a speed boat, gets obliterated almost before it has existed. Yesterday seems infinitely remote—more so than a century ago, and a figure like Mussolini, whom most of us remember in the flesh, is already as fabulous as Tamburlaine. In the horror and fantasy of his end, the seeming solidity of his life tends to be overlooked. After all, he had many admirers besides Sir Oswald Mosley. If Lady Chamberlain, as Ciano records, decked herself out in Fascist insignia, there were many others, like Bernard Shaw and Rabindranath Tagore, who worshipped at the same unlovely shrine. It would, indeed, be a useful and diverting project to prepare an anthology of the various tributes which ostensible champions of freedom and enlightenment have paid to the tyrants of the age—so strangely assorted a couple as George Lansbury and Lloyd George captivated by Hitler, and all the vast and ludicrous company who have at different times seen a new dawn breaking in the Soviet prison-house. Some of these last, incidentally, having grown disillusioned with Moscow, are now at the same game in Belgrade.

In such circumstances, a document like Ciano's Diary is particularly valuable. For those who have eyes to see, its lesson is as unmistakable as its matter and manner (excellently conveyed in Mr. Mayor's careful and sensitive translation) are enthralling. Better than any laboured argument or statement of principles, it demonstrates the ultimate fallacy of power—that those who pursue it as an end in itself cannot but become divorced from reality, and, in becoming so, encompass their own ruin. If Ciano himself, despite his high office, had only a minor part in the working out of this immense tragedy, he was well situated to observe its course, and gifted with a sufficiency of literary talent, and even humour, to leave behind him one of those rare source books out of which history is woven.

MALCOLM MUGGERIDGE

PART I

ITALY JOINS THE ANTI-COMINTERN PACT

ITALY JOINS THE ANTI-COMINTERN PACT

Attacks on shipping in the Mediterranean—Santander captured by Italian and Spanish Nationalist troops—Arrangements for Mussolini's visit to Germany—Schemes for Albania—More piracy and more protests—Invitation to Nyon—British attitude to the recognition of the Italian Empire—The Mediterranean patrol—Revolts in Abyssinia—Mussolini and Ciano in Germany (September 24-9)—A new commander in Spain—Grandi and the Non-Intervention Committee—Perth on Anglo-Italian agreement—Ribbentrop in Rome (October 22-4)—Eden suggests a meeting with Ciano—Hess in Rome—The Anti-Comintern Pact signed (November 6)—Italy sabotages the Brussels Conference—China and Italian mediation—Press war with France—Italy recognizes Manchukuo—Plans for naval construction—Stoyadinovich in Italy (December 5-10)—Italy leaves the League of Nations (December 11)—Standstill in Spain—Lady Chamberlain—Plans for Spain reconsidered.

AUGUST 23. From to-day I mean to resume a regular diary.

The Duce said to me that democracy has the same effect on the Slavs as alcohol has on negroes—complete disintegration. He also talked about the necessity for exceptional régimes following strong revolutionary movements.

Ingram[1] made a friendly *démarche* about the torpedo attacks[2] in the Mediterranean. I replied quite brazenly. He went away almost satisfied.

The Chinese want aeroplanes for Shanghai. I virtually replied 'No'. I reminded the Ambassador of their attitude during sanctions and also later. After that they can't expect our sympathy.

AUGUST 24. I took Suvich[3] to see the Duce. His report on his mission to Washington was commonplace and verbose—verbosity is often a Venetian characteristic.

Bocchini[4] talked to me about various questions, then about his forthcoming visit to Germany. I gave him instructions for the Duce's visit. On the internal situation nothing new.

[1] Edward Maurice Ingram, Counsellor at the British Embassy in Rome, 1935-7. Chargé d'Affaires in the absence of the Ambassador.
[2] In the previous fortnight there had been an outbreak of submarine and air attacks on Spanish Republican and other vessels, including the British steamship *British Corporal*.
[3] Fulvio Suvich, Italian Ambassador in Washington.
[4] Arturo Bocchini, Chief of Police.

I received Medici[1] to talk about his row with Balbo[2] and Colonna.[3] I advised absolute calm. Even if he is right, he mustn't annoy the Chief! Decided to send the *Montecuccoli*[4] to China.

Good news from Spain. The offensive continues victoriously. Telegraphed to cut off Santander's water supply in order to hasten the surrender, which is now very near—possibly to-morrow.

Starace[5] telephoned me, furious with Badoglio[6] for some remarks he made to the *Federale* of Asti.[7] Some remarks criticizing the Spanish enterprise and personally hostile towards me and Russo.[8]

AUGUST 25. Santander fell to-day before the blows of our Legions. I gave the Duce the news at the airport, while we were waiting for the airmen on the Damascus–Paris race. He was pleased. He said he was expecting good news from me to-day. It is a great victory we have won. I believe there will be more than 50,000 prisoners. My mind goes back to the Guadalajara days. People were getting frightened. We talked to Russo about the situation and nearly made each other's hair turn white. But we had faith.

I have persuaded the Duce to give 60 millions to Albania over the next four years, for works of various kinds. My visit to Tirana convinced me of the necessity for taking good care of this sector of the front. We must create stable centres of Italian influence there. Who knows what the future may have in store? We must be ready to seize the opportunities which will present themselves. We are not going to withdraw this time, as we did in 1920. In the south we have absorbed several hundred thousand Albanians.[9] Why shouldn't the same thing happen on the other side of the entrance to the Adriatic?

At the sea I read a chapter about the Peace of Amiens. Very interesting, on the eve of my negotiations with Great Britain. It made me think of many analogies.

AUGUST 26. The victory of Santander has assumed major proportions. It is not the beginning of the end—the end is still a long way

---

[1] Marchese Giacomo Medici del Vascello, Under-Secretary of State under the President of the Council (Mussolini).

[2] Air Marshal Italo Balbo, Governor-General of Libya. One of the quadrumvirs of the March on Rome. Killed in an aeroplane over Tobruk in June 1940.

[3] Prince Ascanio Colonna, a member of the distinguished Roman family. Italian Ambassador in Washington, 1938.

[4] *Montecuccoli*, an Italian cruiser.

[5] Lieutenant-General Achille Starace, Secretary-General of the Fascist Party, 1928–39. Chief of Staff, Fascist Militia, 1939–41. Shot with Mussolini in April 1945.

[6] Marshal Pietro Badoglio, Duke of Addis Ababa, conqueror of Abyssinia. Chief of General Staff until December 1940. Prime Minister after the fall of Mussolini, from July 1943 to June 1944.

[7] A. Tosi, Federal Secretary of the Fascist Party for the Province of Asti.

[8] Luigi Russo, Chief of Staff of the Fascist Militia.

[9] Albanians settled in southern Italy and Sicily in large numbers in the fifteenth century and later.

away—but it is a heavy blow to the Reds in Spain. I have given orders for the aircraft at Palma to bomb Valencia to-night. This is the moment to terrorize the enemy. The Duce said to me that he will make the defeatists of Guadalajara pay—an allusion to Balbo. But he will forgive him or, as usual, do nothing about it.

Russo has sent me a fine letter in the name of the Militia, showing gratitude for my work and my support in bad times. I wrote a reply with my own hand.

Had an exchange of telegrams with Bastico.[1] Received Federzoni,[2] back from America. His account of his visit was full of personalities and boring.

AUGUST 27. Telegraphed Bastico to secure for us, tactfully, flags and guns captured from the Basques. I envy the French their Invalides and the Germans their Military Museum. A flag taken from the enemy is worth more than any picture.

Ingram informed me that Drummond's[3] return is to be delayed, hence also the beginning of the conversations (upon the results of which I now have many doubts). I advised him to let the press know that the delay is caused by the death of the Ambassador's brother. Otherwise there will be the usual speculations.

I promised Hotta[4] that we will not supply arms to China and that we will support the Japanese in their requests.

I am personally making arrangements for the Duce's visit to Germany. To-day I approved the first draft of the programme. I have entrusted the choice of the suite to Starace, Alfieri,[5] and Sebastiani.[6] Pay attention to the uniforms. We must appear more Prussian than the Prussians.

AUGUST 28. Filippo[7] is back from Bled, where he handed Stoyadinovich[8] the photographic proof of the Franco-Czech conspiracy against him. He will arrive at the Little Entente meeting purple in the face. My tactics have succeeded.

The Duce has gone to Riccione.[9] I saw Cupini on his return from his flying triumph in Paris. He asked me for a command in Spain, which I immediately agreed to.

---

[1] General Ettore Bastico, Commander-in-Chief of the Italian troops in Spain.
[2] Luigi Federzoni, President of the Senate. A journalist.
[3] Sir Eric Drummond, British Ambassador in Rome, 1933–9. Succeeded the brother whose death is here alluded to as Earl of Perth. Secretary-General to the League of Nations, 1919–33.
[4] Masa Aki Hotta, Japanese Ambassador in Rome.
[5] Dino Alfieri, Minister of Propaganda.
[6] Osvaldo Sebastiani, private secretary to Mussolini.
[7] Filippo Anfuso, chef de cabinet to Ciano.
[8] Milan Stoyadinovich, Yugoslav Prime Minister and Foreign Minister, June 1935 to February 1939.
[9] Riccione, on the Adriatic coast, near Rimini.

Conde[1] complained about the obstructionism of the Navy over the delivery of the two destroyers and two submarines. I put an end to the legalistic resistance of our sailors by blowing up Cavagnari[2] on the telephone. The Duce approved. This Spanish enterprise is constantly opposed by a policy of passive resistance on the part of the Navy. The Air Force is magnificent. The Army does its job. The Militia is enthusiastic. But, fundamentally, the Duce and I have the sole responsibility—I should say, the sole merit. One day people will realize what they owe to us.

AUGUST 29. Sunday in Rome. Rain—alone in the hotel—read a book. I had the feeling (enhanced by this hotel life) of having gone back ten years. A bachelor Sunday—not a thing I feel any nostalgia for.

AUGUST 30. Papa's[3] birthday. I telephoned good wishes. May God long preserve him.

Decided, in principle, to send 5,000 men to Spain—we can't maintain the formations we already have there without them. I fear reactions in Europe may be violent. There is also a serious risk of wrecking the negotiations with London.

Rosso[4] told me this morning that the Russians want to disentangle themselves from Spain because of the Chinese situation, and that they will reduce their aid to a minimum. It would help a lot, if they did.

I sent for Russo and Pariani[5] to talk about the mobilization and the training of the volunteers.[6]

Received Revel[7] about the Albanian question. He authorized the expenditure for the building of the Legation. Even the way in which we are represented in Tirana must emphasize our predominance. Something in the style of the British High Commissioner in Egypt in the old days.

I saw Stein,[8] just off to Geneva. I confirmed our points of view and gave him a faint smile. On the eve of a possible recognition of the Empire we must nurse Russia's hopes of weakening the Axis. Afterwards, the Duce's visit will completely destroy the illusion.

AUGUST 31. I am glad the Duce is back in Rome. He is, at this moment, more than ever necessary.

[1] Pedro Garcia Conde, Spanish Nationalist Ambassador in Rome.
[2] Admiral Domenico Cavagnari, Under-Secretary for the Navy (the Minister was Mussolini) and Naval Chief of Staff.
[3] Admiral Costanzo Ciano, President of the Chamber of Deputies. A hero of the First World War and an early Fascist. Created Count of Cortellazzo in 1928. Died in 1939.
[4] Augusto Rosso, Italian Ambassador in Moscow.
[5] General Alberto Pariani, Under-Secretary for War (the Minister was Mussolini) and Army Chief of Staff.
[6] The units of the Italian army fighting in Spain were known as the *Corpo Truppe Volontarie* (Corps of Volunteer Troops).
[7] Count Paolo Thaon de Revel, Minister of Finance.
[8] Boris Stein, Soviet Ambassador in Rome.

The naval blockade is producing striking results: four Russian or Red steamers sunk, one Greek captured, one Spanish shelled and obliged to take refuge in a French port.

Lunch at the sea with Revel. The Prince[1] was there and had asked for me to be present. Very polite, as he has been for some time, but a feeble, disconnected, boring conversation.

Medici told me that he spoke to him frankly this morning on the subject of Balbo and opened his eyes to our Ferrarese friend's very dubious loyalty to the monarchy. He praised my loyalty by contrast, he says, and the Prince nodded assent.

Apropos of Balbo, Bastianini[2] told me about a conversation he had with him in Tripoli. Briefly, Balbo made a profession of love and loyalty towards me, speaking in the name of his friends as well as his own. *Timeo Danaos.* What is behind these declarations? Oaths of loyalty are made to the Chief—when they are made between comrades they smack of conspiracy. And that I violently repudiate.

Visit from Ricci,[3] who is, deservedly, nearing the end of his days with the *Balilla*. The Duce told me so, when he came back from the manoeuvres. Visit from Bottai,[4] to make contact.

Magistrati[5] gave me the definitive programme for the Duce's visit to Germany. A solemn event. All is well, and the draft of the press communiqué is excellent.

To-night I go to Viareggio by train. To-morrow is Deda's[6] birthday and I see the children and my parents.

SEPTEMBER 1. Viareggio. Ponte a Moriano. All well.

SEPTEMBER 2. The Duce has approved the programme for his visit to Germany and has given me, for translation, the text of the speech he is to make in Berlin. It is excellent.

The navy is very active—three torpedoings and one prize. But international opinion is getting worked up. Particularly in England,

[1] Umberto, Prince of Piedmont. Exercised the royal prerogative on behalf of his father from June 1944 until May 1946, when his father abdicated and he become King. Left Italy in June 1946 after a plebiscite which resulted in a vote against the monarchy.
[2] Giuseppe Bastianini, Under-Secretary at the Foreign Ministry. Ambassador in London, 1939–40.
[3] Renato Ricci, Under-Secretary of Education and Chief of the *Balilla*, the Fascist organization for the training of boys between the ages of 8 and 14. Under-Secretary for the Corporations, November 1937. Leader of the Republican Fascist Militia in 1943.
[4] Giuseppe Bottai, Minister of Education.
[5] Count Massimo Magistrati, Counsellor at the Italian Embassy in Berlin. Married to Ciano's sister Maria.
[6] Ciano's wife Edda, Mussolini's eldest child. Ciano's family was staying at Viareggio, a seaside resort twenty-five miles north of Leghorn. His parents lived near by at Ponte a Moriano (renamed after his father's death Ponte Ciano). The Ciano family originally came from Leghorn and still possessed important interests there.

as a result of the attack on the destroyer *Havock*,[1] fortunately not hit. It was the *Iride*. The row has already started.

The Duce pretends to have a bone to pick with Egypt about her armaments. When I proved to him that they only exist on paper, he replied that he meant to provide himself with a subject of dispute for the right moment. 'Egypt will serve my purpose. We must begin now to say that it is Egypt who is troubling the waters.'

Arrighi, Doriot's[2] confidential agent, is asking for the subsidy to be continued and wants arms. He foresees a winter of conflict. He considers La Rocque[3] a traitor in the service of the *Front Populaire*.

Received von Hassel[4]—unpleasant and treacherous.

I have ordered Buti[5] and Pietromarchi[6] to prepare a plan of action for Geneva. I am not very confident, but we must leave nothing untried. If the Empire is not recognized now, the question will drag on until next autumn. A serious complication.

SEPTEMBER 3. Full orchestra—France, Russia, Britain. The theme —piracy in the Mediterranean. Guilty—the Fascists. The Duce is very calm. He looks in the direction of London and he doesn't believe the English want a collision with us. He gave me the reasons for this conviction. Napoleon, before setting out for Russia, had a study made of the meteorological phenomena of the previous twenty-five years, in order to find out when the snows begin. He was unlucky: that year the snow came a month early. Mussolini, before beginning his Abyssinian enterprise, studied the composition, by age-groups, of the English people. He found that for 22 million men there are 24 million women, and that there are 12 million citizens over the age of fifty, the age limit for bellicosity. Hence a predominance of the static elements over the dynamic elements of youth. Hence a quiet life, compromise, peace.

He told me a very pretty story: Baldwin was so absorbed in reading a detective story that for a whole Sunday afternoon he did not open the envelope containing the instructions about the Hoare-Laval plan. The delay was enough to set fire to the controversy in France and wreck the plan.

To return to the present, we are keeping calm and we have a plan ready for any eventuality. But this storm will pass like the others. I

---

[1] The British destroyer *Havock* was attacked off the Mediterranean coast of Spain on September 1 by an unidentified submarine, which was in fact the Italian submarine *Iride*.

[2] Jacques Doriot, leader of the totalitarian *Parti Populaire Française*.

[3] Colonel Casimir de la Rocque, leader of the extreme right-wing *Croix de Feu* movement.

[4] Ulrich von Hassel, German Ambassador in Rome, 1932–8. Executed for complicity in the attempt on Hitler's life on July 20, 1944.

[5] Gino Buti, Director-General of the European and Mediterranean Department of the Foreign Ministry.

[6] Count Luca Pietromarchi, head of the 'S' (Spain) Office at the Foreign Ministry.

have received authorization for the reinforcements to be sent to Spain after the decision in Geneva about the recognition of the Empire. Either they refuse to recognize us, and we are free to act. Or they recognize us, and we are equally free, because of the Fascist rule that once a thing is done it's done.

As for Doriot, we will give him money, but no arms.

SEPTEMBER 4. A full day. Many conversations, morning and evening. Poliakoff[1]—I got the impression that in London they have no clear idea of the question of the recognition of the Empire. Without recognition there is no possibility of agreement. Pol. took note of this and will mention it to Chamberlain.

I have ordered Cavagnari to suspend naval action until further orders. But the storm looks like subsiding.

Conde brought me a telegram from Franco saying that if the blockade continues throughout September it will be decisive. True. However, for the moment we must suspend it.

Exhibition of the *Fasciall' Estero*.[2] Good progress. The crowd applauded the Spaniards and, for the first time and warmly, also the Germans.

SEPTEMBER 5. Parade of Starace and his Young Fascists. Very successful. The younger generation must be entirely dominated by the Party. I said so to the Duce, who already holds this view.

Afternoon—Viareggio and Ponte a Moriano. The children are two adorable treasures. Papa is better. Deda well.

Conversation with Balbo. He offered me not a branch, but a whole forest of olives. At the moment he was even sincere.

SEPTEMBER 6. The Duce let fly at America, country of niggers and Jews, the forces which disintegrate civilization. He wants to write a book: Europe in 2000. The races playing an important role will be the Italians, the Germans, the Russians, and the Japanese. Other countries will be destroyed by the acid of Jewish corrosion. The Jews even refuse to breed because it costs pain. They don't realize that pain is the only creative factor in the life of a nation. And also in the lives of men.

I saw Ingram and dropped a hint about getting rid of the Abyssinian stumbling-block at Geneva. I consider that essential for the resumption of talks.

I have received the Soviet accusation.[3] The Duce has approved of my plan. The Russians want to sabotage the conference.[4] Realizing

---

[1] Vladimir Poliakoff, a journalist of British nationality.

[2] *Fasci all' Estero* (Fasces Abroad), the Fascist organization concerned with Italians abroad.

[3] The Soviet note attributed to Italy the responsibility for the sinking of two Soviet ships and demanded compensation.

[4] On September 6 the French and British Governments addressed to all the powers concerned an invitation to a conference, to be held at Nyon, near Geneva, to discuss measures against piracy in the Mediterranean.

that a Mediterranean conference was about to be decided on, they have
fired another torpedo, aimed this time at international understanding.
I harangued Blondel[1] and Ingram on this theme. Ingram evidently
shares my view. They both seemed to me shaken.

We are waiting for the Russian counter-move. The atmosphere is
darkening again. The Bolsheviks have made a false step, and we have
scored a point.

SEPTEMBER 7. Very busy, a lot of people. Spoke to Massimo,[2] to
settle the terms of our reply to the French and British Governments.
We agree in principle. The note was drafted to-night. I shall show it
to the Duce to-morrow. As I foresaw, London and Paris are discon-
certed by the Soviet gaffe. We must turn it to our advantage—force
towards Russia, smiles for the rest.

I received the judges in the Poets of Mussolini competition. A comic
scene—the Sarfatti[3] didn't want to award a prize to the excellent poem
of Fanny Dini, whom she accused of plagiarizing her work. How frightful these literary women are!

Farinacci[4] wants to go to Germany with the Duce. The Duce has
apparently agreed, but does he really want him? And what is the
pretext to be?

SEPTEMBER 8. Of course the Duce doesn't want Farinacci in
Germany, and he has told me to arrange for him not to go.

The note, my draft of which was approved at the Palazzo Venezia,[5]
has been adopted in all essentials by the Germans as well. No Nyon
—but we are ready to discuss things in the Non-Intervention Committee in London. The formula has advantages: it is not simply a
refusal, it is also constructive. Albania is following in our wake;
Bulgaria and Yugoslavia are concerting their moves and may perhaps
join us.

I told Ingram that I had drawn the inspiration for my proposal from
our last conversation. Now, because of his share in its birth, he too is
bound to defend it. The limp, insincere British official was weak
enough to be flattered into accepting this. Touch a man in his personal
vanity and you can't go wrong.

Conversation at the sea with Helfand, the Russian Chargé d'Affaires.
This intelligent and subtle Yid realizes his Government's gaffe (there
is a second note to-day, clinching the accusation), but he has to defend

---

[1] Jules Blondel, French Chargé d'Affaires. Secretary-General for Foreign Affairs in
de Gaulle's National Committee of Liberation, 1942. There was no French Ambassador in Rome from October 1936 to November 1938.
[2] Massimo Magistrati.
[3] Margherita Sarfatti, friend and biographer of Mussolini.
[4] Roberto Farinacci, a member of the Fascist Grand Council. Former Secretary-
General of the Fascist Party. Shot with Mussolini.
[5] Palazzo Venezia, Mussolini's official residence in the centre of Rome.

Moscow, and he does it with dignity. He spoke of overwhelming evidence against us—from deciphered telegrams, I expect. I faced him with calm contempt. He said I was treating Russia as I would not treat Lithuania. I replied that, while I could not do so, the Duce can.

Saw Castellino[1] and Malaparte.[2]

Meeting with Guarneri[3] and Lessona[4] about the economic situation and the Empire's international trade.

Decided to resume the subsidy to the Rexists[5] (250,000 lire a month).

SEPTEMBER 9. The note has been delivered. A long conversation with Cerruti,[6] over-optimistic about the feelings of the French towards us. He makes out they are dying to throw themselves into our arms. I don't believe it. Not just now, at any rate.

Ingram left a memorandum about British intentions with regard to the recognition of the Empire. Rather negative. But without this preliminary the possibility of an agreement with London becomes remote. A pity!

Galli[7]—Turkey, as usual, is waiting for the English to make up their minds. In these circumstances my visit to Ankara will be put off until better times.

Had a long talk with Appelius[8] about Abyssinia—the old days and the present. Nostalgia for the war.

We won't answer the Russians. There is a precedent: Venice used to accumulate unanswered papal bulls.

SEPTEMBER 10. Grandi[9] is getting ready to return to London. I have given him instructions for resuming contact. The situation is becoming difficult again—we shall have to give battle once more.

Berti[10] and Gambara[11] have made a long report on the situation in Spain. To-morrow I shall take them to the Duce. We are still in mid-ocean, and victory may elude us once more. We must hurry up and win. For many reasons.

Marinotti[12]—a first-rate man, but with a touch of pompous verbosity

[1] Nicolò Castellino, Deputy. President of the Federation of Newspaper Editors.
[2] Curzio Malaparte, the well-known journalist and novelist.
[3] Felice Guarneri, Minister of Trade and Currency.
[4] Alessandro Lessona, Minister for Italian Africa. Dismissed in November 1937.
[5] The extreme right-wing party in Belgium, led by Leon Degrelle.
[6] Vittorio Cerruti, Italian Ambassador in Paris.
[7] Carlo Galli, Italian Ambassador in Ankara.
[8] Marius Appelius, a journalist. War correspondent of Il Popolo d'Italia in Abyssinia.
[9] Count Dino Grandi, Italian Ambassador in London, 1932-9. Proposed the anti-Mussolini Order of the Day in the Fascist Grand Council on July 25, 1943. Condemned to death, in his absence, with Ciano and others, in January 1944.
[10] General Francesco Berti. Succeeded General Bastico as Commander-in-Chief in Spain in October 1937.
[11] Colonel Gastone Gambara. Succeeded General Berti as Commander-in-Chief in Spain in October 1938.
[12] F. Marinotti, an industrialist.

which comes from being sure of success. On the whole, a man not to be lost sight of. He may be useful.

SEPTEMBER 11. Conversation between Grandi and the Duce. The Duce summed up the situation. If possible, he still wants agreement. But if Great Britain sticks to an aggressive policy, he is prepared to go to any length of firmness.

Afternoon—conversation between the Duce and Berti. Taking stock of the situation in Spain—on the whole, satisfactory. The Duce means to wait a few weeks before deciding whether to send more troops. If there is no winter lull and Franco acts, the Duce will help him.

The Duce is furious at the first news from Nyon. Bova's[1] last telephone call soothed him a bit.

Received Bocchini—nothing new.

SEPTEMBER 12. Fascist Girls' ceremony. Went off very well.

Flew to Pisa. The races at Leghorn, with Edda and Ciccino.[2] Papa is well.

SEPTEMBER 13. Ingram and Blondel have given us a copy of the Nyon decisions. I have prepared a reply in which, without advancing a claim to take part, I affirm our right to parity. It will certainly embarrass them. Either we co-operate, or the scheme fails and they are to blame. I am waiting for approval from Berlin before delivering my reply.

Ricci produced a splendid parade. But the *Balilla* can't continue as it is now.

Teruzzi,[3] back from Spain, is very critical of Bastico and his staff. He believes a decisive operation is possible for the middle of October. Frankly, I don't.

The Duce is annoyed about the revolt in Gojjam,[4] which is of a considerable size.

SEPTEMBER 14. The Duce telephoned at 7 a.m. to add to our note the request that Germany too should take part in the Mediterranean patrol. Berlin has refused. The Duce's idea—it has to be admitted—would have put the whole question in the melting-pot again. As things are, Nyon is settled.

Zenone[5] is to be a director of S.N.I.A.[6] A Fascist in certain industrial circles is useful.

[1] Renato Bova-Scoppa, Italian representative at Geneva.
[2] Ciccino (Fabrizio), Ciano's son, born in 1931.
[3] General Attilio Teruzzi, a commander in Spain. Appointed Under-Secretary for Italian Africa (under Mussolini, as Minister) in November 1937. Shot with Mussolini.
[4] Gojjam, a district in Abyssinia, to the north of Addis Ababa.
[5] Zenone Benini, Deputy. Vice-President of the Corporation for Metallurgy and Engineering.
[6] Società Nazionale Industria Applicazioni Viscosa, an important rayon manufacturing firm in Milan.

Teruzzi with the Duce. The Duce was in good form—aggressive and anti-British. His comment on the English was that they have their minds in the seats of their trousers.

SEPTEMBER 15. Franco is asking for four submarines to be put at his disposal. Two will go at once and the other two shortly.

Our note is considered very clever, but opinion is definitely against us. Bova telephones from Geneva that Eden and Delbos[1] are ready to accept our demands, but would like us to take the first step. Impossible. We mustn't move an inch. They will come to us.

Marriage of Farace[2] and Catherine of Russia.[3] Many royalties at the wedding, some taking part in the service. In his address the priest invited the bride to follow the example of her great ancestors, and mentioned the celebrated lady who once bore her name. The bridegroom wasn't too pleased.

Lunch with the Prince of Piedmont. Feeble conversation. I sat next to Princess Mafalda.[4] She has neither looks nor intelligence nor personality. But she likes men. After all, all women do.

SEPTEMBER 16. Nothing new on the London-Paris-Geneva front. They are waiting for a move from us, but they won't get one.

Lunch with Volpi,[5] Cini,[6] and Pirelli.[7] Considerable anxiety in industrial circles. They say our 'stocks'[8] are exhausted and we could only keep a war going for a short time.

Complete confidence about victory in China. I agree. Sooner or later the Chinese will run. And when they begin to run, nobody can stop them. Anti-Communist agreement is speeded up.

The Duce is worried that the French police may be on the track of the authors of the Paris outrages.[9] Em.[10] tells me it is impossible. In any case, it's nothing to do with us. They are Frenchmen.

SEPTEMBER 17. The Duce announced to me that Ricci is to be liquidated, on the principle of 'Whoso is against the Party, is against

[1] Yvon Delbos, French Foreign Minister.
[2] Ruggero Farace, an official in the Foreign Ministry.
[3] Catherine of Russia, a distant cousin of the last Tsar and niece of the Queen of Italy.
[4] Princess Mafalda, daughter of the King of Italy, married to Prince Philip of Hesse. She died in a German concentration camp.
[5] Count Giuseppe Volpi di Misurata, Minister of State. President of the Federation of Industry.
[6] Vittorio Cini, Senator. Venetian industrialist.
[7] Alberto Pirelli, Minister of State. President of the International Chamber of Commerce, 1927–9.
[8] In English in the original.
[9] Two bombs had exploded in the Paris offices of two Employers' Associations on September 11. One of the bombs killed two policemen.
[10] Colonel Santo Emanuele, chief of a section of S.I.M. (Servizio Informazioni Militari), the Italian intelligence service.

me and will get his neck broken.' He added that he had told the news
to Alfieri, who is a 'chatterer', so that it may be passed on to the
ever-restless Balbos and Bottais.

He also talked, more optimistically, about the situation in East
Africa. The revolt is not spreading and measures to suppress it—
including gas—have been ordered.

Ricci was wearing the Camper's Medal. He said nothing and I
followed his example.

I wrote to Grandi, reporting the situation and asking for detailed
information.

Lunch, by chance, with Balbo, joined afterwards by the long-winded
Cini. Cini passes for an intelligent man. I wonder whether he really is,
or whether by any chance he is simply a great intriguer.

SEPTEMBER 18. Ingram and Blondel brought me the additional
agreement about seaplanes and surface vessels, and took the opportunity of trying tentatively to resume the conversations about Nyon.
I have prepared a conciliatory reply and have succeeded in getting the
Duce to accept it, though he is still extremely uncompromising. Meanwhile we must let it be known that they made the first gesture. However,
the press must avoid talking about 'Canossa' or 'genuflections', otherwise they will stiffen again. I shall deliver the note to-morrow.

Libohova[1] brought me a letter from King Zog. He is pleased with
the recent pro-Albanian measures.

SEPTEMBER 19. With the Duce I watched the funeral of Prospero
Colonna[2] from the window of the Palazzo Venezia. The Duce was in
a good humour and kept making comments. The weather was warm
and rainy. Good weather for a funeral—in the sun nobody thinks
about death. He told me that Tittoni[3] used to refuse to attend funerals
in winter, for fear of following the corpse into the grave.

I gave the note to the two Chargés d'Affaires. A weight seemed
lifted off their shoulders. I added a few conciliatory words.

The Duce is constantly telephoning to learn the latest developments
in the diplomatic battle now in progress. Meanwhile he is preparing
military action. Bruno[4] will go to Parma on the 22nd, and with him
the whole of Biseo's squadron. I envy them. But, for the present at
any rate, I am nailed to this desk.

SEPTEMBER 20. No official reactions from Paris or London. The
press is good. As for the reply, we shall see to-morrow.

Doucich[5] paid a farewell visit. He is a vain, pompous poet and has

---

[1] Erkem Libohova, Albanian Foreign Minister.
[2] Prince Prospero Colonna, former *Sindaco* (Mayor) of Rome.
[3] Tommaso Tittoni, former Foreign Minister and President of the Senate.
[4] Bruno Mussolini, the Duce's second son. Killed while flying as a test pilot in 1941.
[5] Yovan Doucich, Yugoslav Minister in Rome.

never believed in agreement between Rome and Belgrade. At the moment he is behaving like a long-lost friend. Stoyadinovich, who is pretty shrewd, has liquidated him, quite rightly.

Buffarini[1] gave me the usual review of Italian affairs. All in order. He intimated that yesterday at Lucca Edda was not too warmly received. I am sorry. She is an excellent creature, but she is too free and easy, and she doesn't love the mob. Consequently she isn't loved herself. A pity, because she has rare and great qualities.

SEPTEMBER 21. Blondel and Ingram handed me a note which gives us virtual satisfaction, though the word 'parity' is carefully avoided. The Duce has approved my reply and the press communiqué: we agree to a technical conference to modify the Nyon clauses in accordance with our wishes. It is a fine victory. From suspected pirates to policemen of the Mediterranean—and the Russians, whose ships we were sinking, excluded!

I am angry with Parini.[2] He sent a proclamation to the Italians in Germany entirely without my knowledge. He has lost all sense of proportion. He is ripe for a move. I may replace him by De Cicco,[3] an old and tried comrade.

Nicolas Franco[4] is returning to Spain. He is pleased with his work and hopeful about the situation. He foresees the end of the war next spring. Let me add that he has been mistaken before now.

SEPTEMBER 22. A day of absolute calm.

Good reactions to the conclusion of the Nyon negotiations. The Duce, without saying so, showed that he is very pleased.

SEPTEMBER 23. Preparations for the visit to Germany are complete. I have supervised even the details myself. The Duce told Alfieri that the arrangements I have made come close to his ideal.

Opening of the Augustus Exhibition and the Exhibition of the Revolution. For the latter the Duce ordered that the part dealing with the intervention[5] and the war should be kept small, so that the Exhibition can come down as far as the creation of the Empire. It is his idea of permanent revolution.

Talked to Parini. He is to go as Minister to Cairo. Ghigi goes to Vienna. Salata[6] comes home.

[1] Guido Buffarini-Guidi, Under-Secretary at the Ministry of the Interior (the Minister was Mussolini).

[2] Piero Parini, Director-General of Italians Abroad.

[3] Attilio De Cicco, an official in the Foreign Ministry.

[4] Nicolas Franco, brother of the Generalissimo, was in charge of military negotiations between Nationalist Spain and Italy.

[5] The Italian intervention in the First World War on the side of the Allies in 1915 was the first important event in which the influence of Mussolini was felt.

[6] Francesco Salata, Minister in Vienna, 1936–   In Vienna again on a special mission at the time of the Anschluss.

Lessona reported on the situation of the Empire. Numerous revolts, but localized. I fear, however, that at Mascal[1] something on a larger scale may break out. If the whole country flared up, it would be very serious. But I don't think it will. However, what is happening is hindering demobilization and that is a burden on our finances.

SEPTEMBER 24. Departure for Germany.

SEPTEMBER 25. Munich.

SEPTEMBER 26. Manœuvres at Mecklenburg. Interesting, but I was expecting more.

SEPTEMBER 27. Essen. Visit to Krupp's. The industrial potential is very impressive.

Arrival in Berlin. Triumphal.

SEPTEMBER 28. Potsdam. The tomb of Frederick the Great. Sans Souci. The New Palace. Napoleon too stayed here. He got here by fighting.

Meeting on the Maifeld.[2] Choreography superb—much emotion and much rain.

SEPTEMBER 29. Departure.

As far as formal results go, the visit has added nothing to the Berlin Protocols.[3] But in effect the Duce's presence in Germany has popularized friendship for Fascism—I dare not yet say for Italy. Mussolini's personal success is unquestionable. His magnetism, his voice, his impetuous youthfulness captured the German crowds.

Will the solidarity between the two régimes suffice to form a real bond of union between two peoples drawn in opposite directions by race, culture, religion, and tastes? No one can accuse me of being hostile to the pro-German policy. I initiated it myself. But should we, I wonder, regard Germany as a goal, or rather as a field for manœuvre? The incidents of the last few days and above all Mussolini's fidelity to his political allegiance make me incline towards the first alternative. But may not events develop in such a way as to separate our two peoples once again?

We shall see. The Rome-Berlin Axis is to-day a formidable and extremely useful reality. I shall try to draw a line from Rome to Tokyo, and the system will be complete.

As for the more distant future, there is no point in making prophecies.

[1] Mascal, the Abyssinian feast of the Finding of the Holy Cross, celebrated at the end of September.

[2] Hitler and Mussolini addressed a crowd of 650,000 on the Maifeld, the polo ground of the Olympic Games. Mussolini spoke in German. In spite of Ciano's comments, his success was very doubtful.

[3] The Berlin or October Protocols, a secret Italo-German agreement, were signed by Ciano after his first visit to Berchtesgaden in October 1936.

SEPTEMBER 30. Return to Rome—triumphal. But they should have spared themselves the arches and the laurel. These symbols are reserved for conquerors in war—not for someone coming back from a visit by train.

The enthusiasm of the people was magnificent. They were happy to have their Duce in their midst again. Everybody felt that the country's most precious possession had been lent abroad. And the joy of the masses was, this time, the sum of every man's individual satisfaction.

OCTOBER 1. Ciccino's birthday.

Went to Ponte a Moriano—a family day with Deda, the children, and my parents.

OCTOBER 2. The Duce went to Rocca.[1]

In the afternoon I received Blondel and Lord Perth, and they handed me their note. I don't think we can agree to take part in a conference without Germany. I am waiting for the Duce's opinion and decisions.

Conde asked, in Franco's name, that Bastico should be recalled. We shall consent. Bastico talked to me about the situation in Spain. Franco's position is good, but the issue is still undecided. He wants reinforcements for the corps of volunteers, which in its present state he doesn't consider fit to carry out decisive operations. The withdrawal of the volunteers would endanger the Nationalist position. Cavagnari put before me the decisions for the Mediterranean patrol—good.

OCTOBER 3. Sunday at Castel Fusano. A fine Mediterranean autumn day, warm with a slight haze.

OCTOBER 4. Sent the Duce a draft of our note in reply to the Franco-British move.

In the morning I received the Duke of Aosta,[2] who gave me an account of his visit to England. According to him, agreement ought to be possible. But if we get tough with her, England may still fight and fight well. He was repeating phrases of Grandi's.

Three visitors in the afternoon. De Vecchi[3]—long-winded. Buffarini —cordial. Guarneri—discouraging about the currency situation.

Went to the sea—a fine bathe by myself.

OCTOBER 5. De Vecchi went on with the next instalment of his story. He is intolerably boring.

[1] Rocca della Caminate, Mussolini's country house in his native province of Romagna.

[2] Amedeo of Savoy, cousin of the King of Italy. Appointed Viceroy of Italian East Africa in November 1937. Commander-in-Chief Italian Forces, 1939–41. Died of tuberculosis in Kenya in 1942.

[3] Count Cesare Maria De Vecchi di Val Cismon, Governor of the Dodecanese. Quadrumvir of the March on Rome.

A long conversation with Pariani about the situation in Spain. He would like to send Alpine troops in force to break through to Valencia. But how would France and Britain react? Is it advisable to embark on action which may lead to a conflict? I say No. In the first place, because Germany is not ready. In three years she will be. Secondly, we are short of raw materials and munitions. Finally, a conflict of this kind would bring us into general odium. However, the Spanish situation is serious and requires a rapid solution. I shall talk to the Duce about it.

I had a long discussion with Helfand. The Russians are still finding the Rome Berlin Axis hard to swallow. They hope for an improvement in relations. At the moment I don't see it happening. On the contrary....

OCTOBER 6. I informed Berti that he is to assume command in Spain. He talked at length of how he sees the situation. Still a very long struggle before us—that is the gist of it. Perhaps more than a year, unless we send an entire expeditionary corps and, most important, Alpine troops capable of surprise movements in the mountains during the winter. If we can't do this, he wants us to withdraw the infantry and reduce our contribution to technical services, artillery, engineers, and the air. I shall talk to the Duce to-morrow. My impression of Berti is that, though we shan't regret sending him, he hasn't any brilliant surprises in store for us. He asked for Teruzzi's scalp, and he may get it.

Talked to Bocchini—information about Russian espionage and a diatribe against Balbo. Nothing I hadn't heard before.

Saw the Duce on his return from Rocca. He gave me the text of the note with a few alterations. We shall hand it to the French and British representatives on Saturday.

Galli is going back to Turkey. I have instructed him to drop the project of my visit to Ankara. The time is not ripe.

OCTOBER 7. Conversation with Berti and the Duce. The new commander is to make a report by Saturday 16th with a comprehensive appreciation of the situation and his proposals for dealing with it. Decisions will be taken on the basis of this report, for meanwhile we shall have been able also to study further international developments. Teruzzi will not go back to Spain. I shall talk to the Chief to-morrow about his receiving some recognition for his work, so that he won't be pursued by the usual howls of criticism.

Lord Perth and Blondel asked me for the reply to their note. I told them that the delay has been caused by Azcárate's[1] speech at Geneva, saying that Valencia will not get rid of the Red volunteers. Our note

[1] Pablo de Azcárate y Florez, Spanish Republican delegate at Geneva and Ambassador in London.

is now in Berlin. We shall deliver it as soon as we have their agreement to the formula. We must always give the impression of Axis solidarity. The Japanese are beginning to buy aeroplanes from us.

OCTOBER 8. (I have replaced Parini by De Cicco and made other changes.)

A day with nothing important. The note will be delivered to-morrow. Meanwhile tension has increased. There is no doubt that the Spanish problem is moving towards an international crisis—rupture or clarification. Many anti-Fascist forces are working for the first alternative. But the peoples don't want war at present.

OCTOBER 9. I presented the note to Lord Perth and Blondel at midday. No comment, just a few words to arrange about the time of publication. Blondel seemed rather shaken by our refusal. Lord Perth showed no emotion and said nothing, apart from asking me for the name of a cure for rheumatism, which I recommended to him last year and which, it seems, did him good. A real Englishman.

Turati[1] spoke to me about living conditions and progress made in the Empire. Nothing to be pleased about. But the Minister is more to blame than the Viceroy.[2] We must have faith and leave the man on the spot free to act—or else replace him. But not torment him with questions of detail and keep his hands tied.

OCTOBER 10. Sunday at the sea. Nothing important.

OCTOBER 11. Nothing particularly outstanding. We are waiting for the Franco-British reaction to our note. So far there is little in the press and nothing official. Grandi told me on the telephone that it has been a day of clarification. Now the atmosphere is clearer.

The Duce is following events very closely, calmly but with formidable resolution. He sent for me a second time to-night and talked about various questions. He thinks that a committee of six powers (Italy, France, Great Britain, Germany, Portugal, and Russia) might be able to solve the question of volunteers and also that of belligerency. Meanwhile he wants fresh impressions of Spain, which he will shortly get from Anfuso. I suggested to him that it might be fitting to withdraw our Ambassador from Paris, as a reprisal. He agrees. He thinks of taking this step when twelve months have elapsed since Chambrun's[3] departure.

OCTOBER 12. Visit from Starace, who announced the imminent liquidation of Lessona. I had already realized this myself from something the Duce had said.

[1] Augusto Turati, former Secretary-General of the Fascist Party.
[2] Marshal Rodolfo Graziani. Resigned in November 1937. Commander of the Italian forces in Libya, 1940-1.
[3] Comte Charles de Chambrun, former French Ambassador in Rome. Recalled in October 1936.

The Duce insists on withdrawing Cerruti. He is right. I have already sent a good Counsellor, Prunas, to Paris, to prepare for an interregnum.

The Franco-British reaction to my note is flabby. Delbos's *passez à l'action* is already losing its bite. I think they will confine themselves to continuing the exchange of views.

Berlin is to make a declaration of non-aggression to Brussels. Perhaps we ought to do the same, so as not to be left out of the game.

I saw Russo on the subject of the new contingents of Black Shirts for Spain. For the present I am against sending them. Too dangerous.

OCTOBER 13. I took Teruzzi to the Duce, who promised him a job. I am glad that this faithful old soldier is to be rewarded—he did well in Africa and in Spain.

Lowentau[1] sent me a telegram, asking for a frank declaration on our policy towards China. I replied that we are and will remain neutral, but that the Chinese attitude towards us prevents more active manifestations of sympathy.

Conversation with Dupuy[2] of the *Petit Parisien*. Spectral analysis of Franco-Italian relations. On our side goodwill and the desire for an improvement. But in Paris they don't want to do anything positive in that direction. It is a long time since official France made a gesture of sympathy towards us. What could we do to alter the present situation? However, we mustn't break all links or close all doors.

OCTOBER 14. Edda is back.

The fundamental ideas in our note have been accepted in London and Paris. I am surprised. After the threats of the last few days this withdrawal is enough to make one speculate about the decline of the French and British peoples. The moment will come, it has perhaps already come, when we shall be able to stake all on the final throw.

Volpi talked to me about his visit to Yugoslavia. Not about Yugoslavia, but about himself in Yugoslavia. Hence quite uninteresting. He is aiming at the Ministry of the Colonies, though he denies it with the blushes of a bashful child. He would be a good Minister and would do well. With all his faults he is an able man.

Revel confirmed that the tax on investments is to be put into force at the next Council of Ministers. The stock exchange has been wildly unsteady for the last few days, in anticipation of the financial legislation. The Duce attributes this to fear of war and wants to close the exchanges, which he describes as 'hotbeds of anti-Fascism'. The legislation seems to me to go too far. The experts are against it.

---

[1] Lowentau [*sic*], possibly Marvin Lowenthal, a prominent member of U.S. pacifist organizations.
[2] Pierre Dupuy, editor of the *Petit Parisien*.

Fagiuoli[1] asked me what to do with Visconti.[2] Liquidate him. Valentino[3] is pleased with our position in Poland. He suggests that Beck[4] should visit Rome. Why not, provided the Germans are in favour of the idea? I think they should be. I will talk to the Duce about it.

OCTOBER 15. I have given Grandi his instructions for the Non-Intervention Committee. We must make some concession. I therefore underlined three points: we are ready to discuss the plan for the withdrawal of volunteers—the parties in the conflict should be asked to state their intentions on the subject and, if they are favourable, a plan should be fixed for the withdrawal—at the same time they should be given recognition of their belligerent status.

I talked in a conciliatory sense to Lord Perth, which pleased him very much. He has staked on agreement with us and he wants to bring it off. He asked me about our forces in Libya. I replied that we will talk about that within the framework of Anglo-Italian negotiations.

The Duce took me with him to the Villa Torlonia.[5] He was very cheerful and is taking a close interest in the development of events.

Lugosianu[6] brought me a Roumanian decoration. There was no reason for me to be given it, except the desire for a *rapprochement*.

OCTOBER 16. Took Ciccino to school for the first time. How time passes! I remember going myself, as if it were yesterday, and how I cried at leaving old Emilia and only stopped when the caretaker's husband, in a scavenger's uniform, threatened to arrest me. And yet that's almost thirty years ago! Ciccino will be a good scholar. He has great self-respect and is very proud.

Grandi has watered down my instructions too much, but his pronouncements have had a good effect. Our diplomatic position is clearly advantageous.

I saw the Polish Ambassador, who came to tell me, in Beck's name, of the frankly anti-Italian activities of the French at Geneva. There is nothing to be done about it. Internal politics form a barrier between the two peoples. And also French jealousy.

The Greek Minister came to make a profession of loyalty towards us (in the Greek sense of the word, of course), after having worked against us at Nyon. He protested a little about the intrepid De Vecchi, who is

[1] V. Fagiuoli, director of the Spanish-Italian mercury cartel.
[2] E. Visconti, former *Podestà* (Fascist local governor) of Leghorn. Director of the Siele mercury mine.
[3] Baron Pietro Arone di Valentino, Italian Ambassador in Warsaw.
[4] Colonel Joseph Beck, Foreign Minister of Poland since 1932.
[5] Villa Torlonia, Mussolini's private residence on the outskirts of Rome.
[6] Ion Lugosianu, Roumanian Minister in Rome.

persecuting the Greeks and is said to have introduced the castor oil
method in the Dodecanese. He is an old fool and we shall have more
trouble from him.

I went home with the Duce and gave him a full report on the
situation. He is pleased. He had prepared an *Informazione Diplomatica*[1] directed against Belgium, but I persuaded him to give it up.
It would have been tiresome, from the point of view of Germany as
well.

OCTOBER 17. Nothing special. Filippo[2] is back from Spain. He
repeats what we more or less knew already, i.e. that our troops are
tired and that Franco can hardly wait for them to clear out, though
he wants to retain the air force and the artillery. He is jealous of our
successes and afraid of those that are still to come.

OCTOBER 18. Police review and in the afternoon manœuvres.
Splendid. It is a perfect little army, equipped with all the most modern
weapons. With such a police force, assuming that it is loyal, a popular
upheaval is no longer conceivable—any riot would be crushed in a
matter of minutes. The truth is that the modern State always has the
means to defend itself, provided that the man in command is determined to make use of them.

Himmler was present and full of admiration.

I received Ricci and said a few kind words to him. He has made
certain mistakes, but all the same he is a good organizer and loyal.

I confirmed to Blondel, who questioned me on the point, that I had
had a conversation with Dupuy.

OCTOBER 19. Council of Ministers. The law for a 10 per cent
company tax was approved. Medici and Benni[3] were not enthusiastic.

Franco is asking for a division in order to liquidate the northern
front. We have agreed.

OCTOBER 20. Raumer, Ribbentrop's[4] *chef de cabinet*, was brought
to see me by von Hassel. The object of his visit was to propose the
adherence of Italy, with the status of an original signatory, to the pact
between Germany and Japan. This is a consequence of my contacts
with Tokyo. I expressed myself, in principle, in favour, but asked that
we should be informed of and, if necessary, participate in the secret

[1] *Informazioni Diplomatiche* (Diplomatic Bulletins) were published at irregular inter-
vals. They were usually written by Ciano or Mussolini and contained important
statements on foreign policy.
[2] Filippo Anfuso.
[3] Antonio Benni, Minister of Communications.
[4] Joachim von Ribbentrop was at this time Ambassador in London and did not
become Foreign Minister until February 1938, but he already played an important
part in the direction of German foreign policy, sometimes, as on this occasion, in
opposition to the German Foreign Ministry.

agreements which I have reason to believe exist between Berlin and Tokyo.

Mais il y a quelque chose qui cloche. Neurath[1] seems to me not to be pulling his weight. And von Hassel, notably, agrees with him. They don't want to do something which will disturb London, and then they are afraid of Ribbentrop's personal success.

OCTOBER 21. As I foresaw, the plot is thickening in the Ribbentrop affair. Neurath, playing a different game, sent for Attolico.[2] He was hoping that we would not accept. As we have accepted, he is trying to discourage us. He talked about possible repercussions in London. Then he went to Berchtesgaden. Then he went back to Berlin. Conclusion: Ribbentrop will be here to-morrow, but his mission has not received Neurath's blessing. Attolico, an ex-mason, immediately fell in behind Neurath. The Duce is right, as he always is. You can't change the way these old men's minds work. You must change *them*. It is deplorable to see how in Germany the Foreign Minister fails to act on the Führer's instructions. This is made overwhelmingly clear by Neurath's telephone call to von Hassel.

I was much touched to-day by the story of a girl who begged me to help her. She told me in a simple and unmistakably truthful way of how she was driven to prostitution.

Saw the film about the life of Zola. Technically good, but its contents are poisonous. It is the glorification of anti-militarism. I shall have it banned.

OCTOBER 22. Conversation with Ribbentrop, in the presence of von Hassel and Raumer for the latter part. Then a conversation *à trois* with the Duce. I have written a report of the two conversations elsewhere.[3] In principle, it is decided that we adhere to the pact between Germany and Japan.

Meanwhile from Berlin, at the instigation of Neurath, Attolico has been urging us not to join. And von Hassel here has been very much against the idea. When Ribbentrop arrived, he said to one of my secretaries at the airport, 'To-night I shall write one of the happiest pages of my diary.' These cross-currents in German foreign policy are dangerous.

Good news from Spain—Gijon has fallen. This will enable Franco to concentrate our forces on the Aragon front and, let us hope, accelerate the progress of this cursed war.

---

[1] Constantin von Neurath, Foreign Minister. Dismissed from Foreign Ministry in February 1938.

[2] Bernardo Attolico, Italian Ambassador in Berlin. Recalled at the request of the Germans in April 1940. Ambassador to the Holy See, 1940–2.

[3] Ciano wrote reports of the more important diplomatic conversations in which he took part. These reports, usually referred to in the diary as *verbali* (Minutes), have been published in *L'Europa verso la Catastrofe*, Mondadori, Milan, 1948. English translation in *Ciano's Diplomatic Papers*, Odhams Press, 1948.

OCTOBER 23. I have summoned the Prince of Hesse[1] to Rome, and I am sending him to the Führer to find out what he thinks about the Tripartite Pact.

In London the situation has been complicated by Russia's refusal to accept the plan for Spain and by the ambiguous attitude of France and Britain. The Duce, on my advice, has drafted *Informazione Diplomatica* No. 4 himself.

I received the Japanese Ambassador in connexion with the tripartite agreement. I made a Minute of the conversation.

Gerbore[2] tells me he has learnt that the German police are suspicious of Magistrati's ideas. This may be due to something Renzetti[3] has done. I have sent Gerbore to Berlin to inform Massimo. It is a tiresome business, because, considering the way in which I am related to Massimo, it is proof of a generally suspicious attitude. It is hard work undoing our former reputation in German eyes.

A tearful appeal from Signora Patrone about her son languishing in a Russian prison. I will do what I can to hasten the exchange with Grigorieff.[4]

Dinner in honour of Ribbentrop at the Villa Madama.

OCTOBER 24. Drafted instructions for Grandi for the meeting of the Committee next Tuesday. We cannot give way on the question of unanimity—otherwise we shall be giving Russia an obvious advantage. Besides, if we give way, we shall find France and England more and more unyielding. Ribbentrop agrees—his feelings for England are those of a woman for a faithless lover. In a conversation I had with him last night he preached the necessity of a military alliance between Italy, Germany, and Japan, in anticipation of the inevitable conflict with the western powers. He told me of Hitler's advice that we should never again give up Majorca, our formidable new pawn on the Mediterranean chess-board.

Sunday afternoon—played a war game with Ciccino and Dindina[5] and their soldiers. We put the whole neighbourhood to flight with the noise of our gunfire!

OCTOBER 25. Ribbentrop telephoned to say that the Führer sees no objection to the agreement being signed in Rome and not in Munich, as Ribbentrop himself had proposed in view of his position as Ambassador in London. The Duce approves and wants the signature to take place as soon as possible. If the Japanese are not too pernickety, we can sign on the 6th. There will follow an unexpected meeting of

---

[1] Prince Philip of Hesse, husband of Princess Mafalda of Savoy. Acted as special emissary between Hitler and Mussolini.

[2] Pietro Gerbore, an official in the Foreign Ministry.

[3] Mario Renzetti, Italian Consul-General in Berlin.

[4] Grigorieff, a Soviet agent arrested in Italy.

[5] Dindina (Raimonda), Ciano's daughter, born in 1933.

the Grand Council, at which it will be decided to leave the League of Nations on the 18th, the second anniversary of sanctions. This is how Italy remembers and takes her revenge. In any case, the anti-Leaguers are already so numerous that we might think of founding a league of the nations not belonging to the League of Nations!

I protested to Drummond about the activities of British agents among the Abyssinian *émigrés* in Jerusalem. If they continue, we shall allow our Arabic radio service freedom of action again. Drummond, who is a genuine convert, is also going to telegraph to support our point of view at the London Committee.

OCTOBER 26. Talked to Hotta about drafting the agreement. Nothing else important.

OCTOBER 27. In the morning I received Henry Gris, a Lithuanian journalist, who wrote an abusive article about me some months ago in *Esquire*. He was very embarrassed and blushed, particularly in his ears and his chin. I spoke to him politely and at some length, which had the effect of making him even shyer.

Conversation with Hess,[1] who has arrived with the rest of the delegation. I made a point of telling him that in Italy the most Fascist-minded Ministry is the Foreign Ministry. I knew that this was going to flutter the dove-cots. He immediately went off into a tirade against Neurath and German diplomats in general and their links with International Diplomacy. I took the opportunity of asking for von Hassel's scalp—he has been playing a double game for too long. I produced evidence to show why we mistrust the man. Hess agreed and is going to talk to the Führer. He asked for my advice about a successor. I said that a Party man would be the thing. The alliance between the two countries is based above all on the identity of political régime, which determines a common destiny. *Simul stabunt, simul cadent.*

OCTOBER 28. The demonstration in the Foro Mussolini was magnificent and picturesque—the finest demonstration I have ever seen. Starace is a great stage manager. The Germans were moved by the Duce's speech and the demonstration and dazzled by our colours and our sun.

In the afternoon I talked to Stein about the release of Markoff.[2] Not much politics but, as usual, apocalyptic prophecies about what will happen if we continue our friendship with Germany. If the agreement with Japan comes off as well, there is to be a universal deluge.

Something new—a written message from Eden, delivered by Perth, that he would be glad to meet me in Brussels.[3] It is interesting that Eden should have made this move. I think I ought to go. I telephoned

---

[1] Rudolf Hess, Hitler's Deputy.

[2] Markoff, a Soviet agent arrested in Italy.

[3] A Nine Power Conference, convened by the League of Nations, was to meet in Brussels on November 3 to discuss the question of the Far East.

the Duce and he agrees. It is a good way of shelving the question of the 'Far East'[1]—all the spotlights of world publicity will be focused on the Eden-Ciano meeting.

OCTOBER 29. In the morning there was a presentation of medals to the widows of those who have fallen in Spain. The ceremony was a success. But as I watched these men and women in mourning file by and looked into their eyes red with weeping, I examined my conscience and asked myself whether this blood has been shed in a good cause. Yes, the answer is Yes. At Malaga, at Guadalajara, at Santander, we were fighting in defence of our civilization and our Revolution. And sacrifices are necessary in order to forge the bold and strong spirit of a nation. The wounded were full of courage. One of them, who had lost both hands and an eye, said, 'All I want is another hand to go back to Spain with.' It sounds like a phrase in an anthology, but it came from the lips of a boy of twenty, maimed by the enemy's steel but happy because the Duce had stopped for a moment to talk to him. The Germans who were with us have learnt something.

The Duce isn't keen for me to go to Brussels. All things considered, he is right. Without preparation, a conversation with Eden would be useless and possibly harmful because of the disappointment which would result from it. If necessary, we can always find an opportunity later. I spoke to Perth, who was not very convinced by my arguments. He personally was in favour of the meeting, which would in his opinion have done much to clarify the situation.

OCTOBER 30. In the morning I had a conversation with Philip of Hesse on his return from Berlin, where he had seen Hitler. The truth is that Hitler was very angry with Ribbentrop, not because of what has happened—Hitler approves of the Tripartite Pact and claims to have originated it himself—but because, contrary to his instructions, Ribbentrop had kept the whole thing a secret from Neurath. Now the question is settled—Ribbentrop will be Neurath's successor.

Hess asked to see me outside my office, so I saw him at the Grand Hotel. He was excited and nervous. He told me that von Hassel's wife had spoken in a very hostile way about Italy in conversation with him. Hess was loyally indignant. He wanted to go straight to Berlin to ask for Hassel's scalp. This would be all the easier, as Hassel himself was going to Berlin to complain about Ribbentrop. The Führer would be able to liquidate him as a result of his own complaint. I advised him not to go, but to write. Any sudden and unexpected journey on his part would give rise to other interpretations. The row would seem to be between him and us, not between him and his Embassy. He has written. Hassel really is hostile to Fascism and an enemy of the

[1] In English in the original.

Rome-Berlin Axis. He goes about telling a story that Streicher,[1] when passing through Rome, visited the German school and showered praises on a girl whom he picked out as the most intelligent and best-looking. She was the only Jewish girl in the school. . . .

OCTOBER 31. Inaugural ceremony at Guidonia.[2]

A great commotion in Paris as a result of Cerruti's departure. It was a situation which had to be cleared up. We have now cleared it up and it was the right thing to do. If we are going to get France to recognize us, it will certainly not be by smiles and concessions, which is what Cerruti wanted. The Germans are very favourably impressed by our gesture.

NOVEMBER 1. Tokyo has agreed to the formula of the Tripartite Pact. The signature will take place on Saturday at 11 a.m. Working out details is a lengthy and meticulous business with the Germans and the Japanese, and they wanted to settle even the most minute questions of form. Something very important has happened. The alliance of three military empires the size of Italy, Germany, and Japan throws an unprecedented weight of armed strength into the balance of power. England will have to reconsider her position everywhere.

Conversation with the King of Greece. Polite, modest, fairly frank. He was anxious to talk about politics, though he doesn't like the subject. I gave him an outline of the European situation and said, very calmly and very firmly, that, while we wish for peace, we are prepared for any eventuality if we cannot obtain recognition of our rights and national interests. The Rome-Berlin Axis is, unequivocally, a force to reckon with. Others must make up their minds to be its friends or its foes. As there is nothing to separate Italy and Greece, I count on Greek friendship. He was impressed, and was even more impressed when I told him that in the Balkans we can already count absolutely on certain states. My allusion to Yugoslavia was obvious. In any case the line of advance drawn by destiny is Salonika for the Serbs, Tirana and Corfu for us. The Greeks know this and are frightened. I don't think my kind words succeeded in effacing the idea from his mind. It is, after all, an idea for the realization of which I have for some time been working.

NOVEMBER 2. A very hostile speech from Eden. It was only to be expected. He can't reconcile himself to his loss of face over Abyssinia and is trying to land us a kick on the shins. I have drafted *Informazione Diplomatica* No. 5, which is a good reply. An even better reply will be the signing on Saturday of the Tripartite Pact, anti-Communist in theory, but in fact unmistakably anti-British.

[1] Julius Streicher, editor of the anti-Semitic paper, *Der Stürmer*.
[2] Guidonia, a new town in the Sabine Mountains, designed as a centre of aeronautical research. Named after the Italian air pioneer, Alessandro Guidoni.

Conversation with Balbo. As always, sour and treacherous. He is sniping at the Party and at the same time trying to save his stooge, Lessona.

NOVEMBER 3. The Duce was making fun of Grandi to-day. Grandi really is backing the Non-Intervention Committee too heavily. He sends the Stefani Agency[1] announcements which the Chief describes as 'Dispatches from Austerlitz'.

Aldrovandi[2] has read his speech to the Nine-Power Conference in Brussels. It was apparently received with chilly silence, though they all realized it was the only realistic speech.

The Japanese Ambassador asked me again for assurances about our attitude towards Russia. The facts speak for themselves. Our torpedoes have also spoken.

Admiral Bernotti, who has come back from the exercises at Biserta for the implementation of the Nyon agreement, told me that, while the English Admiral was polite, the French Admiral was extremely dis-agreeable. The French staff officers had more sympathy for the Spanish Nationalists.

NOVEMBER 4. Mass at Santa Maria degli Angeli and the usual ceremony in honour of the Unknown Soldier.

Anniversary of Victory Day.[3]

NOVEMBER 5. I met von Ribbentrop at the station. Hassel was green with rage.

Conversation with the Roumanian Cabinet Minister, Irimescu.[4] I alluded to the pact which is to be signed to-morrow and said that it concerns Roumania very closely. Simply for the reason of her alarming proximity to the Bolsheviks, Bucharest must orientate her sympathies towards the powerful new anti-Communist system.

Conversation with Ribbentrop, Hotta, and Hassel. We fixed a few details for to-morrow's ceremony. The English, it seems, have shown the Japanese that they are very worried at the signing of the pact. They feel that the system is closing against them.

I told the Turkish Ambassador that I will not go to Ankara until the preliminary conditions for such a visit are realized, that is to say, until the Empire is recognized. I was pretty snubbing.

NOVEMBER 6. We signed the Pact this morning. One was conscious of an atmosphere definitely unlike that of the usual diplomatic cere-mony. Three nations are embarking together upon a path which may perhaps lead them to war. A war necessary in order to break through

---

[1] Stefani, the official Fascist press agency.
[2] Count Luigi Aldrovandi-Marescotti, leader of the Italian delegation at the Conference. Former Ambassador in Berlin.
[3] The armistice between Italy and Austria was signed on November 4, 1918.
[4] Radu Irimescu, Roumanian Minister for the Navy and the Air.

the crust which is stifling the energy and the aspirations of the young nations. After the signature we went to see the Duce. I have seldom seen him so happy. The situation of 1935 has been transformed. Italy has broken out of her isolation: she is in the centre of the most formidable political and military combination which has ever existed.

In the afternoon there was a conversation à trois—Duce-Ciano-Ribbentrop. An extremely interesting conversation. I have summarized it in a Minute.

In the evening there was a grand dinner at the Palazzo Venezia. The two Japanese Military Attachés, both good Fascists, were radiant. They are in favour of a military pact. They were delighted when I said to them, in the Duce's presence, that they ought to occupy Vladivostok, that pistol pointed at Japan.

NOVEMBER 7. The Duce deplores that Aldrovandi should have given his consent to the sending of a second invitation to Japan to take part in the Brussels Conference. He is right—we might have spared ourselves these few steps in the League ballroom. The Duce hates the reputation which Italy used to have, and wants to efface it by means of a policy as straight as the blade of a sword. Moral: I have telegraphed Tokyo to say that, as soon as the Japanese have refused, we will withdraw from Brussels. That will blow the conference sky high.

Ribbentrop has gone. Hotta, Hassel, and I were at the station. The Duce has asked Ribbentrop too for Hassel's scalp.

I am sad about Papa, who is sinking hourly. I had good hopes of a recovery, but it seems that the treatments are useless. This strong, generous, heroic man is now tired and old. It is a great grief to me—he loved me more than anyone and he made great sacrifices for me. May God bring about a miracle.

NOVEMBER 8. The following scene took place in my office this morning. Stein came in and said: 'I am instructed by my Government to inform you that it considers your participation in the Tripartite Pact as contrary to our Pact of 1933 and as an unfriendly gesture towards the Soviets. I have nothing more to say.' I replied: 'I take note of what you have told me, and I will report it to the Duce. I have nothing more to say.' I rose and showed him to the door, where we both prostrated ourselves in a profound and chilly bow.

The Brazilian Ambassador is going to advise his Government to join the Tripartite Pact.

The Hungarian Minister has been instructed by Kanya[1] to ask for a meeting of the signatories of the Rome Protocols.[2] I see no objection in principle. It might well take place in Budapest, in January. I agree

[1] Kalman Kanya, Hungarian Foreign Minister.
[2] An economic agreement between Italy, Austria, and Hungary, signed in March 1934.

that we must give the impression that the Rome bloc is really solid.
The Duce came back in the afternoon, and I had a short conference
with him.

NOVEMBER 9. Echoes of the Pact continue. I have been thinking
a lot about future developments. We must not go about asking little
states to join—it must remain a pact of giants. But three countries
interest me: Spain, representing the prolongation of the Axis to the
Atlantic; Brazil, in order to shake the whole democratic system in
South America; and Poland, as a line of defence against Russia. For
Spain we must wait. Brazil requires immediate attention and I have
telegraphed to Lojacono.[1] For about a year I have been subsidizing
the Integralists[2] to the extent of 40 contos a month. If in these days
of struggle it is necessary to intervene on a larger scale, I shall place
the sums at our Ambassador's disposal.

Dined with Wysocki,[3] where I met Beck's wife and had a long talk
with Lugosianu, who has resigned in the hope—very possibly a vain
hope—of getting the Foreign Ministry in the next Cabinet. I proved
to him that Roumania now has no alternative but to align herself with
our formidable anti-Russian system. The Russians are her danger,
even more as allies than as enemies. The Roumanians may as well
waste no time in making sure of our friendship and protection.

NOVEMBER 10. The Duce has personally drafted *Informazione
Diplomatica* No. 6 in reply to Chamberlain.

Pertinax[4] has made a fierce attack on the governing clique in Poland.
I have instructed Ansaldo[5] to take up their defence. They will be
grateful. An attack on a country is merely unpleasant, an attack on
personalities produces a change of heart. That is the moment to set to
work. Meanwhile Russia is making things easier for us. The cry of
'Halt!', by which Russia tries to deter Poland from joining the Tripartite Pact, only makes it clearer to her that her place is with the Fascist
states.

I have summoned for Monday the Committee which is to make
arrangements for Hitler's reception. The visit will be in May, but we
must think ahead if we want to do things properly. I am particularly
concerned about the decoration of the streets. Hitherto we have
always done it in a commonplace, countrified, Humbertine[6] sort of
way.

---

[1] Vincenzo Lojacono, Italian Ambassador in Brazil.
[2] The Brazilian totalitarian party. It was dissolved by the Vargas Government in
December 1937.
[3] Alfred Wysocki, Polish Ambassador in Rome.
[4] Pertinax, pseudonym of the French journalist André Géraud.
[5] Giovanni Ansaldo, editor of Ciano's paper, *Il Telegrafo*, of Leghorn.
[6] The Italian equivalent of Victorian (Umberto I was King of Italy from 1878
to 1900).

Talked to Solmi,[1] who would like to have a legal congress. It seems to me a harmless idea.

NOVEMBER 11. I have had another request from Eden for a meeting in Brussels. I sent for Drummond and told him I thought I could not accept, partly because of the place, partly because of the faint League atmosphere of the setting, partly because of the moribund condition into which the conference has now sunk. But it must not be deduced from this that I do not want to meet Eden. On the contrary, I should be only too pleased. But somewhere else, and after suitable preparation, in order to ensure that the meeting does not lead to illusions, controversy, and disappointment.

Anfuso has patched up a blunder of Salata's in Vienna. Salata, who had been instructed to put before Schuschnigg two British documents which compromise Schmidt,[2] began asking for confrontations, withdrawals, etc. The scandal would have compromised our intelligence service. Anfuso drew a veil over the whole affair. Schuschnigg has told him that, if and when we wish, he will sack Schmidt. A very good thing, because he is a treacherous man.

NOVEMBER 12. The press has made a lot of noise about my interview with Perth. God knows what would have happened if I had consented to meet Eden. However, it is worth registering the fact that something is happening and there has been a partial thaw.

Hotta thanked me for our attitude at Brussels. But he asks us not to withdraw our delegation, as it is still useful in obstructing decisions hostile to Japan.

Received the Brazilian Ambassador. I told him of our sympathy for the policy of Vargas,[3] and promised him the support of the Italians in Brazil, who are indeed (particularly those in San Paolo) for obvious reasons of local interest not much in favour of Integralism.

Conversation with Phillips.[4] A long explanation of the background and the results of the Tripartite Pact. He has been impressed by Delbos's book, Expérience Rouge, in which he talks about the Russian preparations for the revolution in Spain.

NOVEMBER 13. An interesting talk with the Duce. He was set off by a remark of mine and launched full tilt into an attack on the bourgeoisie and their persistent anti-Fascist tendencies. In fact for some days now the Argentina theatre has been the scene of anti-Fascist meetings, for that is what the acting of Pagnol's[5] play Napoleone Unico

---

[1] Arrigo Solmi, Minister of Justice.
[2] Guido Schmidt, Austrian Under-Secretary for Foreign Affairs.
[3] Getulio Vargas, President of Brazil, 1930–45.
[4] William Phillips, United States Ambassador in Rome, 1936–41.
[5] Marcel Pagnol, the French dramatist.

amounts to—the situations, characters, and jokes have obvious analogies. He accused the intellectual and bourgeois classes of cowardice, inertia, and love of a quiet life, and declared that as long as he is alive he will keep them on the move 'to the tune of kicks on the shin'. 'When Spain is finished, I will think of something else. The character of the Italian people must be moulded by fighting.' He has banned the play. Plato was prepared to ban the *Odyssey* and even music if it seemed flabby and depressing.

Barella[1] talked to me about the *Popolo d'Italia*. He can't get the circulation to increase—a phenomenon which ties up with the anti-Fascism of the bourgeoisie. Even the Duce's articles don't send the sales up, unless thousands of lire are spent on newsboys and the Party's forces are mobilized. To think that the Duce believes that the Italians are waiting impatiently for these articles of his. The bourgeoisie often makes one sick.

And it is this bourgeoisie which is at the moment wildly happy because of the non-existent negotiations with London. I feel inclined to get back to the truth of the situation by publishing an *Informazione Diplomatica*.

NOVEMBER 14. A strongly anti-Japanese motion has been prepared in Brussels. The threads of the plot against Tokyo are beginning to be unravelled. Nothing could be more dangerous than to fall for this technique of collective security. If your finger gets caught in the machinery, you lose your whole arm. I have drafted the announcement of our negative vote, which Aldrovandi will make to-morrow, and shown it to Hotta. Hotta, for his part, has told me that Tokyo is preparing to recognize Franco and has asked me for information about the state of affairs in White Spain. At the same time he asked whether we are ready to accord formal recognition to Manchukuo. I myself have no objection, in the present state of affairs, but we shall have to come to an agreement with Berlin.

Conde talked to me on the subject of the handing over of the *Pepe* and the *Poerio*[2] to the Spanish navy. Cavagnari is making difficulties because the September instalment of the price of the two submarines hasn't been paid yet. Our sailors have always been obstructive about the Spanish enterprise. They hate anything which may possibly mean danger to as much as a motor-launch of their fleet. . . . They are admirable cultivators of that international law which, in order to wage war properly, they ought to despise.

Don Juan, the heir to the Spanish throne, has asked to see me. We

---

[1] Giulio Barella, editor of *Il Popolo d'Italia*, the daily paper founded by Mussolini in 1914.
[2] *Pepe* and *Poerio*, two Italian destroyers.

must be very cautious, although I myself believe in the necessity for the restoration of the monarchy.

NOVEMBER 15. A long conversation with Chen Kung-po.[1] I found him aged and, away from his own world, much less brilliant than I remembered him to be. I expounded the following thesis. Japan will overwhelm you militarily and the democracies will not give you any practical assistance. Your only salvation is to be found in direct negotiations through the mediation of Italy and Germany. And the sooner the better. I gathered that the Chinese are relying upon the vast size of their country, but they forget that China's vital points are on the sea or the rivers and that the Japanese navy can operate unopposed. I have sent a telegram to Chiang Kai-shek setting out my point of view.

In the afternoon there was a meeting of the Committee for the reception of the Führer. I intend that everything shall be perfect. That is why I have started the organization six months in advance. Yesterday everybody responded with enthusiasm. The most delicate problem is relations with the King—the Führer got Hess to tell me that he did not want to stay at the Quirinal.[2] But at least he will have to go there one day. I am thinking of splitting the visit into two parts, a visit to the King and a visit to the Duce. We shall have to exercise a lot of tact. It is a difficult subject and people will be only too ready to criticize.

NOVEMBER 16. Mussolini was very pleased with Aldrovandi's statement in Brussels—a downright No. 'At last I have the kind of diplomacy I like,' he said to me. He talked at length about the necessity for redeeming Italy's reputation as a faithless nation. Bismarck used to say that you can't have a policy with Italy when she is faithless both as friend and foe. Demonstrations like yesterday's prove that Fascist Italy is no longer the Italy of intrigues who prostituted herself to the democracies.

Chen Kung-po has asked me to sound Tokyo, in my name, about conditions of peace. He gave me to understand that the recognition of Manchukuo might be conceded.

Von Hassel talked to me against Schuschnigg, who is said, in conversation with one of his ministers, to have declared himself in favour of an agreement with Prague and therefore with the western democracies. I said I didn't believe the report—Schuschnigg knows that that would mean being abandoned by us, which would be the end of Austria.

I took Don Juan, future King of Spain, to see the Duce. The Duce said to him that it is easier for monarchies than for republics to frame a social policy, because they need to make fewer compromises. He advised him to base his régime on the support of the rural masses, as

[1] Chen Kung-po, Chinese Minister for Press and Propaganda.
[2] Quirinal, the royal palace in Rome.

they are more loyal and less neurotic than the urban population. He said Spain should be given an imperial spirit. The present civil war is the consequence of the psychological collapse of 1898, which resulted in the vivisection of the Spanish soul and despair for a future no longer worthy of the past.

NOVEMBER 17. Went with Cerruti to the Duce on a farewell visit. At least it had the atmosphere of one, though in theory that is not the position. The Duce attacked French policy towards us. Cerruti defended it, with remarkable courage. He said we owed it to Laval that sanctions were not applied on oil during the Abyssinian war. The Duce said that sanctions on oil would have meant war. That was the only reason why France didn't want them. We shall not forget all that London did, and Paris connived at, two years ago. When Cerruti said that for France Italy is enemy No. 1, Mussolini replied: 'A great honour. I want to be feared and hated, rather than tolerated or protected.' When the subject of the French army was raised, the Duce quoted Paul Allard's book and advised Cerruti to read it. At the end of the conversation everybody's opinions were unchanged. And France's stock had shown no signs of rising.

NOVEMBER 18. Nothing worthy of note, except the opening of the Textiles Exibition. A prodigy of Fascist will.

NOVEMBER 19. Lessona informed me that the blow has fallen. He was very sad. He asked for it. He has never been frank or friendly to those who have helped him. He has always tried to make trouble. Now he has fallen into his enemies' hands and they will go on kicking him after he is down. Teruzzi is considered a loyal but mediocre executive—in fact more loyal than mediocre.

Conversation with the Duce and Chen Kung-po. The Duce repeated more or less what I had already said to old Kung-po. The only way out is German-Italian mediation. There is nothing to hope for from Chinese arms—still less from military aid from abroad. Kung-po is going to telegraph to his Government. It may be that they are on the way to mediation. They are depressed at Shanghai. Cora[1] telegraphs that for the first time he has seen T. V. Soong[2] depressed. That is striking, because T. V. Soong is a brave man. I have telegraphed to Cora to talk to him on the lines of the instructions I sent on October 28 and of my conversations with Chen Kung-po.

NOVEMBER 20. The Duce has taken steps about a blatantly pro-French article in the *Tribuna*. He described the author, Scardaoni,[3] as 'a son of slaves'.

[1] Giuliano Cora, Italian Ambassador to China.
[2] T. V. Soong, former Minister of Finance. Brother of Madame Chiang Kai-shek.
[3] Francesco Scardaoni, Paris correspondent of *La Tribuna*.

I received the Japanese envoy, Baron Okura,[1] and took him to see the Duce. He said nothing of much importance but confined himself to expressions of gratitude for our solidarity with his country.

Volpi pretended to be delighted that the 'lot hadn't fallen on him' to go to the Colonies. But his face fell when I told him that the present situation is destined to last a long time. He was still hoping. . . .

The Brazilian Ambassador had nothing new to tell me about his country. Vargas is looking for a formula for Brazil. He will have to find one. Otherwise his movement will rapidly collapse. The secret of dictatorships of the right—and their advantage over other régimes—consists precisely in having a national formula. Italy and Germany have found theirs. The Germans in racial ideology. We in Roman imperialism.

NOVEMBER 21. Was delighted to see two good Fascist faces at the Palazzo Venezia—Teruzzi and Ricci.

Halifax's[2] visit to Germany is a new proof of the anomalies in the Reich's foreign policy. Too many cocks in the hen-house. There are at least four foreign policies—Hitler's, Goering's, Neurath's, Ribbentrop's. Without counting the minor ones. It is difficult to co-ordinate them all properly. All the time Neurath has to be dragged along behind and slows things down.

Here am I thinking of recognizing Manchukuo. Neurath puts on the brakes. If the Führer knew, he would approve. But the Wilhelmstrasse is the most obstinately *ancien régime* organization. In Italy, after all, it took us fifteen years to conquer the Palazzo Chigi. And only I know what a struggle I have to make these goats keep step to the Fascist march.

Conversation with the Duce and General Visconti-Prasca.[3] Prasca is very pro-French—he studied in France and believes in the French General Staff and French military efficiency. In the course of the conversation, which covered familiar ground, the Duce expounded two interesting ideas. (1) An army must be political. Not go in for political activity. But every soldier must be the bearer of a fragment of a political ideology. Otherwise you get not soldiers but employees kept by the state. On this way of thinking Badoglio considers the Reich's present army more powerful than the Kaiser's army, though inferior to it in equipment, discipline, and training. (2) The shrinking of the French population has its origin in the two and a half million dead of the Napoleonic wars, and the law which abolished primogeniture and thus put a premium on only sons.

[1] Baron Okura, an industrialist, one of a number of prominent Japanese sent to Europe and America to counteract Chinese propaganda.

[2] Lord Halifax was at this time Lord President of the Council. He succeeded Eden as Foreign Secretary in March 1938.

[3] General Sebastiano Visconti-Prasca, Italian Military Attaché in Paris.

NOVEMBER 22. The Duce raised doubts about the political relia-
bility of Alessandro Pavolini.[1] I replied that I should reject every
suspicion unless it were documented in an absolutely unquestionable
fashion.

My conversation with the Duce was short. Decided in principle on
the building of the new Ministry for Foreign Affairs. I am sorry to
leave the Palazzo Chigi with its Mussolinian tradition. But the new
building must play its part in the creation of the Duce's Rome.

In the afternoon I had a conversation with Guarneri and Revel.
Both very pessimistic about the currency situation, which, in their
opinion, is a reason to avoid action which may lead to war. They ask
for two years of tranquillity and ten years of peace. It seems to me
too much.

On the Duce's orders I sent a telegram to Attolico, to inform the
Führer of our intention to say good-bye to Geneva on the 25th of
next month. A gesture of this kind, made by us after the virtual failure
of Halifax's visit to Berlin, will help towards the strengthening of the
Axis, or better still of the triangle. We won't have a meeting of the
Grand Council. A telegram from me to the Secretary of the moth-
eaten League will be enough.

NOVEMBER 23. Received a letter from Neurath, giving an account
of Halifax's visit. The results seem to me to be absolutely nil. We did
well not to go to Brussels.

From Paris, Prunas reports that there have been outrages upon the
graves of the Italians who fell at Bligny.[2] If Francophile hearts still
exist in Italy, I think the publication of this piece of news will be
enough to cure them for ever. I told Alfieri, who has a brother buried
at Rheims, and he reacted with a violence scarcely compatible with his
gentle character. I have already sent copies of the report to Del Croix[3]
and Rossi.[4] Should the outrages continue, we shall ask for the bodies
to be repatriated. And we shall send the French theirs.

NOVEMBER 24. The Führer is, in principle, in favour of our
quitting Geneva. But he doesn't want our action to be tied up with
the anti-Communist Pact. He prefers that it should be explained by
the non-recognition of the Empire. About Manchukuo they are still
wavering in Berlin. The pro-democratic rein of the Wilhemstrasse still
exercises too powerful an influence over the Führer.

I have given Ghigi instructions for his mission to Vienna. He was
not very well up in the situation and seemed to me rather frightened.

[1] Alessandro Pavolini, President of the Federation of the Professions and Arts.
[2] Bligny, on the Marne front, was the scene of fierce fighting in July 1918, in which
the Italian Second Army Corps suffered heavy casualties.
[3] Carlo Del Croix, President of the Association of War Wounded and Invalids.
[4] Amilcare Rossi, President of the National Association of ex-Combatants.

I defined the task of the Italian Minister at the Ballplatz as that of a doctor who has to give oxygen to a dying man without the dying man's heir noticing. In case of doubt we are more interested in the heir than in the dying man.

NOVEMBER 25. We have decided for an attack on France apropos of Campinchi's[1] speech. I am not altogether certain of the authenticity of the text, but the Duce wants to fire away. As a spare cartridge, he has in reserve the outrages upon the Bligny graves.

The Duce thinks of leaving Geneva on December 18, with a Grand Council for the occasion. Not earlier, in order not to give offence to Stoyadinovich on the eve of his visit to Italy.

Meanwhile Berlin informs us that for the present they do not mean to proceed to the recognition of Manchukuo, though they leave us liberty of action. We shall recognize. In a few days—not to-day, in order not to spoil the German-Japanese anniversary.[2] We have the additional motive of having to do something in return for the recognition of our Empire.

Anfuso has gone to Vienna. He is taking Schuschnigg a Czech document containing serious statements of Hornbostel[3] (Schmidt?) against the Axis and in favour of the western democracies. I have given the Chancellor my opinion that it is a dangerous game. I have also sent a copy of the document to Göring.

NOVEMBER 26. The Duce has read in a British intercept that Pirelli is spreading poisonous rumours against autarchy. I had warned him about Pirelli's uncertain political colour. Now I am proved right.

At the Duce's request Franco is giving us 100,000 tons of steel. A good thing, because meanwhile production can be speeded up by Ilva.[4] Besides, it is evidence in favour of the sincerity of Franco's sentiments towards us. Many people are beginning to have doubts. I, honestly, have none. I do, however, have considerable doubts of the honesty of Sangroniz[5] and the rest of the Foreign Ministry. They too belong to international diplomacy.

Dinner in honour of Okura at the Japanese Embassy. Hotta told me that our conduct at Brussels has definitely convinced Tokyo of our sincerity and that consequently it will be possible to start talking about a pact for military consultation again. I gave him to understand that we will recognize Manchukuo. Japanese military men are fanatically pro-Italian. The Military Attaché was talking last night about war

[1] César Campinchi, French Minister for the Navy.
[2] The original Anti-Comintern Pact, between Germany and Japan, was signed on November 25, 1936.
[3] Theodor Hornbostel, Director of the Political Department of the Austrian Chancellery.
[4] Ilva, the most important group of Italian steel foundries.
[5] J. A. de Sangroniz, Chief of the Spanish Nationalist Diplomatic Cabinet.

with England. As he lives in Via Addis Ababa, he said that he is hoping to move soon to Via Tunis and Via Cairo and, in Tokyo, to Via Singapore. The Naval Attaché asks us not to deliver to the U.S.S.R. the very swift cruiser now being built by Orlando.[1] The Japanese would be prepared to buy it. They are afraid of its speed, if it is sent to Vladivostok.

NOVEMBER 27. The defenestration of Schacht[2] is excellent—the thorough nazification of the government is beginning. Let us hope he will soon be followed by some more.

Saw Cini, Marziali,[3] Felicioni,[4] Baroni.[5]

To-day again we have found in a British intercept evidence of the gloomy pronouncements Guarneri is making about the financial situation. The Duce told me that he is keeping an eye on him because of the Federation of Industry circles to which he belongs. I mentioned to the Duce my conversation with Guarneri of a few days ago. I confess that I am quite calm about the situation. But even if I were not, I would become so by my contact with Mussolini's imperturbable serenity. He has always been right. And this time, into the bargain, he is associated with the conquerors on every front: Spain, China, Africa. . . . In a very few days, perhaps on Monday, we shall recognize Manchukuo. A policy of realism. And even as regards the Chinese it is the best moment to take this step. They are in such distress that they won't be able to react. Besides, if the war continues, China will soon cease to exist. It was hard enough to conduct operations from Nanking —from Chungking, with the country invaded, with no communications and no revenue, it will be impossible. There are many indications that the break-up of China is at hand. To avoid it, they ought to make peace—on any condition.

NOVEMBER 28. We recognize Manchukuo to-morrow. I informed Hotta to-day and he was very pleased. We are gaining ground. Whereas any uncertainty or vacillation would keep people away, the loyal and helpful policy we are carrying out cements our friendships. Our conduct at Brussels won the day with Japan. To-morrow's stroke will be another success.

Sunday at the sea with Edda. For the first time the children ate at table with us. That very much gives one the feeling of a family. For that reason I like it.

The Duce has authorized me to give the Japanese a copy of the plans

---

[1] Orlando, a Leghorn firm of shipbuilders.
[2] Dr. Hjalmar Schacht, President of the Reichsbank. He had just resigned from the post of Minister of Economic Affairs.
[3] Giovanni Battista Marziali, Prefect of Naples.
[4] Felice Felicioni, President of the *Società Dante Alighieri*.
[5] Guido Baroni, a journalist.

of Singapore which Perego[1] sent. We must present the gift graciously, as a proof that we are now actively co-operating.

NOVEMBER 29. I sent for Blondel to show him a disgraceful cartoon in *Aux Écoutes*. After explaining that I was speaking in a purely personal capacity, I told him that insulting the sacred person of the Duce was not the way to re-establish good relations between our countries.

Opening of the Chamber. A great welcome for Papa, who seemed in pretty good form, though rather pale and much aged. No enthusiasm in the Chamber for the recent ministerial nominations.

I told the Duce about Anfuso's conversation with Schuschnigg. The Chancellor admitted the authenticity of the words used by Hornbostel, but defended him so far as Italy is concerned—he talks against the Axis because he is anti-Nazi. The Chancellor was very impressed by the effectiveness of our intelligence service. He asked if we spent enormous sums. On the contrary, we spend very little, but we have in Emanuele a most valuable man.

NOVEMBER 30. Conversation with the Chinese Ambassador. He wanted explanations about the recognition of Manchukuo. He was afraid that a step of this kind might make it difficult for us to mediate in the conflict. I said that on the contrary it should make it easier. In order to make peace, China will have to recognize Manchukuo. Italy's action has made this easier for her.

Talked to the Pole about the general situation. He asked his usual unintelligent questions.

Nothing else.

DECEMBER 1. The Duce has gone off the deep end with the Ministry of Popular Culture for sending the film *Squadrone Bianco* to Egypt. It was an idiotic thing to do. If we have a pro-Arab policy, what is the point of serving up to the Egyptians the spectacle of Arabs being scientifically massacred by our troops?

I gave the Japanese Military Attaché the plans of Singapore. He was much impressed by this gesture. We must actively work on the Japanese General Staff, in order to arrive at the military agreement which alone can decide the issue with England. England is evidently not disarming. Percy Loraine[2] told a diplomat in Istambul that, when England is ready, she will destroy us and smash the Duce. He is exaggerating. And it isn't altogether necessary for us to wait for this state of perfect readiness, about which I am in any case a little sceptical. Perhaps the arms will be ready, but what about the men?

DECEMBER 2. Nothing particularly important.

[1] Alberto Perego, Italian Consul in Singapore.
[2] Sir Percy Loraine, British Ambassador in Ankara. Succeeded Lord Perth as Ambassador in Rome in May 1939.

At dinner the Duce told stories about his youth with great zest. He said that his father was fond of his debts and, even when he was able to liquidate them, he kept them, at least in part, on principle. The father's last debt was paid by the Duce two days ago.

When the Duce starts to talk, he is delightful. I know nobody who uses such rich and original metaphors.

Gave Grandi instructions to protest about some anti-Italian remarks of Sir Percy Loraine. He will have to see Chamberlain in person.

DECEMBER 3. Conversation with Bocchini. Nothing new. He is busy preparing for the visit of Stoyadinovich. There was a danger of a Croat outrage, but the man has now been identified and will be arrested. I will tell the Yugoslav Minister about this at the end of the visit.

Conversation with the Duke of Aosta. He is very conscious of the weight of his responsibilities, which is a good sign. But he still seems to me rather bewildered. He is a sympathetic man, and I wish him success with all my heart.

The Jews are flooding me with insulting anonymous letters, accusing me of having promised Hitler to persecute them. It is not true. The Germans have never mentioned this subject to us. Nor do I believe that we ought to unleash an anti-Semitic campaign in Italy. The problem doesn't exist here. There are not many Jews and, with some exceptions, there is no harm in them. And then the Jews should never be persecuted as Jews. That produces solidarity among Jews all over the world. There are so many other pretexts for attacking them. But, I repeat, the problem doesn't exist here. And perhaps in small doses Jews are necessary to society, just as leaven is necessary to bread.

DECEMBER 4. The Duce informed me of his decisions about the new building programme for the Navy. I am delighted. I have written in my own hand to Göring, who since January has been insisting on the construction of the two new 35,000-tonners.

A very interesting conversation between Grandi and Eden. I believe that really, particularly since the Tripartite Pact, London wants to come to an understanding with Berlin and is prepared even for great sacrifices. And France? In any case, in a few days we shall throw our bomb and quit Geneva. And as the Führer is pledged to announce that Germany does not intend to return to the League, the British attempt at negotiations is not going to make any headway. As far as we are concerned, I have sent Grandi instructions similar to those of last summer: either complete agreement, with recognition of the Empire, or better wait.

The Pope has given me the Piana Grand Cross. Pizzardo[1] wrote me a very affectionate letter, and I replied with equal warmth.

[1] Monsignor Giuseppe Pizzardo, Vatican Secretary for Extraordinary Affairs. He was made a cardinal a few days later.

DECEMBER 5. Neurath's meeting with Delbos at the station in Berlin is now seen in its true proportions as a purely formal gesture. The preparations for Stoyadinovich's visit are complete. He arrives at 9.50 to-night. I shall be at the station with the Duce. I have taken pains about even the smallest details of the visit. This man has shown himself a genuine friend, and I want him to have an exceptional welcome. In the first place, because I regard the Belgrade Pact[1] as fundamental for our policy. The alliance with the Slavs allows us to view with calmness the possibility of the Anschluss. After the signature the King told me that he considered this action to be the most important effected by the régime. And then I have a personal liking for Stoyadinovich. Strong, sanguine, with a resounding laugh and a vigorous handshake, he is a man who inspires confidence. He has confidence in himself and he is right. Of the politicians I have met so far in my European peregrinations he is the one who interests me most. The French and English find it hard to swallow this visit. From an intercepted telephone conversation between the British Press Attaché and a journalist it appears that the British Embassy is spreading a rumour that we mean to tie up Stoyadinovich more closely than ever with us by exploiting his weakness for pretty women. There is an element of truth in this. The Duce laughed when I told him that, besides the official receptions, I have laid on a few dances with the prettiest women in Roman society.

I informed Hotta of our new naval programme and hinted vaguely at our leaving Geneva. It is to happen on Saturday 11th.

DECEMBER 6. Very busy with S.'s visit. He had a conversation with me and afterwards with the Duce. At first he was very embarrassed. Then he relaxed and talked with his usual open frankness. The meeting between the two men went well. They have made real contact.

Anfuso contacted the French nationalists for the first time at Turin yesterday. The Duce approves of the setting up of arms depots at the frontier.

DECEMBER 7. The visit continues. Second conversation with the Duce. Minutes made of both conversations. All well.

DECEMBER 8. Visit to the towns in the Pontine Marshes.[2] Stoyadinovich enters more and more into the spirit of the thing. He is getting to like the idea of dictatorship. He has taken up the Roman salute and wears his cloak with the leather lining outside, because it is 'more military'.

[1] The Belgrade Pact, a political agreement between Italy and Yugoslavia, was signed by Ciano and Stoyadinovich on March 25, 1937.
[2] The new towns in the reclaimed Pontine Marshes, south-east of Rome, were one of the showpieces of the Fascist régime.

DECEMBER 9. Visit to Milan. The working masses, who are intelligent, appreciate the significance of the event, and gave the visitor a very warm welcome. I too was given an affectionate welcome. It is a good plan to end a foreigner's visit at Milan. He has a chance of seeing the city's ardent, creative rhythm. And then contact with the workers makes him realize that the régime has really permeated the masses and destroyed the Marxist strongholds. It made a particularly deep impression on the Yugoslav journalists, especially those of the opposition.

Parenti[1] is doing good work. He is a comrade made after the image and likeness of Starace, and for that reason admirable for the present phase of the Party. The *Podestà* is a fool who will have to be liquidated as soon as possible.

DECEMBER 10. Departure of Stoyadinovich. The net results of his trip are good. It ended this morning with a visit to the local Fascist headquarters and the laying of a wreath 'in honour of the martyrs of the Fascist Revolution'. Not bad for a Yugoslav Prime Minister! S. will go back to build up his party on the basis of a dictatorship. He has four years before the King comes of age. But even after that he will continue to exercise control in conjunction with Paul.[2] He liked the Mussolinian formula 'force and consent'. King Alexander only had force. S. wants to make his dictatorship popular. Nothing new has been put on paper. But there is now much more between the two countries than the Belgrade Pact. The conversations of the last few days have even laid the foundations of a possible alliance. An alliance which might be aimed in various directions. Possibly northwards even, one day. In the afternoon there was a shooting party at the Crespis'.[3] Back to Rome in the evening.

DECEMBER 11. Reported to the Duce on the visit to Milan. He was pleased and already sparkling in anticipation of the Grand Council to-night. I have communicated our decision to the German Chargé d'Affaires and our Embassy in Tokyo. But the news was already expected in political and journalistic circles. There has been a leakage. From what the Chief told me, the police are on the right track and actually have proofs against the culprit, who is, however, not a member of the administration. I shall find out the name from Bocchini.

Grand Council. Lasted two minutes. The Duce said that the arguments in favour of leaving Geneva are universally known. There could not be a more favourable moment than the present, if only because of Japan's crushing victory. He opened the debate. Starace proposed

---

[1] Rino Parenti, *Federale* of Milan.
[2] Prince Paul, Regent of Yugoslavia. Brother of Alexander I (murdered at Marseilles in 1934).
[3] The Crespi brothers were prominent Lombard industrialists.

approval by acclamation. I rose first, then Farinacci, Grandi, and Buffarini. Then all the rest. The Duce spoke from the Palazzo Venezia. I was expecting a stronger speech. On the contrary, it was very measured and prudent throughout. As always, the Duce is right.

DECEMBER 12. There is something like joy in the world over our decision of yesterday. Such desperately alarming rumours had been spread that many people regard our departure from Geneva as a simple administrative measure.

Talk with Grandi. I tried to cheer him up, as he was rather worried. He sees no hope of an understanding with London. I told him that on the contrary I am just as optimistic about one as I was before, and that in any case our situation allows us to contemplate even the possibility of a clash with perfect serenity. Naturally I too prefer an agreement with London. Though I fully agree with the Duce that on the historical plane a conflict between Italy and Great Britain is inevitable.

DECEMBER 13. I was cheered by the Senate when I entered the Chamber!

Conversation with the Polish Ambassador (Minute made) about the visit of Delbos to Warsaw. It was a failure.

Bocchini put me in the picture of the Engely[1] plot to prevent our leaving Geneva. A stupid, low farce, which will bring one or two people up before the Special Tribunal for the Defence of the State. I hope nobody connected with the administration will be indirectly compromised.

Received Röder.[2] He is the best of the Hungarians. I informed him of our conversations with Stoyadinovich. He is very pleased about the split between Yugoslavia and the other two states of the Little Entente. If Hungary wants a victory she should concentrate her forces against Czechoslovakia, come to a thorough understanding with Belgrade, and find a *modus vivendi* with Bucharest. I talked to him on these lines, and he expressed agreement.

DECEMBER 14. I mentioned to the Duce that Balbo had attacked the Rome-Berlin Axis at the Colonnas'. Reliable information—reported by d'Ajeta,[3] who was present. The Chief was very indignant. Then he said apropos of Balbo: 'I won't guarantee the future of that man.'

Otherwise nothing new.

DECEMBER 15. Council of Ministers for the approval of the budget. I received Balbo and asked him whether it is true that he is opposed

[1] Giovanni Engely, an Italian journalist. Rome correspondent of the Swiss Telepress Agency.
[2] General Wilhelm Röder, Hungarian Minister for War.
[3] Marchese Blasco Lanzo d'Ajeta, one of Ciano's secretaries.

to the policy of the Axis. Reluctantly he confirmed in all essentials that
he is. He says that he doesn't trust the Germans. That one day they
will let us down. That they may well turn against us. Altogether he
said a lot of commonplace things. He does this from a spirit of *fronde*.
But he took offence when I told him he is the Prince de Condé. He
didn't know who he was. A poor intellect, large ambitions, completely
treacherous, capable of anything—that is Balbo. We must keep an
eye on him.

I learnt from Delia di Bagno[1] that Balbo has advised certain people
not to go to Abyssinia because of the 'conditions of grave insecurity in
the country'.

Otherwise nothing new.

DECEMBER 16. The Japanese Ambassador expressed his regrets for
the death of Sandri.[2] I took note of the fact but made no protest. I
went so far as to say that I consider such incidents normal in the framework of a full-scale war. If the Americans don't want bombs, they
must get out. He was surprised and touched by this attitude of ours.

Engely will be arrested to-day. An S.I.M.[3] document has also
brought to light overtures made to the English Embassy by Pilotti.[4]
Bastianini is implicated too. I don't believe it. He is an ass, but loyal.
He may, however, have talked out of naïvety. At the root of many
actions you find stupidity rather than bad faith.

I mean to ask for Guido Schmidt's scalp. He has talked to the
English about the intercepts which I brought to the notice of Chancellor
Schuschnigg. This, naturally, transpires from another intercept.

I told the Egyptian Minister not to insist about the question of the
Coptic Church. Their press campaign won't alter our decisions and
will only have the effect of worsening relations between the two
countries. And, particularly for them, good relations are desirable.

DECEMBER 17. I took Viola[5] to see the Duce. The interview did
not produce any new results, except the confirmation of the withdrawal
of the volunteers on January 15, whether the battle is over or not.
Viola is hopeful about the situation—he thinks that Franco will be
loyal to us and that our credits will be repaid. As a concrete proof of
loyalty Franco ought, at the end of the war, to join the Tripartite Pact,
say good-bye to Geneva, and make a really solid pact with us, confirm-
ing the secret one of last November. Viola thinks that Franco will
agree to these requests.

[1] Wife of an official in the Foreign Ministry.
[2] Sandro Sandri, an Italian journalist killed in a Japanese air attack on the U.S.
gunboat *Panay*.
[3] *Servizio Informazioni Militari*, the Italian intelligence service.
[4] Massimo Pilotti, Deputy Secretary-General of the League of Nations, 1932–8.
[5] Count Guido Viola, Italian Ambassador to Nationalist Spain.

Van Zeeland[1] came to see me. He is in Rome for the preparation of his economic report. I wouldn't dislike him if I didn't remember that at Geneva he wanted to go as far as total sanctions. He expounded his ideas for the recovery of international trade. I replied that our economic policy had followed that of other countries. Beginning with the so-called democracies. Now other considerations, and our recent experiences, impel us to follow the path of autarky to the end. Sanctions mean something in our national life. History may be too far off to be master of our lives, but personal experience is bound to influence us.

DECEMBER 18. Birth of Marzio.[2]

I told the Czech Minister that our relations with his country depend on those between Prague and Berlin and Prague and Budapest. We ourselves have nothing either for or against the Czechs. We are not interested, except indirectly. But I want to give them a piece of advice: not to trust in collective security and not to rely on geographically distant friendships. The Minister reminded me of my predictions about China and drew a parallel.

A conversation of minor importance with Berger[3] and Villani,[4] in preparation for the meeting at Budapest, which is itself of little importance. The Rome Protocols have been superseded. I said that I should be glad if Schuschnigg were there. That is to say, I don't want Schmidt.

The economic agreement with Germany is signed. A tough negotiation—the German bureaucracy is still putting spokes in the wheels. Hassel has thrown up the sponge. Perhaps he is already aware of the torpedo coming his way. Hesse tells me that the present Ambassador in Tokyo will come here. I don't know him.

DECEMBER 19. People have tried to find a political and prophetic significance in the choice of the name Marzio, as suggesting war. But do they really think the two sides will wait for a solution for as many years as it will take for Marzio to arrive at military age? I sometimes wonder whether it isn't up to us to force the pace and put a match to the barrel ourselves. I have had telegrams of good wishes from Hitler, Göring, Hess, Stoyadinovich, Goebbels, Daranyi,[5] Kotta[6] (Albania), and others of less importance. And, in the Royal Family, from the Prince of Piedmont (most friendly), the Queen, the princesses, and the Duke of Aosta.

[1] Paul van Zeeland, former Belgian Prime Minister. He had been invited by the British and French Governments to inquire into the possibility of reducing obstacles to international trade.
[2] Ciano's second son.
[3] Egon Berger-Waldenegg, Austrian Minister in Rome.
[4] Frederick Villani, Hungarian Minister in Rome.
[5] Koloman Daranyi, Hungarian Prime Minister, 1936–8.
[6] Constantin Kotta, Albanian Prime Minister.

After Vienna, Filippo[1] is to go to Spain to carry out an inquiry into the activities of our officers, who are said to be speculating in currency and collecting valuable objects. The Italians have acquired the military spirit, but how much longer is it going to take to give them a sense of national dignity?

Mussolini was furious about the failure of the Italian Exhibition in Berlin. He said that *he* hadn't wanted it. It had taken place nevertheless and it had been a failure. 'This is the epitaph I want on my tomb,' he said. 'Here lies one of the most intelligent animals who ever appeared on the face of the earth.' The Duce is proud of his instinct, which he considers, as it has indeed shown itself to be, infallible.

DECEMBER 20. The news from Spain is not good. The Guadalajara offensive is put off indefinitely because of the spiritual vacillations of Franco's commanders and the preventive offensive of the Reds at Teruel. Our generals are restless, quite rightly. Franco has no idea of synthesis in war. His operations are those of a magnificent battalion commander. His objective is always ground, never the enemy. And he doesn't realize that it is by the destruction of the enemy that you win a war. After that it is a simple enough matter to occupy territory. Berti wants to come here for consultations. He will propose the withdrawal of a large proportion of the volunteers. After sixteen months many of them are tired. We must bear in mind that only an *élite* can understand and feel the aims of an ideological war, fought far from home, without direct or immediate profits.

Saw von Hassel in the evening. A conversation to pick up the threads after his visit to Berlin. At the end he said that his Government is preparing to withdraw him because 'the Italians are tired of him'. He had made a similar announcement yesterday to the Duce, who replied that he knew nothing about it. I did the same. Still it was a difficult situation, and the scene was a flop.

Marconi's daughter[2] came to me to ask for help for herself and her brother. They are reduced to living in a slum. Without money and without work. He must have been a great genius, but I only knew him when he had gone to pieces.

DECEMBER 21. The Duce has sent for Berti for consultations. I told him about an article in *Action Française*, in which it is said that the totalitarian states may not wait until 1941 to attack. Mussolini replied: 'As a matter of fact I am preparing a very great surprise for the Italians. As soon as Spain is finished, I shall issue an announcement which will become historic.' I remember his wanting to make a

---

[1] Filippo Anfuso.
[2] Degna Marconi, daughter by his first marriage of Guglielmo Marconi, the inventor, who died in July 1937.

surprise attack on the Home Fleet[1] at Alexandria and Malta in August 1935. He said to me then: 'In one night the course of history can be changed.' However, he didn't do it, because we had no precise information about the efficiency of the English fleet and because our Navy put on the brakes.

But ever since he has been meditating and maturing a plan of that kind.

A double conversation, at the Palazzo Venezia and the Palazzo Chigi, with Nakano, head of the Japanese Black Dragon. He was the bearer of a message from Prince Konoe[2] to the Duce. Various points were discussed in the conversation with the Duce, but interest centred on one question—relations with England. Nakano is an extremist. He says that there can never be friendship between the Japanese people and Great Britain. In her struggle in China, Japan sees as her greatest obstacle the Jewish-British plutocracy, which wants to arrest the march of the young peoples. Mussolini hinted at the possibility of closer agreements. I had myself mentioned the subject to the Military Attaché two days ago. I think we shall be able to arrive at a pact of consultation, which I regard as very valuable for our mutual interests.

Received the Foreign Press Directorate. They want to improve the information service.

DECEMBER 22. Took Mizzi[3] to see the Duce. A very pessimistic picture of the situation in Malta. The British policy of denationalization is being intensified—time is against us. Large-scale British military preparations. Mizzi is convinced that Great Britain is preparing to have her revenge in a second round as soon as possible.

Lady Chamberlain[4] sang a very different tune to me at lunch. Understanding, agreement, friendship. I replied that for our part we are ready—the most complete agreement, without a shadow, and meant to last. Otherwise, better wait for favourable conditions to ripen. Meanwhile Eden's speeches of yesterday and the day before have not been very encouraging from the point of view of reopening negotiations. Though I didn't say so, it is my opinion that we had better sharpen our swords. Lady Chamberlain wears the Fascist badge. I am too much of a patriot to appreciate such a gesture from an Englishwoman at the present moment.

---

[1] Home Fleet, in English in the original. In fact no units of the Home Fleet were in the Mediterranean at this time, when it was already clear that an Italian invasion of Abyssinia was imminent. The Mediterranean Fleet moved from Malta to Alexandria towards the end of August.

[2] Prince Fumimaro Konoe, Japanese Prime Minister.

[3] Enrico Mizzi, leader of the Italian Nationalist party in Malta.

[4] Lady (Ivy) Chamberlain, widow of Sir Austen Chamberlain, half-brother of Neville Chamberlain and former Foreign Secretary.

DECEMBER 23. I got tough with the Greek Minister. We have had a copy of the conversation between Eden and the King of Greece. After his visit to Rome he went to London and incited the English to attack us. He spoke ill of me and called me, ironically, the super-Metternich. The Greeks of the Dodecanese *will pay for this.*

With the King for the signing of papers. He talked mostly about the various sovereigns who have visited him during his long reign, describing in lively words several Oriental potentates who distinguished themselves by their ludicrous behaviour. The King is a very interesting and agreeable conversationalist. Occasionally he makes the mistake of going into too much detail—this lowers and deadens the tone of the conversation.

The Duce is anxious about Spain. Without over-estimating the Red action against Teruel, he believes, rightly enough, that it will have the effect of raising Red morale. He said that the Spaniards, thanks to their Arab descent, don't understand war on a large scale—they have no idea of synthesis and make war as individuals, in patrols or at most in tribes.

Long conversation with three leaders of the Falange. They don't think the Teruel situation is very important. They believe that in a few months the revolution may emerge into complete victory. They are monarchists. Anti-British. They talk of recovering Gibraltar and say that from the time of Philip the Second onwards all Spain's miseries have had an English trademark. I did not fail to encourage them on this wise path and warned them of the dangerous Anglomania of a few old stagers of diplomacy. They know whom I mean and they are keeping an eye on them. Number one is Sangroniz.

DECEMBER 24. The anti-Italian offensive is in full swing again in London. Crolla's[1] conversation with Eden has also been without significance or results. The Duce is calm. He showed me this morning the new programme for rearmament in the air—in June we shall be building 300 aircraft a month and we shall have a fleet of 3,000. We must tighten our belt and arm. Everything suggests that the struggle is inevitable. In that case we must not lose our greatest advantage—the initiative.

I have made Pignatti[2] raise with Pacelli[3] the subject of Cardinal Verdier's[4] pro-Communist attitude. The Church is too equivocal in certain of its contacts with the left. I am aware of the difficulties created by the clash with Germany, but the Vatican goes too far and jeopardizes its relations with us. Mussolini says he is ready to break

---

[1] Guido Crolla, Counsellor at the Italian Embassy in London.
[2] Count Bonifacio Pignatti Morano di Custoza, Italian Ambassador to the Holy See.
[3] Cardinal Eugenio Pacelli, Vatican Secretary of State. The present Pope Pius XII.
[4] Cardinal Jean Verdier, Archbishop of Paris.

a few bludgeons on the backsides of the priests. He also says that for us that is not difficult, as the Italian people are not religious. They are merely superstitious.

Anfuso is back from Vienna and has reported on his conversation with Schuschnigg. Schuschnigg tried to shield Schmidt, saying that he knew of Schmidt's letter to Vansittart,[1] which did not, however, betray our secret service. He again affirms that Schmidt is our friend and is trying to save Schmidt's head. He will talk to me about it at Budapest. It seems that ever since our denunciation Schmidt has become neurasthenic. He can't understand how we have so many English documents.

DECEMBER 25. Not a peaceful Christmas. At the Duce's orders I sent for the Japanese Ambassador and addressed him as follows: 'Moderate your behaviour with Washington, be rougher towards London. For two reasons. First, to separate London from America. Secondly, because, in the event of a conflict with the United States, we could do nothing concrete for you, while in case of war with Great Britain we pledge ourselves to give you the greatest possible positive assistance.' The Ambassador, a career diplomat and therefore prudent, reserved, and God-fearing, was left a little disturbed by this announcement. He was already at lunch when I sent for him, and arrived smelling of tangerine. I fear I must have disturbed his digestion.

I have prepared a telegram for Auriti,[2] to keep him informed, but I haven't dared send it yet. You never know with cipher. We are reading everything the English send—are we to believe that other people are less good at the game than we are? Anyhow, even if they are, one should always be on one's guard. Suetonius says you should regard your opponent as an elephant, even if you know very well he is only a flea.

DECEMBER 26. I was right not to send the telegram. Tokyo, or rather the Gaimu-sho,[3] has let us down. So has Berlin. Contrary to everything we had been given to understand, Hirota[4] has entrusted the Germans with a message for Chiang Kai-shek, containing terms of peace. We are only informed two days later and the explanation given is that our bad relations with China make us unsuitable to act as peacemakers. But it is just because of our loyalty to the Japanese that our relations with China are bad! I sent for Hassel and Hotta and told them that we intend to participate in the next phase of the negotiations. Hassel said that it was the intention of his Government that we should. But at bottom he was pleased at the contretemps—every time there is

[1] Sir Robert Vansittart (now Lord Vansittart), Permanent Under-Secretary at the Foreign Office.
[2] Giacinto Auriti, Italian Ambassador in Tokyo.
[3] Gaimu-sho, the Japanese Foreign Office.
[4] Koki Hirota, Japanese Foreign Minister.

friction between us and Berlin, he is delighted. Hotta, who has been a witness of our undeviating and uncompromising pro-Japanese policy, was humiliated by what has happened. He even talked of resigning. He will telegraph to his Government in strong terms. But in Tokyo too the Foreign Ministry is not up to the level of the times. Japan is making heroic history, and her diplomats are carrying on petty chancery intrigues. I can imagine the Butis, Vitettis,[1] Cerrutis, etc., of Japan trembling as ours were here at the time of the Abyssinian enterprise, and as they still are every time Mussolini's heroic impetus overthrows one of the traditional positions of professional diplomacy.

I have had the shiploads of arms being sent by Guarneri to China confiscated. I am against this sending arms—you can't sit on both sides of the fence, and the damage done by certain things getting known is much more serious than the profit of gaining a few millions.

DECEMBER 27. I have stopped the ships containing war material sold to China by Guarneri against my advice. You can't sit on both sides of the fence. The Japanese have got to know of it.

Berti has arrived. He gave me a not very clear account of the situation, from which, however, one thing emerges—he is anxious to liquidate the Corps of Volunteer Troops. I say nothing of other reasons, but there is one which is certainly impressive—we can't gamble Italy's prestige on twenty battalions of infantry. He makes the usual points against the Spaniards—lack of unity in command, inadequate co-ordination, no bite, and no anxiety to finish the campaign.

To-morrow we go to the Duce together. The Duce will hear what I have to say and make a decision. I wonder, however, whether after all the efforts we have made and the sacrifices we have endured we ought to withdraw just when the little check at Teruel has made Franco's star less bright than it was two months ago. Shan't we take upon ourselves the responsibility for a failure of the Whites? And put new heart into the Reds and those who are supplying and supporting them? And perhaps give the Spaniards themselves a chance of liquidating too cheaply the debt of gratitude which they feel, and should feel, towards us? The Duce will answer these questions to-morrow. The problem merits the most careful consideration. Every decision has its unfavourable aspect. This Spanish business is long and burdensome.

DECEMBER 28. I have thought a lot about yesterday's conversation with Berti. I get the impression that he is out of his depth. He doesn't believe in the Spanish enterprise, and lack of faith is the first factor in failure. I talked to Pariani, who shares my point of view. He too

[1] Leonardo Vitetti, Director-General of General Affairs at the Foreign Ministry.

thinks we can't withdraw now. He believes we should replace Berti by Frusci.[1] I reported my conversations to the Duce and expounded my opinion in favour of staying in Spain. To the arguments I noted yesterday I added that our voluntary withdrawal would encourage and confirm those who say that Italy is exhausted and can't stand any further military efforts. That would be most serious—as regards both friends and enemies.

In the four-sided conversation (Duce-Ciano-Pariani-Berti) we heard once again Berti's arguments for withdrawing our troops. The Duce opposed him. He agreed with me on all points. So we are to stay in Spain. Only the Duce will write a letter to Franco to impress upon him that time is a factor of the first importance for us and that we cannot continue to be tied up in a war which drags on for ever. He must work for a speedy conclusion—a military conclusion, without relying too much on an internal collapse of Red Spain. There will be another meeting of the four of us at the Palazzo Venezia to-morrow morning.

Received von Hassel. I announced to him the confiscation of an anti-German publication and at the same time asked for measures to be taken about a recently published book which is disrespectful towards our army.

As head of the Military Mission to Bolivia they have appointed a colonel five foot high and as round as a ball! It makes me angry. Why do soldiers fail to understand certain things?

DECEMBER 29. Yesterday afternoon the Duce again summoned me, Pariani, and Berti to the Palazzo Venezia and gave Berti his written instructions for Spain. The chief points are: our troops will stay in Spain until victory; they are not to be frittered away but used for decisive action; unity of command is essential. I have informed the Germans of all this and asked them to make a common approach to Franco with us. At the Duce's orders I sent for Berti to the Palazzo Chigi and asked him bluntly in the presence of Pariani whether he wanted to command the Volunteer Corps and lead it into battle. After a lot of chatter he finally said he did. But afterwards he asked to see me again and said that in a fortnight he will send a report on the basis of which we can decide. He does not really believe in the cause—personally I think he ought to be replaced.

The government crisis in Roumania is good. Another country is moving in our direction. The French system of alliances has been blown to bits. That happened on the day I signed the Belgrade Pact. I have drafted a pro-Roumanian *Informazione Diplomatica*, and telegraphed Sola[2] instructions for a progressive *rapprochement*. All this is good as regards the Hungarians too, who have occasional pro-British backslidings.

[1] General Luigi Frusci, an Italian commander in Spain.
[2] Ugo Sola, Italian Minister in Bucharest.

Conversation with Giovanni Preziosi.[1] He wanted my support in organizing an anti-Semitic campaign, but I refused. I have no love for the Jews, but I see no case for action of this kind in Italy. At least not for the present.

DECEMBER 30. Berti had been anxious to give orders for our troops to go into reserve. The Spanish Command is, quite rightly, against this. I have telegraphed to Frusci to do nothing until Berti arrives, which will be to-morrow evening. The Nationalist offensive on Teruel has begun and may lead up to the great battle. Is it really necessary to pull out at this moment?

Micesco, the new Roumanian Foreign Minister, has sent me a very friendly telegram. A clear sign of his intentions.

Conversation with Count Bethlen,[2] who is passing through Rome. Energetic, incisive, a man used to command. We surveyed the European scene, pausing over the Danube and the Balkans. He was anxious to know the true state of our relations with London. He thinks peace between Italy and England would facilitate the solution of the problems of Central Europe. I told him calmly and coldly what our intentions are: peace, if possible; war, if necessary. The Hungarians receive every sort of kindness at our hands—rather with the air of condescension of a decayed aristocrat—but they don't fully realize yet how powerful we are and they have sentimental leanings towards London, produced by two powerful influences: Jewishness and snobbery. I told Bethlen that the democracies will give Hungary nothing beyond fine words.

DECEMBER 31. The offensive in Spain is going well. I telephoned Pariani to ask whether he doesn't think it worth while stimulating Berti to move up our divisions to the front as well, in order to exploit the success. Our aircraft in the Balearic Islands have been reinforced and have orders to hurl tons of high explosive on the area behind Teruel and on the coastal cities, to lower the morale of the Reds.

The Duce in a good mood. He asked Valle,[3] in my presence, the strength of the Air Force. During the year 3,000 machines according to programme, plus 750 extra. He said to me that at this rate, if the English don't come to terms, the day of that famous announcement of his may not be far off.

I made a protest to the Norwegian Minister about the telegram sent by his King to the Negus. I said that such a gesture is bound seriously to compromise relations between our two countries. He knew

[1] Giovanni Preziosi, editor of the anti-Semitic review *La Vita Italiana*. A renegade priest.

[2] Count Istvan Bethlen, former Hungarian Prime Minister.

[3] General Giuseppe Valle, Under-Secretary for Air (the Minister was Mussolini) and Chief of Air Staff.

nothing about it and showed no interest. All he did was to spit copiously. I was not tempted to prolong the conversation. He is an old man of seventy, who preserves traces of a quite remarkable stupidity.

A long conversation with Bigliardi.[1] He talked about the state of mind of the Navy—very calm and full of confidence in the Government's policy. No anxiety at the thought of a clash with the English. On the contrary. . . . The new naval construction programme has been welcomed with joy in our wardrooms. It has got about that I am a supporter of this new programme, and this has increased my popularity, which is, according to Bigliardi, very widespread in the Navy.

[1] Candido Bigliardi, a senior naval officer.

PART II

JANUARY 1, 1938 – APRIL 30, 1938

THE ANSCHLUSS
AND THE ANGLO-ITALIAN AGREEMENT

JANUARY 1, 1938–APRIL 30, 1938

THE ANSCHLUSS
AND THE ANGLO-ITALIAN AGREEMENT

Capture of Teruel—Arms for China—Air raids in Spain—Friction with the Vatican—Von Hassel in disfavour—Ciano confers with the Rome Protocols states in Budapest (January 9-13)—Teruel retaken by the Reds—Subhas Chandra Bose—Radio Bari—The parade step —Mussolini spurs on Franco—Nationalist offensive in Spain—Grandi talks to Eden—Schuschnigg at Berchtesgaden (February 12)— Butenko—Mussolini on the Berchtesgaden Agreement—Italy and Yugoslavia—Grandi sees Chamberlain—Eden resigns (February 20) —Teruel retaken by the Nationalists—Schuschnigg's speech—Death of D'Annunzio—Beck in Rome—Preliminary conversation with Perth—Advance in Spain—The Germans occupy Austria (March 12)—The Duce addresses the Chamber—Negotiations with Perth begin—Thoughts on Albania—The question of Italian troops in Libya—German propaganda in South Tyrol—The League and the recognition of the Italian Empire—Agreement with England— Mussolini receives Perth—The Pact signed (April 16)—The French propose negotiations—More trouble in South Tyrol—Capture of Tortosa—Hore-Belisha in Rome—Ciano in Tirana for the marriage of King Zog (April 25-9)—Report on Albania.

JANUARY 1. Conversation with Lady Chamberlain in the morning. She showed me a letter from her brother-in-law. Nothing new, simply the old complaints about the anti-British propaganda of Radio Bari and the Italian press and a reaffirmation of general goodwill for negotiations with us. We shall see. . . .

In the afternoon I talked to von Hassel, who informed me of various new points in the message which Trautmann[1] is to convey to the Chinese Government on behalf of Japan. It is really only a question of clarification. I took the opportunity of telling von Hassel that Trautmann is not behaving well towards our officials in China. He makes a point of remaining aloof from them. Evidently he hasn't entered into the spirit of the Axis. I am not surprised—he is a career diplomat, of moderate abilities and sombre character. I remember what an anti-Nazi he was in 1932, and how upset he was in 1933 when Hitler got into power.

Just after midnight to-night I was informed by telephone at home of the capture of Teruel. The year couldn't have a better beginning.

[1] Dr. Oskar Trautmann, German Ambassador to China.

57

Frusci's telegrams speak of a disorderly flight of the Reds. It is my impression that, if we go all out, we can win a big success and possibly reach the sea. That would mean the end of the war. But will the necessary drive be forthcoming?

Valle bombed Barcelona yesterday, having taken off from Monte Celio.[1] The flight lasted six hours. Why didn't he tell me? He has promised he will next time.

JANUARY 2. I had a conversation with Host Venturi[2] yesterday, to decide the fate of the *Ischia*, which has on board a cargo of armoured cars for the Chinese and is bound for Hong Kong. As for technical reasons the ship can't be diverted, we had already informed the Japanese of her position and speed, so that they could intercept her. But they didn't want to do this for fear of international incidents. They have left us free to deliver the cargo. But the Duce, who 'intends to make of the Japanese military allies against Great Britain', got me to investigate the best means of preventing the ship unloading. We decided to force her ashore on the island of Hainan. Venturi says this is a simple matter and the Duce has approved. The appropriate orders have been given.

Berti's first telegrams damp any enthusiasm for the victory of Teruel —he still foresees a strong capacity for local resistance on the part of the Reds. I believe he has the evil eye.

The Duce and I examined the agenda for the forthcoming meeting in Budapest. We shall have to demand of the Austrians and the Hungarians a greater political solidarity with us. They are, both countries, only too ready to beg, but also to make themselves scarce whenever they have to assume any responsibility on our behalf. Mussolini is annoyed. He said this morning that when the Spanish question is liquidated he will invite Göring to nazify Austria. I don't love the Austrians, but it seems to me we ought to go gently.

The running aground of the *Ischia* has been called off, as a result of conversations with Ingianni[3] and the shipbuilder Lauro,[4] who are more expert than Host Venturi and drew my attention to all the complications which might arise. I will talk to the Duce again.

JANUARY 3. Conversation with Perth, of which I made a Minute. A conversation, it seems to me, of distinct importance—it indicates that Great Britain does not want to close the door to negotiations. After Crolla's last telegram and Eden's speeches one might have imagined

---

[1] One of the seven hills of Rome.
[2] Giovanni Host Venturi, Under-Secretary for the Mercantile Marine. Minister of Communications, 1939.
[3] Giulio Ingianni, Director-General of the Mercantile Marine.
[4] Achille Lauro, shipbuilder.

that she did. If it were possible to arrive at a complete and durable agreement, then we ought to proceed. Otherwise not.

Received the Japanese Ambassador and Naval Attaché about the question of the *Ischia*. They can seize her—we shall not protest. But to sink her or run her aground would produce a dispute and perhaps an international scandal which might reflect upon our merchant marine. I didn't feel like advising the Duce to do it. If the Japanese don't seize her, she will reach Hong Kong. Fifty armoured cars are not going to change the course of the war in the Far East!

I have given Mazzolini[1] his instructions on his departure for Egypt. Besides the normal political and diplomatic activity, he is to study all possible ways of using the Italian communities in the event of war with England. A few determined action groups could, with the advantage of surprise, get the cities into a state of turmoil, create chaos in the Canal Zone, and perhaps effect military sabotage. He is neither to write nor to telephone, but to come to Italy on the pretext of leave for family reasons.

Valle came to see me about the communiqué announcing his 'raid'[2] on Barcelona. The España Agency reports sixty dead. Berti telegraphs that the Teruel offensive is finished.

I have mentioned to Jacomoni[3] the name of one of the Durini[4] girls as a wife for King Zog. He is determined to get married and he wants an Italian. But after his two unsuccessful attempts he is rather discredited here.

JANUARY 4. The Nuncio[5] spoke to me about his conversation with Buffarini. He was very alarmed, and his alarm has been passed on to the Holy See. Buffarini apparently said that the situation as regards Catholic Action[6] is becoming worse than it was in 1931. I was not in a position to confirm or deny this. But I painted for the Nuncio's benefit a picture of the Vatican's recent international activity. I am aware of the difficulties created by Germany, but they ought not to overdo their flirtations with Popular Fronts and sometimes even with the Communists. That sort of thing may make the Duce more sensitive on the score of the Catholic organizations. And the Holy See should remember that the Axis is fighting against Communism in Spain and that Spain has recently witnessed the massacre of members of the religious orders at the hands of the Reds.

[1] Count Serafino Mazzolini, recently appointed Italian Minister in Egypt.
[2] In English in the original.
[3] Francesco Jacomoni, Italian Minister in Tirana. Lieutenant-General of Albania after the Italian occupation in 1939.
[4] An aristocratic Italian family.
[5] Monsignor Francesco Borgongini-Duca, Nuncio to the Quirinal.
[6] A non-political lay organization concerned chiefly with education and social welfare.

I have sent to Vienna and Budapest the draft of an announcement
pledging the two Danubian countries to a closer adherence to the Axis
and to an anti-Comintern and anti-League policy. It is the right
moment. The Hungarians are too much afraid of a *rapprochement*
between us and Roumania to refuse. The Duce has, however, confirmed to me that he does not intend to make an agreement with the
Roumanians unless the green light shows in Budapest.

O'Kelly,[1] the Irish Vice-President. A polite and friendly little man.
He says his country's next step will be to proclaim a Republic of
Ireland. Very anti-British. I said that our two countries will grow
closer and closer to each other, both for positive and for negative
reasons.

I suggested to the Duce, who agreed, sending Paulucci de Calboli[2]
to Japan as head of the Party mission. He will be pleased. He has
always been an anti-League man and an Anglophobe—he will get on
well with the Japs.

JANUARY 5. The Duce told me about three conversations which he
had at the theatre last night. The first, of which I have made a Minute,
was with Count Bethlen, who emphasized Magyar anxieties with
respect to Germany. To a Little Entente pivoting on Berlin the
Hungarians still prefer one with its centre of gravity in Paris. Mussolini
assured him that we shall not come to an understanding with Roumania
without first getting the approval of Hungary. Bethlen was very
relieved.

Next he talked to von Hassel, who complained about his fate and
softened the Duce's heart—he has told me to intervene again in Berlin,
this time in order to save Hassel. It is not a part which I enjoy playing.
Hassel is an enemy, and I much preferred it when the Duce told me to
ask for his scalp. However, I shall talk to Hassel to-morrow and then
we shall see.

Lastly there was Perth—a brief summing-up of the position of the
two countries and a confirmation of my conversation with him on
January 3. Perth, who is an optimist, said to the Duce that we shall
see agreement before the year is out—possibly, he says, within the next
three months. When the sky turns pink. . . . But there isn't enough
pink in the sky yet to warrant such confidence in the future.

I saw Blondel on his return from leave. He says that government
circles are well disposed, but that distrust of Italy has increased among
the public.

Conversation with the Nuncio. I reassured him—nothing will be

---

[1] Sean T. O'Kelly, Vice-President of Fianna Fail and of the Executive Council
of Eire.
[2] Marchese Giacomo Paulucci di Calboli Barone, a former Under-Secretary of the
League of Nations.

done against Catholic Action. I confirmed, however, all that I had said yesterday about the danger of the Vatican's slidings towards the left.

JANUARY 6. Conversation with von Hassel. I spoke frankly. I told him what reasons we have to be dissatisfied with him—remarks he has made against Italy, and his attitude during the negotiation and the signature of the Tripartite Pact. He denied the first charge. As for the second, he said he was carrying out the instructions sent him. He says he has always been pro-Italian, even when everybody in Germany, including the Party, was against us. He added that he has always set himself to wipe out the memory of 1915 from the mind of the German people. He didn't ask for mercy or pity—if we intervene in Berlin, it must be on our own initiative and because we want to.

It seems to me best to leave him to his fate. He was an enemy in the past; he is now more than ever one. If we saved him, he would be an enemy made more bitter by gratitude. Besides, we can't disavow Hess and Hesse, who acted upon our suggestion. Hassel goes and Hess stays. Therefore I am more concerned about Hess.

Talking of Garibaldi, the Duce said: 'It was his good fortune to be uneducated. If he had been educated, he would have read Clausewitz and lost his battles.' He was in a very good temper and in the mood for paradox.

He has ordered me to liquidate Parini because of the extravagance in the administration of D.I.E.[1]

JANUARY 7. A long conversation with the King. He wanted to talk to me about the work to be done at the Palace for the occasion of Hitler's visit. He hinted at a return visit to Germany. A thorny question. The Duce doesn't care for the idea, as the visit would duplicate his. 'This is an occasion,' he has said to me, apropos of the visit, 'on which the Monarchy shows itself to be a useless superstructure.' 'The Germans,' he added, 'love me partly from Party solidarity. They don't love the King, because they remember that it was he who signed the declaration of war in 1915.' I avoided making a reply to the King— but the visit will have to be made. For reasons of etiquette, and for the sake of the King's prestige. It may, however, be deferred. The King told me not to trust the Germans—in the past Berlin has always been the most treacherous of chanceries. Austria used to be correct. He praised the personal honesty of the Liberals—in the long years of his reign there were only two exceptions, a certain Maury[2] and Nunzio Nasi.[3] He criticized the building of large ships. He doesn't believe in

---

[1] *Direzione degl' Italiani all' Estero*, the department of the Foreign Ministry concerned with the control of Italians abroad.
[2] Eugenio Maury, Under-Secretary for Posts and Telegraphs in 1909.
[3] Nunzio Nasi, Minister for Education, 1900–3. Convicted of peculation in 1908.

them—they are too vulnerable to sudden air and submarine attacks.

The Duce told me to wash my hands of von Hassel. Good. He listened to a report from Anfuso on the situation in Spain. Nothing new—great slowness of movement on the part of the Whites. It seems that Teruel has not been completely occupied, because, when the Generals reached the Archbishop's Palace, they wasted two hours dining with him.

Conversation with Miroinescu, a pro-Italian Roumanian Senator. He said that the Goga[1] Government is a government of transition and compromise as regards Codreanu[2]—a sort of von Papen Government. He thinks a *modus vivendi* with Hungary possible.

Conversation with Perth. In consequence of rumours which are circulating about the cession of Jubaland[3] to Germany, he reminded me of the 1924 Treaty, which gives Great Britain an option. I described the rumours as ridiculous and absurd. He personally thought so too.

JANUARY 8. We discussed with the Duce the Austro-Hungarian counter-proposals for the Budapest meeting. As I foresaw, they are trying to evade all responsibility *vis-à-vis* the so-called 'democracies'. On the other hand, they are trying to slip in a few words likely to disturb Germany and prevent the *rapprochement* with Roumania. The Rome Protocols are shown to be more and more impotent—agreements with a purely economic content necessarily lack profound vitality. The economic background changes too quickly—sometimes from one year to another. In Central Europe a good or bad harvest, for instance, is enough to make the difference. However, we shall see what happens at Budapest.

The Duce is anxious about the Empire—Gojjam is in revolt. The rebels number 15,000. Our garrisons are besieged. It will take two months and strong forces to suppress the movement. According to the Duce it is Pirzio Biroli[4] who is to blame, and also the lack of racial preparedness of the Italians. The behaviour of many Italians has made the natives lose their respect for the white man.

A long conversation with Starace and Buffarini about finding a successor for Colonna[5] as Governor of Rome. It seems we shall have to fall back on G. G. Borghese.[6] It is a bitter pill to swallow—his anti-Fascism is too recent. I mentioned the name of Costantino Patrizi. A bit better. . . .

---

[1] Octavian Goga, Roumanian Prime Minister, December 1937 to February 1938.
[2] Zelea Codreanu, leader of the totalitarian Iron Guard.
[3] Jubaland, formerly part of the colony of Kenya, was ceded by Great Britain to Italy in 1924 and incorporated in Italian Somaliland in 1925.
[4] Alessandro Pirzio Biroli, Governor of the Abyssinian province of Amhara.
[5] Prince Piero Colonna, Governor of Rome. He died a few months later.
[6] Prince Gian Giacomo Borghese, Prince Colonna's successor.

JANUARY 9. *En route* for Budapest. Conversation with Villani, from which I derive the conviction that I shall find the atmosphere rather clouded as far as we are concerned. We shall try to clear it up. Enthusiastic greetings at the station, in spite of the snowstorm.

JANUARY 10. The Conference began for me with two conversations, one with Schuschnigg and one with Schmidt. The principal object of the Austrians was to settle the question of the British documents relating to Schmidt's conversation with Vansittart. At first I was inflexible—though it immediately became clear that the Chancellor was not prepared to sacrifice his Secretary of State to us. There was nothing for it but to relent, but I could—and did—still drive a hard bargain before granting our pardon. In this way I had Schmidt on my side for the political negotiations. He began by revealing to me that Kanya was prepared to recognize Franco, but that he would only do so under pressure from me. The hardest thing for the Hungarians to swallow was the announcement about Geneva. On this point the Austrians were more prepared to yield. On the other hand, they wanted a declaration about the independence of Austria, which out of consideration for Germany I felt we could not make. The Hungarians asked for a declaration about minorities. This request was aimed mostly against Roumania, but, if I had agreed to it, it would have annoyed the Yugoslavs more than anybody.

JANUARY 11. That is what I wanted to avoid. Besides, this talk of minorities, without particularization, would have given the Little Entente a new motive for solidarity just at the moment when it is going through a most acute crisis. The Conference thus began in a climate which was anything but easy. There was friction on many points. I made the usual general survey, with particular reference to our relations with England. This was a subject which particularly worried Kanya. I gave a mildly optimistic flavour to my report—it was absolutely necessary not to alarm the Conference, if I wanted to secure explicit adherence to our policy. Kanya spoke very bitterly about the Little Entente and about the men at the head of the three states. He said that Goga is a double deserter and described Stoyadinovich as a Balkan ruffian. I protested and declared that we in Italy have no reason to complain of the policy of Belgrade. Kanya has a mania about the Little Entente. Especially Roumania. When he wants to insult or disparage, he says 'like a Roumanian', or 'as thievish as a Roumanian', or 'almost as much a liar as a Roumanian'. He is always using expressions like that.

JANUARY 12. In order to arrive at a positive result for the tripartite declaration, I was eventually obliged to use a firm hand. Then they gave way. They virtually accepted all the formulas I proposed, with a few alterations, suggested by them, which, in my opinion, strengthen rather than weaken the document. The negotiations took place in Daranyi's room in the Prime Minister's mansion, with a large portrait in oils of the young Franz Joseph in 1848 on the wall. How history has changed in ninety years!

I found in Hungary an atmosphere on the whole favourable to us among the people and among the young. Those who belong to the past, and there are many of them—Kanya is perhaps typical—do not love us. They share the view of a Princess Esterhazy, the wife of an ex-Prime Minister, who told me quite bluntly at dinner that we Italians were more responsible than anyone else for the mutilation of Hungary, and that, while it is easy enough to pull a country to pieces, it is very difficult to put it together again!

JANUARY 13. But the young are not like that. They love Italy because of her warlike courage and because of her social justice. Feudal Hungary, the Hungary of the great landowners, cannot welcome the advent of a régime which seriously and profoundly improves the condition of the masses.

Turul, a Nationalist youth organization, wanted to appoint me its Grand Master as successor to Gömbös.[1] The Government opposed this on the pretext that it might offend, of all people, Schuschnigg. They will appoint me when there is another opportunity soon. There was also an interesting demonstration at the theatre. When I rose to leave, the entire military college, *although orders had been given not to make any kind of demonstration*, rose to their feet and gave the Roman salute. A clear sign of the times. The return journey went well. Many courtesies from the Yugoslavs. A warm welcome at Trieste. The Budapest Conference has had a good reception in Italy. The Duce sent me a telephone message expressing his satisfaction. That is the reward which counts most.

JANUARY 14. I reported to the Duce on my visit to Budapest. He is pleased with the results and repeated his congratulations.

He was not so irritated as I expected to find him over the capture of Teruel. He regards it as a local success for the Reds of slight importance—to have checked the advance on Madrid seems to him of more significance from the strategic point of view. He would like to have more definite knowledge of Franco's plans. He is also talking of the possibility of a landing at Valencia, to take the Reds in the rear. France and England wouldn't make a move. But to do this it would be necessary to know what is in Franco's mind and to have precise guarantees, perhaps even of a territorial nature. I did not conceal my anxiety. I consider that during the winter the Reds have strengthened

[1] Gyula Gömbös, former Hungarian Prime Minister. Died in 1936.

their position. I should not be surprised by an offensive in the near future which might push back the whole Nationalist front. What would happen then to our thirty thousand men in the interior of Spain?

The present position is, in my opinion, untenable. We must make up our minds—either we strike the blow which will precipitate the crisis, or we skilfully disengage ourselves and rest content with having inscribed upon our banners the names of the victories of Malaga and Santander.

JANUARY 19.[1] Nothing important in the morning. Several minor interviews.

In the afternoon I received Munters, the Latvian Foreign Minister. Not a very significant figure. He claims to be the representative of a Fascist Government, but at heart he is democratic and pro-League. The secret of Geneva, as far as little countries are concerned, is that it serves for their politicians as a stage lit by the spotlights of world publicity. Munters was overjoyed to be able to say that he knows all the more or less great ones of the earth. He drank to the 'King Emperor'. This is a species of recognition of the Empire, slightly disguised but definitely useful as a way of shaking these little northern states.

JANUARY 20. Bose,[2] the leader of the Indian Congress Party, talked to me at length about his party's position. Hitherto they have not been able to accomplish much. Great Britain, from the centre, exercises supreme power. In the provinces a few unimportant departments have been entrusted to Indians. Great Britain has excellent agents in the large and small states, which are governed despotically and rely upon British troops for support. The programme of the Congress Party is the independence of India. The means by which they hope to achieve it are obstructionism and passive resistance. No armed struggle. All they ask of us is to continue to keep Great Britain worried about our intentions and from time to time to inform them about the general political situation. This is to enable them better to orientate themselves. I for my part suggested to Bose that he should direct his Indian sympathies towards Italy and Japan—the two countries which have done most to impair British prestige. He said he will try—but it will be difficult, because the Indian people are governed by sentiment and therefore support China to-day, just as they supported Abyssinia. Personally, from my fleeting visits to India, I have formed the opinion that they are a flabby people, incapable of strong reactions, and that they

---

[1] The leaves for January 15 to 18 are missing from the diary.

[2] Subhas Chandra Bose. In 1942 he formed a Free Indian Government in Singapore which was recognized by the Axis powers. Reported killed in a flying accident in August 1945.

will not get independence until other forces bring about the collapse of Great Britain. And perhaps even then the country will only get a new master.

Meeting of the Committee for the Führer's visit.

JANUARY 23.[1] Nothing new. Sunday at the sea.

JANUARY 24. I am more and more worried about the situation in Spain. The offensive towards Teruel, which should have begun to-day, has been postponed again. I indicated to the Duce that a conversation with Franco might be necessary. We could get him to come to Cagliari by sea and the two of us, Mussolini and I, could meet him there. I think a meeting would clear up our doubts about his intentions and his potentialities and would help us to fix the lines of our policy. For we really must make a decision about Spain.

As there is a lot of talk at the moment about a wireless war with Great Britain, I want to put on record the origin of Radio Bari's Arabic broadcasts. When I was Under-Secretary for Propaganda I was asked to do something for an Italo-Arab, the brother of a bishop, Monsignor Cattan. I took him on at the Ministry and, as he spoke Arabic well, we got him to give a lecture and a news broadcast or two. The thing was a success—letters began to pour in from Palestine, Syria, Egypt— and we developed it. Then we had to dismiss Cattan because, on his own initiative, he was insulting the English, with whom we were then on good terms. But in view of the programme's success I didn't want to stop it and it was continued after Cattan had left. I did not, however, realize that I was striking such a resounding new note of discord with England.

JANUARY 25. A very quiet day.

Conversation with Ruegger,[2] with special reference to the attacks of the Swiss press. Ruegger points out that the papers concerned belong to the extreme left and hate Motta[3] and his Government. He asks us not to exaggerate their importance.

In Spain the Reds have attacked again and the offensive on Teruel is consequently postponed once more.

JANUARY 26. Nothing important has happened.

I was interested by a report from Galli about a conversation with Aras,[4] in the course of which they examined the possible forms which a war in the Mediterranean might take. Galli emphasizes the possibility of Turkish troops being sent to Egypt to defend the Canal, in view of the fact that Great Britain would never be able to raise a large

---

[1] The leaf for January 21 and 22 is missing from the diary.
[2] Paul Ruegger, Swiss Minister in Rome.
[3] Giuseppe Motta, Swiss President and Foreign Minister.
[4] Tewfik Rüstü Aras, Turkish Foreign Minister.

army. It is a new and interesting hypothesis, which I shall mention to the General Staff.

Marzio was baptized by Monsignor Celso Costantini. He received the water and the salt in religious silence, without a tear, which the experts say is almost a miracle.

Hassel went off on so-called leave this morning—an unspeeded guest. I heard this last night from his daughter, who also told me that von Neurath was furious that Hassel had managed to have explanations with the Duce and with me.

JANUARY 29.[1] The Duce is preparing to write a letter to Franco, to stimulate him to do something decisive. I encouraged him to do this. We must get to the end of the Spanish adventure.

Nothing else.

JANUARY 30. No events worth noting.

I have advised the Duce not to let Biseo continue his flight to Argentina, where some kind of hostile demonstration against our airmen was being prepared. There is really no point in exposing equipment and men to the not inconsiderable wear and tear of a three thousand kilometres' flight, in order to give the rabble of a second-class country like Argentina a chance to insult us. The Duce agrees—they will not go. Of all the countries in which I have lived Argentina is certainly the one I loved least—indeed I felt a profound contempt for it. A people without a soul and a land without colour—both failed to exercise any kind of charm on me. For several decades, when all sorts of human wrecks were making their way to South America, the worst of all used to stop at the first place they came to. That was the beginning of Buenos Aires, a city as monotonous and turbid as the river on whose banks it lies. In recent years there has been added to this unpleasant mixture a very plentiful Jewish element. I don't believe that can have improved things.

JANUARY 31. As was to be expected, criticisms of the parade step[2] have started up. The old soldiers are particularly against it, because they choose to regard it as a Prussian invention. The Duce is very angry—he has read me the speech he is going to make to-morrow, explaining and extolling the innovation. It seems that the King too has expressed himself unfavourably. The Duce's comment was: 'It is not my fault if the King is half size. Naturally he won't be able to do the parade step without making himself ridiculous. He will hate it for the same reason that he has always hated horses—he has to use a ladder to climb on to one. But a physical defect in a sovereign is not a good

---

[1] The leaf for January 27 and 28 is missing from the diary.

[2] The parade step or 'Roman step', closely resembling the German goose-step, was introduced by Mussolini after his visit to Germany in September 1937.

reason for stunting, as he has done, the army of a great nation.'
'People say the goose-step is Prussian. Nonsense. The goose is a
Roman animal—it saved the Capitol. Its place is with the eagle and
the she-wolf.'

The Duce has drafted a strong letter to Franco. As Berti will be here
to-morrow, I advised him to have a talk with him before deciding
whether to send it or not.

Renato Ricci is worried about the Carrara marble, now that France
has put on prohibitive duties. Germany, once a large buyer, has closed
her markets. A new marble crisis seems to be on the way.

FEBRUARY 1. A Militia review—the parade step appeared in public
and was much applauded. The Duce addressed the Militia opposite
the Colosseum. He spoke in military fashion, lashing out at the mur-
murers, whom he described as sedentary, paunchy, mentally deficient,
and half-sized. I recognized the allusion, but Badoglio and De Bono[1]
thought he meant them and looked very sour. Particularly De Bono,
who said that after such a speech he had no alternative but to retire.

I took Lady Chamberlain to see the Duce, and she showed him an
important letter from Neville Chamberlain. Two points: Great
Britain is coming round to the idea of a formal recognition of the
Empire; conversations can begin at the end of the month. Mussolini
approved and agreed. Lady Chamberlain will write to her brother-in-
law to inform him of the Duce's reactions, which were definitely
favourable. He showed himself in full sympathy with the project of an
agreement and said that he intends to make one which will be complete
and durable and able to serve as a basis for co-operation between the
two Empires. He dictated to Lady Chamberlain the terms of her letter.

FEBRUARY 2. The Duce had a talk with Berti in my presence.
Berti, who has no power of synthesis and always seems to be gloomy,
had nothing new to say. A sea of futile verbiage and in the midst of it
a few ideas, which we all know by heart, about the inconclusive
character of Spanish generalship. The Duce gave him his letter to
Franco. An admirable, virile document—it reinforces our obligations
if Franco means to fight, but opens the way for us to disengage ourselves
if the Generalissimo is going to insist on a long-drawn war of nerves.

Meanwhile Mussolini has intensified the air raids on the coast, which
are breaking the nerve of the civil population. Information from several
sources indicates that the Red communications are in a very bad state.
A blow from ten Nationalist divisions would be enough. But is Franco
intelligent enough or strong enough to strike? I told the Duce of the
impression made by his military oratory yesterday. He is pleased. He

---

[1] Marshal Emilio de Bono, Quadrumvir of the March on Rome. Executed by the
Badoglio Government in January 1944.

loves a soldier's style, like steel, and has more and more made it his own. Besides, he regards the Italian people as a very tough people, fundamentally dramatic. Perhaps sad too, like Italian songs. Our reputation has been ruined abroad, he says, by Neapolitan singing and dancing.

Conversation with the American Ambassador. He is afraid of war, but I reassured him considerably.

Conversation with the Japanese Ambassador. He told me that the Japanese are beginning to form a series of local governments of a provisional character in China, but that they will end by establishing themselves there permanently.

FEBRUARY 3. Conversation with General Aymonino[1] to settle about the Führer's visit to the Prince of Piedmont. I shall meet H.R.H. when he returns to Rome, and arrange the details with him.

I received Lady Listowel, the wife of a Labour Lord. She is a Hungarian of some charm, appears to be our friend and speaks Italian well. She says that 'feeling'[2] in England is rising against us and that, when rearmament has been completed, there will be a blaze of red-hot nationalist propaganda and we must not be surprised if the English attack us. This is much more likely to happen, if Eden should ever become the head of a Labour-Liberal Government.

Conversation with the Duce and Magistrati. Massimo made light of Germany's flirtation with France and gave an account of a conversation he had had with Göring, in which the latter said that the Nazis want to raise Germany's potential as high as possible and, for this reason, to avoid a war for several years. With this end in view the ball of steel must be given a covering of soft rubber. Anyone coming near now sees and feels the rubber—when the ball is fired, it will be the steel which will strike. Mussolini was interested. He would like at an early opportunity to interrogate Germany about her attitude in the event of an isolated war between Great Britain and us. He said once more that he regards war as inevitable—therefore he does not want to lose the advantage of the initiative. He is satisfied if Germany remains a benevolent neutral.

Bonmartini,[3] who has bought the *Giornale d'Italia*, came with an offer to put it completely at my disposal. He hates Balbo with all his heart. He is, however, an insignificant individual.

FEBRUARY 4. We have agreed to Eden's requests for a stricter surveillance of the Mediterranean in the campaign against piracy. These measures are simply a waste of time.

[1] General Aldo Aymonino, Adjutant to the Prince of Piedmont.
[2] In English in the original.
[3] Bonmartini, an industrialist.

I put before the Duce the plans for the embellishment of Rome for the Führer's visit. He liked them and approved the work that has been done so far.

Meeting of the Supreme Committee of Defence.

Conversation with Lord Lothian,[1] Under-Secretary for the Colonies, on his way back from India. At his request I explained to him our point of view on the possibility of an understanding with England. He seemed to me a sensible man. He approved of the idea of a comprehensive agreement, to include recognition of the Empire. 'Between England and Italy,' he said, 'there can be no half measures—nothing except a return to the traditional friendship or war.' I replied that I agreed. Except that it is no use speaking of the traditional friendship —the understanding must have new foundations which will fully take into account the new power of Italy.

Giacomo Costa, an anti-Fascist lawyer who escaped from Lipari[2] two months ago, has offered us his services as an informer and *agent provocateur* among the *émigrés* in Paris. He is in contact with the journalist Pascazio.[3] We shall use him.

FEBRUARY 5. The changes in the German Government are good. They are making rapid strides towards total nazification, and this is beneficial to the Axis, as one of the strongest reasons for its existence is the identity of régime. The Duce too is very pleased—it is an important event and it gives a knock-out blow to the recent period of flirtation with France. Ribbentrop at the Foreign Ministry is admirable. His conversations with the Duce and with me in October and November last made clear his hostility to the English, who have treated him badly. London was failure for him, Rome success. He made good his claim to the Minister's epaulettes in the Hall of Victory on the day when the Tripartite Pact was signed. I foresee a strengthening of the Axis and the Triangle as a result of what has happened. We shall reach closer and more concrete agreements and we may be able to think of a Conference of the three Foreign Ministers, which might perhaps take place in Addis Ababa.

I have appointed Pavolini President of the Institute for International Trade. He will do well and he is reliable.

Baistrocchi[4] is putting himself forward as a candidate for Commissioner of Munitions, to replace Dall' Olio,[5] who is exhausted. At a meeting of the Supreme Committee Balbo had spoken to me of General Gazzera[6] as a possible successor. I did not lose the opportunity of

[1] Lord Lothian, a former Under-Secretary for India, held no Cabinet office in 1938.
[2] Lipari, an island near the toe of Italy, on which political prisoners were confined.
[3] Nicola Pascazio, a Fascist journalist.
[4] General Federico Baistrocchi, Under-Secretary for War, 1933–6.
[5] General Alfredo Dall' Olio, Commissioner for Munitions, 1935–9.
[6] General Pietro Gazzera, Governor of Jimma in Abyssinia.

mentioning this to Baistrocchi, who, it is well known, hates Gazzera. He is now, I think, not too fond of Balbo either.

FEBRUARY 6. Our compliance with the British requests about piracy has produced a certain *détente* in London. Eden has used calmer language to Grandi and has made a statement to the *Sunday Times* about Anglo-Italian relations—the truth is that it is a very hypocritical statement. I have told the journalists not to make too much of it. I believe it is not so much our compliance as the new German Government which has impressed London.

Franco's offensive in the direction of Teruel has begun. Berti telegraphs that it is making good progress and makes no criticisms of any kind. This leads me to believe that things really are going well. We shall see! Recent events, as well as past history, discourage one from being too optimistic when Spanish generals are in charge.

A long conversation with the Duce. I told him of the pessimism of Guarneri, who said in so many words after the Defence Committee yesterday: 'We are bankrupt.' The Duce knew of this and he does not at all share these exaggerated fears. The situation is really very healthy. We also talked about the Jewish problem. I expressed myself in favour of a solution which will not raise a problem which fortunately does not exist here. The Duce is of the same opinion. He will pour water on the flames, though not enough to suppress the thing altogether.

FEBRUARY 7. Grandi has started off in top gear after his talks with Eden, and wants authorization to begin the conversations. I have drafted with my own hand a telegram, which I read to the Duce, recommending calm and prudence in face of this British zeal for reconciliation, which might after all be a manœuvre of Eden's, now that the change of guard in Germany has shown that the English efforts to weaken the Axis at the Berlin end are not destined to succeed. Calm and prudence—and in any case the conversations must be in Rome. Grandi is trying to push himself forward. He would like to play the part of the man who made peace with England, a part which probably appeals to plenty of Italians. But it won't do. Peace and war are in the grasp of Mussolini and of Mussolini alone. No one is allowed to play a personal role.

I told the Duce of Baistrocchi's wish to succeed Dall' Olio, who is very old and ill. The Duce said he will only appoint his successor 'when he is in his coffin'. He seemed rather sceptical about the name of Baistrocchi, who is active but a muddler.

Philip of Hesse is very pleased with the changes in Berlin. He tells me that Neurath and Ribbentrop knew nothing about them a few hours before.

Good news from Spain. An important break-through has been

effected by three Nationalist columns in the Teruel sector. The advance continues.

FEBRUARY 8. After a further bound the advance now seems to have been checked. With the Spaniards, this is not surprising. We have asked Berti whether the objectives of the present action are tactical or strategic, as, if they are strategic, the Duce intends to resume the air raids on the coastal cities in order to break Red resistance. I have received and passed to the Duce an eyewitness account of the recent bombing of Barcelona. I have never read a document so realistically horrifying. And yet there were only nine S.79s and the whole 'raid'[1] only lasted a minute and a half. Large buildings demolished, traffic interrupted, panic on the verge of madness, and 500 dead and 1,500 wounded. It is a good lesson for the future. It is useless to think of anti-aircraft defence and building shelters—the only method of salvation from air attack is the evacuation of large towns.

I have sent a telegram to Berlin to put an end to speculation about the so-called Anglo-Italian *rapprochement*. Our policy follows and will continue to follow an absolutely straight line. The Führer should bear this in mind in his speech of February 20. I said this in my telegram to Attolico.

FEBRUARY 9. According to Berti's reports the Spaniards have stopped in order to prepare a second wave. The pause ought to be short. The victory just won seems to be important, though only on a tactical level and therefore not decisive.

The press is attempting to speculate about the conversations between Grandi and Eden and, contrary to the facts, to infer an Italian initiative. I have drafted *Informazione Diplomatica* No. 14, which I have passed to the Duce, and I have had the Rome *Piccolo* confiscated, as in spite of the prohibition it continued to build up the reports of the London conversations with huge headlines.

Grandi has telephoned to me—after reading my telegram of the day before yesterday he is beginning to mark time. There is, however, no doubt that it is he who lost his balance. At heart he is dying for a *rapprochement* with London and detests the Germans.

At the Supreme Committee of Defence I raised the subject of the mentality of the Americans, a problem of great and not merely negative importance for us. I should like to know how England, blockaded by submarines, will manage to keep herself supplied with only her own shipping, without being able to count on the help of neutral shipping as in the past.

FEBRUARY 10. Received Berger and Cristich.[2] The latter talked about the forthcoming visit of Spaho,[3] the Minister of Communications,

---

[1] In English in the original.   [2] Bosko Cristich, Yugoslav Minister in Rome.
[3] Mehmed Spaho, Yugoslav Minister of Communications. A prominent Moslem.

and asked me in confidence, on behalf of Stoyadinovich, not to let the press emphasize the visit too much. Spaho is a personage of quite sufficient importance and they do not want to inflate him any further. Cristich is devoted to Stoyadinovich and was very pleased when I said that, six months after his death, Stoyadinovich will still be the head of the Government. He is a strong man and no one will take his power from him.

Pirelli pro-English as ever and anxious for an agreement. He agreed about the spiritual preparedness of the Italians for war, but is worried about the lack of gold. When I said that, like Machiavelli, if I have to choose between gold and iron, I choose iron, he replied: 'That's all right if you have the iron.' Pirelli is a capitalist—he is afraid of war, and thinks about his interests, including those that he possesses in England.

Grandi telephones that in to-day's conversation with Eden a step forward was made. We shall see.

Conversations with Phillips and Hotta—the latter for information about the progress of the London talks. I don't want there to be any suspicions of us in Tokyo.

Goga has resigned—apparently in consequence of a Franco-Anglo-Russian intervention to protect the Jews.

FEBRUARY 11. Agreed with Volpi about various arrangements for the Belgrade Exhibition.

Grandi's report on yesterday's conversation has not yet arrived. But the international press is already pricking the bubble of an imminent agreement between Italy and England.

The meeting between the Führer and Schuschnigg will take place at Berchtesgaden to-morrow. It is an event of great interest. For the present it is secret—really secret. Nothing has leaked out yet. But it proves that the Führer's intentions towards Austria have not altered for the worse recently. Mussolini on the other hand has become more radical. He told me this morning that he is in favour of the nazification of Austria. Anything that is not thorough-going is not safe, as the case of Roumania proves.

I have promised 100,000 lire to Del Croix to raise the tone of the entertainment of the German wounded—he had intended to keep it quiet on the pretext of the scanty financial resources of the Association. I don't like this Del Croix, and I ask myself what sense there is in retaining at the head of so many genuine and honourable wounded a man who may have been unfortunate but has shown no particular signs of heroism. We all know the circumstances in which he was wounded. And it is impossible to forget his attitude in 1924. All the more as he hasn't changed his mind. If ever the barometer goes to 'stormy', he will leave us in the lurch again.

FEBRUARY 12. The Grandi-Eden talks don't seem likely to commit us very far. I believe that Great Britain would like to reach a settlement about Spain—that is why they let us glimpse the possibility of an understanding. In the face of which we have remained colder than they can have expected. Farinacci has replied with a downright attack. He informed me of his intention of writing an article of the kind and I saw no reason to prevent it.

There is an attack on me in *Choc*, saying that I represent the real danger to peace, because I have no feelings of Latinity and want to turn the tragedy to my own advantage. It is very exaggerated, but there is an element of truth in it. My conception of the Fascist Empire is not of something static. We must go on advancing. And it is reasonable enough that the haves should be worried. As for Latin solidarity, it is something invented by the French whenever they want other people to get themselves blown to bits on their behalf.

I have agreed with Wysocki on the essentials of the programme for Beck's visit. Another incident which will not go down well in Paris. Who cares?

The Roumanian crisis is obscure. Meanwhile a man describing himself as Butenko, the Soviet Chargé d'Affaires who disappeared from Bucharest, has given himself up at the *Questura* in Milan. He has no papers which prove his statements. He may be simply a lunatic or a mischief-maker. In any case I am having him sent on to Rome.

FEBRUARY 13. Signora Sarfatti wants to go to America for a lecture tour. I will talk about it to the Duce, though I myself regard her as one of the very few women capable of presenting us in a good light abroad. She talked to me about the Jewish question with obvious anxiety and was pleased to learn my moderate views on the subject. In any case she already knew about the project of making a public announcement of a reassuring kind in the near future.

The first reports of the Hitler-Schuschnigg conversation point to a silent nazification of Austria. The Anschluss is inevitable. The only thing to do is to delay it as long as possible.

Butenko is in Rome and has asked to see me. I will only see him when he has been definitely identified. I have sent for an official of the Legation in Bucharest in order to make certain of his identity.

FEBRUARY 14. A quiet day. The Duce is back from the mountains, but I haven't conferred with him yet. The news from Vienna confirms that the nazification of Austria is in progress as a result of the Berchtesgaden meeting.

I talked to Pariani about our military relations with Germany. He is, it should be understood, convinced of the inevitability of war with the western powers. He regards the spring of 1939 as the most favourable moment for us. We shall have completed our preparations for the supply of *munitions, which for small arms are at present inadequate, and France and England will be going through their period of most acute crisis. Pariani believes in the success of a sudden lightning war. Attack on Egypt, attack on the fleet, invasion of France. The war will be won at Suez and in Paris. I suggested that it might be useful to form immediately a secret Italo-German war committee. He likes the idea and, now that Blomberg[1] has been removed, he thinks it is possible. We shall talk to the Duce about it. I suggested studying plans for an invasion of Switzerland as a means of attacking France. He agrees and thinks it a good idea. I also suggested landing Italian troops at Port Said and Suez, all this as part of the surprise operations. It would be easy to arrange for the presence of troop transports for East Africa at the right moment. He approves and will pass on my suggestions for a technical examination.

Cantilo, the Argentine Ambassador, has become Minister for Foreign Affairs. He is a disagreeable man and no friend of ours.

FEBRUARY 15. Received Manacorda[2] and Pavolini.

The Duce has seen the Austro-German Agreement. He says he regards it as a logical and inevitable development in the relations between two German countries. In commenting on what has happened it is necessary to emphasize that it is a question of two German countries. In order to prove that she is still independent, Austria ought to join the Anti-Comintern Pact.

As regards relations with London, I have sent a telegram summing up our policy: we are ready to treat, on the basis already stated, once the ground is cleared of the Spanish problem. Meanwhile it is interesting to note that Eden's report of his conversation with Grandi is very different from that drawn up by Grandi, in that Eden makes us responsible for some part of the initiative. I shall not send Grandi a copy of the document, as it is not altogether clear what his game is.

The Duce has written *Informazione Diplomatica* No. 14 himself on the Jewish question. He himself describes it, in spite of its almost conciliatory form, as a masterpiece of anti-Semitic propaganda. For my part I have confined myself to observing that the Jewish state wished for by him ought not to be Palestine. On the grounds that we must safeguard our relations with the Arabs.

[1] Field-Marshal Werner von Blomberg, German Minister for War, 1933–8. He had recently made an undesirable marriage, which was made the pretext for his enforced resignation.
[2] Professor Guido Manacorda, a pro-Fascist Catholic writer.

FEBRUARY 16. Butenko has been recognized by the Stefani correspondent from Bucharest. I saw him this morning at the Ministry. He
doesn't seem to me a man of much character. But he was so confused
and frightened that it would be premature to pass judgment on him.
He even asked that the guards, instead of staying in the corridor,
should take up permanent residence in his hotel bedroom. I have
passed on his statements to the *Giornale d'Italia* and by means of the
foreign press, wireless, etc., I am building up the sensational news. It
is a good piece of anti-Soviet propaganda, which must be properly
exploited.

After seeing the Duce I drafted a long letter to Grandi. I am telling
him that he must give a touch of the accelerator to the London negotiations. Whatever the result is to be, it is important to know it. Events
may soon prevent the manœuvres which to-day are still possible—but
perhaps only for a little while longer.

On the Chancellor's instructions Berger-Waldenegg has talked to me
about the results of the Berchtesgaden meeting. I expected to find him
crushed. On the contrary, he was calm and hopeful of genuine collaboration with Germany. I am more sceptical. I advised him to suggest
to Vienna joining the Tripartite Pact. It would be a proof of Austrian
independence.

Conversation with Blondel—a survey of the situation and a hint at
the possibility of a press truce.

FEBRUARY 17. A dinner-party at home yesterday, with many
diplomats. I talked to Cristich about the Austrian situation. We
opened our hearts—Italy and Yugoslavia are in an identical position
with regard to pan-Germanism. They are worse off than we are—
because they are less strong and because they have not such a solid
natural barrier for a frontier. In any case, there is nothing to be done.
But as the Austrian cockerel has found his way—or almost—into the
German pot earlier than necessary, it is indispensable that the bonds
between Rome and Belgrade should be further strengthened, and we
must always bear in mind that Hungary and Poland too are in a
similar situation. Cristich agreed. I think we should forthwith study
the question of an alliance with Yugoslavia. A horizontal Axis will
make possible the existence of the vertical Axis.

A short, incidental conversation with Perth, with whom I used more
or less the language of the letter sent to Grandi. I did the same with
Lady Chamberlain this morning—she has not yet received a reply to
her letter of February 1.

I received Phillips and we made the usual survey of the situation.
He asked me what I thought of the disagreement between Eden and
Chamberlain. I said that I had no precise information, but that in any

case I should have preferred to base an understanding with London on a unanimous 'feeling'[1] rather than on the dissension between these two statesmen.

Wrote *Informazione Diplomatica* No. 15, about Austria.

FEBRUARY 18. The Duce was in a mood of irritation with the Germans this morning, over the manner in which they have acted in the Austrian business. In the first place they ought to have given us warning—but not a word. And then, if, instead of halting at the position they have reached, they should want to go on to a real, proper Anschluss, a general situation would be created entirely different to that in which the Axis was formed, and it would become necessary to re-examine the whole position.

I took the opportunity of finding myself with Hesse, after lunching with him and the Prince of Piedmont, to talk to him as a friend, quite frankly. I have made a Minute of the conversation.

Grandi has been received by Chamberlain, but I have no information on the results of the talk. On the telephone he was very reticent —a reticence, it seemed to me, not inspired solely by the fear of interception.

FEBRUARY 19. Council of Ministers.

I have invited Schuschnigg to publish details of the part played by Italy in all this Austrian crisis. These rumours about desperate appeals from Vienna remaining unanswered must be contradicted. The truth is that we only learnt about the whole thing after the *fait accompli*, when there was no possible alternative and nothing remained for us but to give our approval to what Schuschnigg had done.

I have also telegraphed to Berlin to let it be known that the Führer in his speech should take good care not to put the friendship of Italy on a footing with that of Poland, as certain information of Attolico suggested he might. We should leave no doubt about our reaction to this.

Grandi has taken a step forward in his conversations. It really seems possible that we may begin soon. Nevertheless, on Eden's express orders, Perth has brought me a very forcible protest about a colonial question of quite minor importance. It strikes an odd note, on the morrow of the London conversations. Everything suggests that Eden, seeing that he has lost the game against Chamberlain, is still trying to muddle things and put the negotiations back where they began. This is what Grandi thinks (I have telephoned to him), and he says that the dissension in the Government in London is very acute.

FEBRUARY 20. A hectic day—the Führer's speech in Berlin and a crisis in London over the Eden-Chamberlain split, mostly over policy towards Italy.

[1] In English in the original.

According to telegrams from Attolico and Magistrati the Führer's speech was good as regards us and mostly directed against Great Britain. On Austria too, although the word 'independence' doesn't appear once, his pronouncements seem fairly satisfactory. Austria is considered to be a national entity and not a German province. At least for the present.

In London the crisis is on. The Duce has been telephoning from Terminillo[1] for information every half-hour. The situation is fluid. Eden resigned at 1 p.m. and appeared at the Cabinet after his resignation. The Cabinet meeting lasted until 6.30, when it was adjourned until after dinner. Eden was cheered by the crowd when he left, surly and alone, with shouts of 'Eden Prime Minister'. Labour, Liberals, and left-wing Conservatives have already tabled a motion in favour of Eden. The crisis is perhaps one of the most important which has ever taken place. It may mean peace or war. I have authorized Grandi to take any step which may add an arrow to Chamberlain's quiver. An Eden Cabinet would have as its aim the fight against the dictatorships —Mussolini's first. I am waiting for news at the Ministry. The Duce went to bed at 10. Signs of the times—the English are working on Sunday, while the Italian Chief enjoys his 'week-end'.[2]

FEBRUARY 21. It was at a party at the Colonnas' that I learnt of Eden's fall last night. There was a general cheer at the news. The Prince and Princess[3] of Piedmont were there, and the Prince insisted on drinking several toasts with me. From the Colonnas' I gave instructions for the press not to be too triumphant—we don't want to turn Eden into a victim of Fascism. In fact the papers to-day present what has happened as the normal development of an internal British Cabinet crisis. Perth, who is taking it well, telephoned this morning to suggest that I should do just what I had already done.

Conversation with Lagardelle,[4] back from Paris. The old words and the old schemes—the whole thing out of date now because of this British business.

Grandi telephoned a brief account of his conversation with Chamberlain. I confirmed that we are ready to begin negotiations on the basis already stated. It seems that instructions will be sent to Perth as soon as possible.

I settled the programme of Beck's visit with the Polish Ambassador. The press will have to refrain from giving it an anti-French character —the event itself is sufficiently anti-French, and there is no need to emphasize the fact in print.

[1] Terminillo, a winter sports centre in the Abruzzi.
[2] In English in the original.
[3] Marie José, wife of Prince Umberto and sister of King Leopold of the Belgians.
[4] Lagardelle, a French diplomat.

Sereggi[1] has invited me in the name of Zog to be a witness to his marriage on April 26. I have accepted. I still firmly believe in my programme for Albania and anything that can enhance our prestige and our influence must not be neglected.

FEBRUARY 22. A long Council of Ministers. When I got back to the Palazzo Chigi late in the afternoon, I found Perth waiting in the ante-room. I have made a Minute of our conversation. I want to add that he didn't seem to me at all distressed by Eden's departure—he blushed like a child when I paid him a compliment on the work he has accomplished. It is odd how easily the English blush—much more than we Latins. Shyness or modesty?

Conversation with Lessona, very worried because the Party has started proceedings against him on account of De Bono's accusation about his Diploma of the March on Rome. Lessona has drawn up a memorial in his own defence. Very weak—as the only witness of his participation in the march he cites a dead man, Dario Lupi.[2] He asked me to intervene. He realizes that the battle will end in his defeat. But is he really worth saving?

Ward Price[3] asked for an interview with the Duce or with me. It doesn't seem to me a suitable moment. I confined myself to giving him some general information about the forthcoming negotiations and denying the rumour that we have asked London for a loan.

Things are going well in Spain. Teruel has been retaken and the troops are advancing. Berti thinks it is possible to reach the sea and is asking Franco to use our divisions. The Duce has sent Franco a fine telegram, urging him on to fight and telling him he must choose between using the Legionaries in battle and sending them home.

FEBRUARY 23. Schuschnigg has sent, by way of Ghigi, the fragment of his forthcoming speech which concerns Italy. It is good—for one thing it gives the lie to the rumours of a change in our attitude towards Austria. What in fact could we do? Start a war with Germany? At the first shot we fired every Austrian, without a single exception, would fall in behind the Germans against us. I have thanked Schuschnigg and have also suggested that he should make it clear that the independence of Austria is based on the will and determination of the Austrian people and not on the uncertain guarantees of foreign states. A country whose independence is assured by outsiders is virtually finished.

The struggle in Spain is continuing victoriously. Franco must exploit his success to the utmost and use the favourable situation which has

[1] General Zeff Sereggi, Adjutant to King Zog and Albanian Minister in Rome.
[2] Dario Lupi, Under-Secretary for Education in Mussolini's first Government in 1922.
[3] George Ward Price, of the *Daily Mail*.

arisen as a result of military and political events. If he misses this
exceptional opportunity too, it will be a definite proof of his inade-
quacy. Fortune is not a train which passes every day at the same time
—nor an honest woman who gives herself once and for all. She is a
prostitute who offers herself fleetingly and then passes on to others. If
you can't manage to seize her by the hair, you lose her.

Farewell visit from Cantilo, who is shortly leaving for Argentina,
without much enthusiasm for what he will have to do.

FEBRUARY 24. Talked to Cristich about the Slav minorities in
Venezia Giulia. In order to help Stoyadinovich in a parliamentary
debate, I said that we are still prepared to do something on their behalf,
though what we could do I don't know—they are quiet people and ask
for nothing. If only the Germans in the South Tyrol were equally
docile.

Blondel wanted to survey the European scene, pausing at London
and Vienna. I expounded some of our ideas about Austria. He was
obliged to admit that they are realistic.

Ward Price came to say good-bye to me before returning to London.
Among other things he said that Schuschnigg had said to him that
Italy's protection of Austria was incapable of practical realization,
because, if one Italian soldier set foot on Austrian territory, the result
would be an *union sacrée* against us. He also said that in a recent
conversation Göring gave him to understand that in Berlin Mussolini
had more or less given the Germans a free hand in Austria—which is
untrue. Göring added that in any case it is a German question, in
which other powers are not permitted to interfere—the other powers
including, so Ward Price says, Italy.

The Duce has telephoned to say that Schuschnigg made a strong
speech, on the lines of our suggestions.

FEBRUARY 25. The Duce was very pleased with Schuschnigg's
speech, which he heard on the wireless. He was particularly struck by
the enthusiasm of the Assembly, which has given him more confidence
in the vitality of Austria. He says that Austrian patriotism was re-
awakened yesterday after languishing for twenty years, and that the
setting of uniforms, flags, and banners helped to do this. The Duce
believes in the necessity of revitalizing political life by means of imagination and display. If Schuschnigg had appeared yesterday with a dreary
routine ceremony and the shambling walk of a monk, he wouldn't have
had such a striking success.

Villani asked me for news of our conversations with London and
whether it is part of the programme to discuss Central Europe. I
replied that it is not. And I confirmed that the possible agreement with
London is not intended to replace the Axis but to stand beside it.

Took leave of von Hassel. A brief, cold, hostile conversation. I feel not the slightest remorse at having caused the removal of this man, who was a bad servant of his country and of the cause of German-Italian friendship. He may perhaps have tried to overcome his hostile sentiments, but he did not succeed—he belongs, fatally and inexorably, to the world of Junkers, who cannot forget 1914 and, because they are at heart hostile to Nazism, have no sense of the solidarity of the two régimes. Besides, von Hassel knew Dante too well. I distrust foreigners who know Dante. They try to pull a fast one on us with their poetry.

FEBRUARY 26. The Czechoslovak Minister[1] came to protest about the article in the *Giornale d' Italia* stating that Benes[2] had told a foreign diplomat that as early as 1923 he had recommended 'getting rid of' Mussolini. The information was provided by us and comes from the deciphering of a telegram from the French Minister in Prague. I think that we ought now to release the document to the press, particularly as certain criticisms made by Benes of the other Little Entente countries may lead to a violent controversy, perhaps even a crisis.

Received Spaho, the Yugoslav Minister of Communications.

The Duce is very irritated by the fact that Franco continues to keep our volunteer forces out of action and has not answered his letter. He has given orders for the aircraft in the Balearic Islands to abstain from all operations until our infantry too is used. This idleness is destroying the morale of the troops—cases of indiscipline have become more frequent and for the first time there have been desertions. The country too is tired of the affairs of Spain.

Went to the station to welcome Graziani. The Duce was there, and the whole of the upper hierarchy, civil and military. Only Badoglio was missing. The welcome of the crowd was, on the whole, organized and therefore of a warmth which failed to convince. In the car the Duce said to me: 'Graziani must have been pleased that I embraced him. He fought well, but he has governed badly.'

FEBRUARY 27. Flew to Florence, where I examined the Führer's route and acquainted myself with the preparations. All admirable.

Then to Leghorn, and finally on to Turin.

FEBRUARY 28. Marriage of the Duke of Genoa.[3] Much murmuring in court circles and among the Turin aristocracy against the bride, who is not considered good enough. She is not good-looking and is

[1] Frantisek Karel Chvalkovsky, Minister in Rome, 1932–8. Became Foreign Minister after the Munich Conference.

[2] Edvard Benes, President of Czechoslovakia, 1935–8 and 1945–8. Foreign Minister, 1918–35.

[3] Ferdinando of Savoy, a cousin of the King of Italy. His bride, Countess Maria Luisa Alliaga-Gandolfi, was 37. He was 53.

getting on in years. And as if she wasn't old enough already, the priest, in reading the certificate, added on ten years to her age by mistake! A slip of the tongue which the bride will not forget.

Afternoon with the Fascists—very comradely and friendly.

In the train I had a talk with the Princess of Piedmont.

MARCH 1. Nothing particularly important while I was away.

In spite of our pressure Franco refuses to drive the Teruel action home. He suggests another plan, in the Belchite sector, to be put into operation in ten days. Berti would have preferred to operate at Teruel, but he is not unfavourable to Franco's proposal.

I reported to the Duce on my visit to Turin. He agreed when I told him of my impression that monarchism there is half-hearted—when I spoke of the House of Savoy in my speech there was almost no reaction, while the name of the Duce was greeted with endless acclamations.

I have handed Cristich a copy of the Prague telegrams. It transpires from them that Benes called Yugoslavia and Roumania 'cowardly'. This should make Belgrade sit up and think.

Salata has given me some unpublished and very serious details of the Hitler-Schuschnigg meeting. The violence of the Chancellor was apparently something unheard of. At the slightest sign of resistance he threatened to occupy Salzburg. Schuschnigg is now thinking of holding a plebiscite, on the results of which the decision for the future of Austria would depend. In his opinion, the prognostics should be favourable to the Patriotic Front. But if he is wrong, doesn't it mean an immediate crisis? Is it right to take the risk?

MARCH 2. Last night at the Colonnas' I heard that D'Annunzio[1] had died, and received a message about going to Gardone with the Duce. We left at 8 this morning. I can't say that the Duce was very moved. He considers that D'Annunzio had an enviable fate—a glorious and heroic life, ending in sudden death at an age which it is natural to regard as the term of life. He told me that the news came to him by way of a telephone call from Prefect Rizzo,[2] who used literally these words: 'I am sorry to have to give you some good news!' A slip of the tongue which betrays the feelings of the policeman glad to be quit of his job at last.

The Duce was full of praise for D'Annunzio's activity as soldier and politician, and also for his heroic poetry and some of his plays, but critical of his novels, which he regards as gloomy relics of the nineteenth century. He said that D'Annunzio on the whole behaved well as regards the régime, in spite of the fact that for the first seven or eight years he made no overt act of adherence. If, however, he had taken

---

[1] Gabriele d'Annunzio, the famous poet, statesman, and warrior.
[2] Giovanni Rizzo, a Prefect placed at the disposal of d'Annunzio.

a stand against us in 1924, he would, the Duce thinks, have been a dangerous opponent because of his large following among the young.

I received a telephone call at Brescia in the evening, telling me that Lord Halifax will be obliged to receive the Negus and that he asks me not to attach any importance to this and not to start a press attack. So be it—nevertheless the interview will create a bad impression. I have had this made clear to the English Embassy.

MARCH 3. The funeral took place this morning. I went with the Duce by car and throughout the journey he did nothing but remark on the large quantities of scrap iron to be found in the countryside. He believes that the total for Italy must be five or six million tons. He thinks of requisitioning this 'open-cast mine' in the event of an emergency. It might suffice to provide iron for a year of war.

On the journey back I had a long conversation with De Bono, who talked at length about the Matteotti[1] affair and told me the real truth. He, De Bono, knew nothing about it. As for the rest of the story, I shall remember it without putting it on paper. But why did the old man talk to me? Perhaps because he has full confidence in my discretion. Personally, in his place, I should have held my tongue—on principle.

The visit of the ex-Negus seems to have no significance. Meanwhile we learn from the English that they are going to get into touch with Berlin as well, with a view to a general pacification.

MARCH 4. Franco has replied to the Duce with a very comprehensive letter, in which he sets forth the reasons for the postponement of the grand offensive. The truth is that the Red forces in Asturias had not been liquidated rapidly enough and there were still strong centres of resistance there, which required the presence of Nationalist troops. Now the machine is in gear and Franco's forecast for the future is pretty optimistic. He believes that the Reds have no capacity for resistance left and that at the first serious shock they must collapse. He attributes great importance, moral and material, to the presence of our volunteers. Both the contents and the form of the letter pleased the Duce. He will reply to-morrow, with an assurance that he is taking steps to retain the volunteers in Spain. The Duce was very amused when I pointed out a howler in the statement on D'Annunzio's death drawn up by the Academy: 'His lips and his hands were never weary of dictating. . . .' He attributed it to Formichi,[2] whom he describes as a 'chronic enthusiast'.

[1] Giacomo Matteotti, a Socialist Deputy and one of the last outspoken opponents of Fascism. After accusing the Fascists of frauds and illegalities during the elections of April 1924, he was abducted and murdered. De Bono, at the time of the murder Chief Commissioner of Police for Rome, was accused of complicity in the crime but acquitted by a judicial committee of the Senate. The three survivors of the actual murderers were tried and sentenced to 30 years' imprisonment in 1947.

[2] Carlo Formichi, a professor of Sanskrit.

Grandi has confirmed what I more or less knew already about things in London. He agrees with me in believing that, if we don't get an agreement within two months, within three Eden will be head of the Government, and within four we shall all be wearing uniform.

I received the Prince of the Yemen,[1] De Vecchi, the Portuguese Minister, and the Dutch Minister, with his credentials in order. He seems to be a classic diplomat, with a monocle and many professional reminiscences.

Berlin has given us the report of the Hitler-Henderson[2] conversation. The Führer was very hard and the results absolutely negative.

MARCH 5. The Duce has replied to Franco with an admirable telegram—good wishes for victory and a promise to give all further assistance within the limits of our economic capacity and within the framework of international relations.

The news from Austria gets worse and worse—in Styria the Nazis are in control of everything, the streets and the barracks. In the other provinces they are making rapid progress. People are beginning to talk of Seyss-Inquart[3] as Chancellor, with the specific task of digging the grave of Austrian independence. The Duce is now strongly critical of Schnuschnigg's speech, which he finds wanting in tact towards Germany and the Führer. Schuschnigg talked big without having any possibility or means of doing anything.

Lunch at the Palace. The King again spoke ill of Berlin and told me not to trust the Germans—they are, in his opinion, always wanting in loyalty and always telling lies.

In the afternoon I saw Volpi about the Belgrade Exhibition and other minor matters. He is very pleased at the improvement in relations with London. In view of what he has been told by Schacht, whom he says that he respects but does not like, he believes that Germany will be obliged to make war by her shortage of fats. The way to avoid a war is to help Germany to get back her old colonies.

MARCH 6. The Duce had a moment of human grief this morning. He told me that he misses D'Annunzio. It is true that the old man meant very little recently, but he was there, and from time to time there would be a message from him. The Duce admitted that D'Annunzio had counted for a lot in his life. Undoubtedly he helped to fix the characteristics of Fascism.

Federzoni announced to me this morning that he is to be President of the Academy. He isn't too pleased to be leaving the Senate, but he accepts it with a good grace.

[1] Prince Seif al Islam Hussein, second son of the Imam Yayha.
[2] Sir Nevile Henderson, British Ambassador in Berlin, 1937–9.
[3] Dr. Artur Seyss-Inquart, Austrian S.S. leader. Governor of Holland during the German occupation.

I received Beck at the station. The Chief, without knowing him, has a lively antipathy for him, through that curious gift which men have for hating or loving without ever having seen. I am bound to say that as usual his instinct is right—at first sight Beck is an unsympathetic character, who produces a chill around him. The reception was solemn, perhaps more so than I myself would have wished. But Bastianini, who is out to sell us Poland, had caused the attendance to swell. Beck's wife was exuberantly happy. He was very stiff. However, I do not want to pass judgment on him before I have listened to him and got to know him better. The few words he has uttered so far did not seem to me very pro-German.

MARCH 7. Received Beck. He is a measured, prudent man, obviously rather timid. He doesn't strike me as particularly strong or remarkably intelligent. Above all, he lacks the gift of exposition. His arguments do not convey ideas with geometrical clarity—instead he loses himself and wanders away to something neither essential nor precise. Nothing new will result from the visit, beyond a proof of friendliness between the two countries and a demonstration of the possibility of a closer understanding. We touched a little on every subject, with an almost impersonal interest. He particularly wanted me to realize that Poland intends to maintain a position of equilibrium, without compromising herself in any direction. He repeatedly said that the alliance with France will not operate in the event of a war provoked by the Czech problem. As regards the Anschluss he displayed a lack of interest which seems to me out of proportion to the importance which the problem may assume for Poland.

In the afternoon he was received by the Duce. The conversation was desultory. Finding no intelligent response, Mussolini did not bother to make real contact. They more or less went over the ground already covered with me.

The Duce has had two interviews with the Austrian Military Attaché. He has told him to advise Schuschnigg against the Austrian plebiscite.

MARCH 8. Lunch at the Palace, with Beck. I sat next to the Princess of Piedmont, who does not like the Polish Minister. She finds his face equivocal, the sort of face you might well see in a French newspaper as that of a ravisher of little girls. Perhaps she exaggerates. But one should not ignore these feminine instincts.

The King talked to me about the politicians of before the March on Rome—he has most praise for San Giuliano.[1] Of Giolitti[2] he says that he had a formidable knowledge of the private lives and interests of all Italians, particularly in the parliamentary world. Something like the

---

[1] Antonino Paternò-Castello, Marchese di San Giuliano, twice Foreign Minister between 1905 and 1914.

[2] Giovanni Giolitti, five times Prime Minister between 1892 and 1921.

mayor of a small town. But this gave him his strength in governing through intrigue and corruption, though personally he was honest. The King does not, however, credit him with any real greatness.

In the afternoon I had a conversation with Perth, of which I made a Minute. My first impressions are not too bad, though the point of departure for the discussions is rather remote. However, Chamberlain is more interested than we are in achieving agreement—this is the card on which he has staked his political future, if not that of the whole Conservative Party.

MARCH 9. Conversation Duce-Ciano-Grandi. The Duce has approved of the objections recorded in my Minute of yesterday's conversation. Not that he believes in eternal peace. But he thinks that we shall need the five years between now and the end of the Universal Exhibition[1] in order to rebuild our economic structure.

Conversation with Beck. I informed him of Schuschnigg's decision to hold the plebiscite next Sunday. He regards this as a very dangerous policy—it is, however, the *ultima ratio* of Austria. This led us to examine the Anschluss problem more deeply than we had in our previous conversations. We left each other with the following formula: taking it as settled that understanding with Germany is a fundamental element in the policy of our two countries, we must strengthen the bonds existing between us and equally those which unite us to other countries with a similar political situation and interests, viz. Yugoslavia, Hungary, and Roumania. With this end in view we shall employ our united efforts to facilitate an agreement between the two last-mentioned countries.

He has invited me to go to Poland. I accepted, but did not commit myself to any definite date.

MARCH 10. I reported my conversation with Beck to the Duce, who showed great interest in it. Then I accompanied our Polish guest and his wife to the station. They were both moved and Cittadini[2] tells me that, after the train had started, they wept.

Lunch at the Volpis', with the Duchesse de Guise[3]—an insignificant, painted old thing. She showered me with commonplace questions, to which I could make nothing but commonplace replies.

I prepared my speech for the Grand Council, where I spoke for two and a half hours. It went well. The Duce praised me several times —this so overwhelms me that I am incapable even of thanking him. The truth is that one only works in order to please him—to succeed in this is the greatest satisfaction.

Good news from Spain—the Aragon offensive is proceeding surely

---

[1] A Universal Exhibition was to have been held in Rome in 1942 to celebrate 20 years of Fascist rule.

[2] Cittadini, an official in the protocol department of the Foreign Ministry.

[3] Isabelle, wife of the Duc de Guise, pretender to the French throne.

and swiftly. This time it may perhaps be the decisive battle. The volunteers are fighting wonderfully.

Bad news from Austria. As was to be expected, the Nazis are rising to resist the plebiscite. At any moment blood may be running in the streets. That would justify a German attack. Schuschnigg has made a fatal mistake. It was clear to us from the first moment—but the plebiscite bomb was fated to explode in his hands.

MARCH 11. In Spain it is full speed ahead. The communiqués and the dispatches confirm the crushing advance of our forces. So far few losses and only one division in action.

A hectic day for Austria. From hour to hour telephone messages have confirmed the mobilization on the Bavarian frontier and the German decision to attack. At midday Schuschnigg accepted the post-ponement of the plebiscite, but the Germans did not consider that enough and wanted him to resign. Through Ghigi he asked us what he should do. I have conferred several times with the Duce. We cannot from here assume the responsibility of advising him one way or the other. He must act according to his own conscience. The French Chargé d'Affaires asked to come and see me, on instructions from Paris, in order to form a concerted plan for the Austrian situation. I replied that we have no intention of consulting with anybody. If he had nothing else to say, he need not come and see me. In fact he did not come. After sanctions, the non-recognition of the Empire and all the other miseries inflicted on us since 1935, do they expect to rebuild Stresa in an hour, with Hannibal at the gates? Thanks to their policy, France and England have lost Austria. For us too it is not an advan-tage. But in the meantime we have acquired Abyssinia.

6 p.m. Schuschnigg resigns and Seyss-Inquart takes his place. An independent Austria no longer exists.

MARCH 12. At 9 last night Hesse asks to see me. I was eating dinner at my office desk. He is the bearer of a letter from Hitler to Mussolini. We go together to the Palazzo Venezia. The letter is important—it contains an explanation of what has happened and a precise declaration about the recognition of the Brenner as the frontier of Italy. The Duce is pleased and tells Hesse to inform the Führer that Italy is following events with absolute calm.

Grand Council. Balbo expresses fears for Trieste and criticizes the proceedings of the Germans. Naturally he does this behind the scenes and in whispers. Mussolini speaks out at him. He says: 'If we had eight million Italians on our frontiers, we should do just the same. At least I should. I have in fact done it.' He is thinking of the annexation of Fiume. I read the reports which prove the enthusiasm for the Nazis in Austria. From Spain there is much good news, which is greeted by the Grand Council with cheers. After the session the Duce and I prepare the framework of a public announcement which the Grand Council will approve.

This morning I drafted it and the Duce passed it. Through Hesse we have asked Berlin for permission to publish the letter. It took several hours to get through to the Führer. He agrees, but asks for two passages against Czechoslovakia to be suppressed, which is reasonable enough. Conversation with Perth. Minute made. I am left with the conviction that Great Britain will accept what has happened with ·indignant resignation. Conversation with the Duce and Hesse. In Germany they are delighted with our line of conduct.

Lunch with the pirates—the Duce assembled at his table the staff officers of the ships which conducted the piratical operations against the Reds. He made a brief address, praising the work of the Navy in the Spanish war.

MARCH 13. Last night at the Grand Council I spoke briefly about the events of the day and submitted the Order of the Day dealing with Austria for approval.

To-day all is calm again. The fatal event has reached its conclusion. It has not been pleasant for us—far from it. But one day the world will realize that all this was inevitable. The Duce says that one ambiguity has been removed from the map of Europe. And he enumerates three others still in existence, which will, in his opinion, one after another and in the following order, have to go the same way: Czechoslovakia, Switzerland, and Belgium.

Cristich wanted to hear our views. I spoke frankly to him. I added that, when I signed the Pact with Yugoslavia on March 25 of last year, I was already thinking of all that has actually happened in the last few days. And I discussed the possibility at length with Stoyadinovich. I am now thinking of the second pact which we shall have to forge with Yugoslavia, which will unite the destinies of the two countries in the common defence of our respective worlds—but without altering our friendship with Germany. So long as there are eighty million Germans in the heart of Europe, for Rome and for Belgrade German friendship is a fatality, oppressive perhaps, but very real. One of these days—for obvious reasons not too soon—Stoyadinovich and I will have to have a holiday at the sea or a little stag-hunting together. . . .

In Spain we continue to advance rapidly and victoriously.

MARCH 14. Good news from Spain—our troops are progressing with incredible speed.

Beck came to see me on his way back from Naples. We discussed the situation produced by the Anschluss and confirmed everything we had said in our conversation of March 9.

Received Berger, who told me he has had instructions to hand over the Legation to Plessen.[1] On the pretext of bronchitis he is going to stay in Italy some weeks longer, he says. The truth is that he fears for himself and his family. He was a Minister under Dollfuss and Schuschnigg, and it actually fell to him, as Minister of Justice, to sign the death warrant for the murderers of Dollfuss. Naturally he is still *bouleversé* by what has happened, but he recognizes the errors of the federal Government, and above all he assures me that Schmidt intended to betray everybody—including us. He says he will give me proof of this. Berger too maintains that Italy could not have acted differently —if a single Italian soldier had entered Austria, the whole population of the country, with the exception of the Jews, would have fired on us.

I soothed the anxieties of that presumptuous cretin, Ruegger, who told me he foresaw great danger for us and the rest of the universe. I replied that our frontiers, the Brenner included, are defended not by treaties but by the breasts of 45 million Italians. This being so, we have nothing to fear.

MARCH 15. The Duce is preparing his speech for the Chamber on the Austrian problem. It is necessary, because the country was pretty severely shaken and wants to hear what the Chief has to say.

Conversation with Villani. I spoke again of the need for a policy of still closer ties with Hungary.

Conversation with Perth. Minute made. On the whole things are going well, but I should be sorry if our overwhelming advance in Spain produced a reaction against Chamberlain in England. Chamberlain himself is inflexible. But he has already been shaken by the accomplishment of the Anschluss.

The Duce has read me his speech. It is splendid—Mussolini at his best.

MARCH 16. Impatience to hear the words of the Duce filled the day. A magnificent speech, leaving a profound and decisive impression, with incalculable echoes. The Duce spoke with the natural flow of passion, at times restrained and at times bursting forth. Seldom have I 'lived' one of his speeches as I did to-day. The country has felt the touch of his whip, and pessimists are now skulking in isolation.

All goes on very well in Spain—it may not be long now before the collapse sets in. There are rumours, not verified, of assistance which France might be inclined to send at this eleventh hour—men and aircraft. I don't believe it. Nevertheless I have telegraphed to Berlin, saying that, if this should happen, we should resume our liberty of action and intervene in force.

I made arrangements with Del Croix for the visit of the German

[1] Baron Johann von Plessen, Counsellor at the German Embassy in Rome.

ex-combatants. In spite of the murmuring of the last few days they will be given a good welcome.

MARCH 17. The Duce and I have received a lot of anonymous letters in the last few days, varying in tone, but all against the Anschluss. Now they are falling off. The Duce pointed out that they all came from Milan and that, on the contrary, he didn't have a single one from the South at the time when the coasts of Sicily were threatened by English guns. He attributes this timidity to the wealth of the North. 'A people must be poor in order to be proud,' he concluded.

The reaction to his speech in Germany is admirable. The Führer will speak to-morrow night and will solemnly confirm his friendship for us and his pledges for our frontiers.

I received instructions from the Chief for the negotiations with England. In principle he has accepted two formulas, with deferred obligations, for Spain and for the recognition question, which should make a swift settlement possible. I believe it is important to hurry, because the situation is fluid and I haven't too much confidence in Chamberlain's position.

I told the Nuncio that in a conversation with Magistrati Göring displayed a better attitude towards the Church and even spoke of a general amnesty. For obvious reasons I should like, if it will be possible, to promote such a *rapprochement*.

Wrote a letter to Attolico about the Anglo-Italian talks.

In Spain the offensive is going well.

MARCH 18. My thirty-fifth birthday. Half the journey. . . .

The Duce received the German ex-combatants. Their leader, the Duke of Coburg,[1] is an insignificant man. A really unfortunate physique—which is enough to prove that not all Germans are the giants described by Tacitus. In Germany too, as I noticed during my visit there, there is a considerable percentage of midgets.

At the Chamber, with the Duce and Starace, we talked about Balbo and mentioned certain instances of his behaviour. The Duce hates him. He said he will make him end up where Arpinati[2] is. But, for that, gossip is not enough—we need an incident, a scandal to catch hold of. I asked Starace whether he had taken the hint. He said he had, and thinks of using Consul-General Giannantoni.[3] I think rather of Muti,[4] who is intelligent and reliable and would do admirably to trip up Balbo.

---

[1] Leopold, Duke of Saxe-Coburg, President of the German Association of ex-Combatants. A grandson of Queen Victoria.

[2] Leandro Arpinati, Under-Secretary for the Interior, 1929–33. Subsequently confined as a political prisoner.

[3] Ettore Giannantoni, commander of the Teramana Legion in the March on Rome.

[4] Ettore Muti, Consul-General in the Fascist Militia. Secretary-General of the Fascist Party, 1939–40.

Took leave of Berger. At least for the present, he is not going back to Austria.

Conversation with Perth. Everything proceeds in good order.

MARCH 19. Nicolas Franco is asking, in his brother's name, for the *Taranto*[1] and two destroyers to be transferred, as he admits that the loss of the *Baleares*[2] has left the Nationalists in a position of inferiority as regards naval forces. Discussion *à trois* with the Duce. I spoke against the idea—it would be impossible to conceal the transfer, which would provoke a scandal and perhaps a disastrous change in the situation with England. Chamberlain is much less strong than he was ten days ago—we must not create new difficulties for him. The Duce virtually agreed, while reserving for himself a more detailed study of the question. I believe that instead we might increase our air force in the Balearic Islands and, if suitable, transfer a submarine or two, which would more easily evade the patrols.

Franco is optimistic about the situation, though he doesn't believe that the Red Republic will collapse like a house of cards. He foresees resistance in Catalonia and the necessity for action on the River Segre, in order to deprive Barcelona of its electric power.

The offensive was resumed to-night. No official news yet, but the most joyous hopes of success are encouraged by a dispatch. It is just a year since I went through my worst day: Guadalajara.

I went back to the Duce again to settle the formulas for Palestine and Arabia, which are to be included in the agreement with Great Britain. It is absolutely necessary to safeguard our prestige and our position as regards the Arabs.

MARCH 20. Talking to Grandi the other day, I said that the European situation might perhaps interfere with Anglo-Italian relations. Sure enough this morning Perth handed me a note calling attention to the air raids on Barcelona and added that they might produce a state of opinion hostile to the continuation of the Anglo-Italian negotiations. I replied that operations are initiated by Franco, not by us—we might, therefore, exercise a moderating influence, but we could make no promises. As Perth hinted at the possibility of French intervention, I made it clear that we would immediately take very strong action. The truth about the air raids on Barcelona is that the orders for them were given to Valle by Mussolini in the Chamber a few minutes before he made his speech on Austria. Franco knew nothing about them, and asked yesterday that they should be suspended for fear of complications abroad. Mussolini believes that these air raids are an admirable way of weakening the morale of the Reds, while the

[1] *Taranto*, an Italian cruiser.
[2] The Spanish Nationalist cruiser *Baleares* was torpedoed and sunk on March 6.

troops are advancing in Aragon. He is right. He wasn't very worried when I informed him of Perth's *démarche*. In fact he said he was delighted that the Italians should be horrifying the world by their aggressiveness for a change, instead of charming it by their skill at playing the guitar. In his opinion this will send up our stock in Germany too, where they love total and ruthless war.

In Spain the offensive is making good progress—heroic and victorious.

MARCH 21. Approved the plans for the New York Exhibition.

Our troops in Spain have halted on the positions they have reached, in order to allow the Nationalists to join up on their flank and then push on with the offensive together.

No news from the other fronts.

I have telegraphed to Germany to ask for a measure of clemency for Neumann, the great Viennese Jewish scientist, who has been thrown into prison by the Germans at the age of nearly eighty. His release would be a humane gesture, which will cost little and produce very favourable reactions. I hope the Nazis are not being too heavy handed in Vienna and in Austria in general. It would add to the difficulties of the process of amalgamation, which is always pretty rough work. It was with us too, with the Piedmontese and the Neapolitans. The Piedmontese used the strong arm. They said they meant to impose even their errors of grammar. And in fact they succeeded pretty quickly in their intentions. Their toughest task was the repression of brigandage, which was a political rather than a social phenomenon. The measures they employed were expeditious—in some villages they shot the entire male population, beginning with the mayor.

Grandi telephones from London that there is a pretty strong movement to make trouble, but Chamberlain is remaining firm.

MARCH 22. We are being asked now from too many quarters to intervene in favour of people arrested in Vienna by the Nazis. We must restrict our interventions. First, in order not to assume a governess attitude, which always arouses resentment. And also, in order not to cheapen our recommendations, which would cease to have any effect if they were too widely spread.

Berlin has asked for our *agrément* for Mackensen[1] and naturally we have given it at once. I met him in Budapest and got a good impression of him. Those who know him believe him to be our friend.

I received the Party Mission which is going to Spain. They have no precise ideas of what they are to do. I recommended one thing

---

[1] Hans Georg von Mackensen, Ambassador in Rome, 1938–43. Previously Minister in Budapest and Secretary of State at the Foreign Ministry.

particularly: not to mix themselves up in the domestic questions of the Spaniards.

MARCH 23. Nothing worthy of note.

Conversation with Perth. He promises me a more precise statement on the various points under discussion for next Saturday.

MARCH 24. I said to Cristich, who is leaving for Yugoslavia, that a thousand reasons impelled me to make the Belgrade Pact—to-day there are a thousand and one reasons for consolidating it. I want to get together with Stoyadinovich. We might meet at the Venice Lido in July.

The American Ambassador came to ask us to join in the formation of an international committee with the object of assisting the emigration of political refugees from Germany and Austria. I replied that such a request was in conflict not only with our line of action in international affairs, but with our political morality. Phillips was surprised at my reply. He sees the proposal in a humanitarian light, I only in a political. The abyss of incomprehension between us and the Americans is growing steadily deeper.

Wysocki thanked me in Beck's name for our attitude during the crisis between Poland and Lithuania. I replied that we disinterested ourselves in the fate of Lithuania, because the problem does not concern us. We refused to put pressure on the Warsaw Government, I said, because we know from our own experience how intolerable governess governments are, that is to say governments which always feel obliged to tell you that your actions will create this or that impression. Finally, we are friends of Poland, and it is our habit to back up our friends, simply because they are our friends, even when they are in the wrong. But this, I added, is not the case. . . .

MARCH 25. Long conversation with the Hungarian Minister. He wanted to know what diplomatic instrument we intend to put in the place of the Rome Protocols, between Italy and his country. I haven't thought about it yet, but the question does not appear difficult. However, we must not be in too much of a hurry, in order not to alarm the Germans unnecessarily. My advice to him was that Budapest should form stronger ties with Belgrade. Kanya must overcome his hostile prejudices against the Serbs. The Ballplatz mentality of 1914 cannot be allowed to linger on in the Budapest of 1938.

The Chinese would like to entrust me personally with the task of mediating in the Japanese war. I must tread very carefully. It is a difficult undertaking, perhaps impossible. What is certain is that, if it succeeded, it would send our prestige in the Far East leaping up to inaccessible heights.

Cantilo has left. He has not been our friend as Ambassador—I do

not know whether he will be as Foreign Minister. He is a democrat,
a League man, a fathead—in fact a League man because he is a
fathead. He is worth precious little but full of presumption. He is, in
short, a perfect Argentino.

MARCH 26. A report from Jacomoni on the situation in Albania.
Our penetration is becoming steadily more intense and more organic.
The programme which I traced after my visit is being carried out
without a hitch. I am wondering whether the general situation—particularly the Anschluss—does not permit us to take a step forward
towards the more and more complete domination of this country,
which *will be* ours. It seems that Belgrade is anxious for a military
alliance—Albania might well be the price of it.

I talked to Nicolas Franco about our aid for 1938. They want a
billion lire's worth of goods, payment to be mostly in kind and very
problematical. We must keep our tempers. We are giving our blood
for Spain—do they want more?

The new Belgian Ambassador[1] handed me a copy of his credentials,
addressed to the King Emperor. I was very friendly, partly on account
of this political gesture he was making. He is a great mountain of a
man, with a slight limp, rather verbose. Not unsympathetic at first
sight. If I had to put him into one of the two categories into which
Baudelaire divided the Belgians—the guzzlers and the obscene—I
should choose the first.

Conversation with Perth. We are advancing laboriously, very
laboriously. Nevertheless, we are advancing. I made a Minute of the
conversation.

I have asked the Holy See not to make difficulties about King Zog's
marriage—his bride is a Catholic.

MARCH 27. Libohova, the Albanian Foreign Minister, brought me
the official invitation to act as witness at King Zog's marriage.

With the Duce I made a thorough examination of the various points
in the Anglo-Italian agreement, on the basis of the results reached in
yesterday's conversation. By and large the situation is fairly satisfactory, and we can go ahead. In fact to-day I was able to satisfy Perth
on a number of points, including the evacuation of our forces from
Libya at the rate of 1,000 men a week until the two Army Corps are
reduced to peace strength, guarantees for the departure of all our
volunteers from Spain at the end of the war, and an *Informazione
Diplomatica* in favour of Chamberlain. There still remain numerous
formulas to be settled, above all that relating to the recognition of
the Empire. If there are no unexpected obstacles, I think we should
be able to sign the agreement between April 10 and 20.

[1] Comte André de Kerchove de Deuterghem.

An aeroplane of French make, but with no number and camouflaged, crashed into a mountain near Iglesias[1] last night. Presumably it was coming from Spain and going in the direction of Rome, which suggests some sort of demonstration on the part of the Spanish Reds. I told Perth about it, adding that any action of this kind would be the signal for war.

In Spain the advance, resumed yesterday, is proceeding slowly on account of strong enemy resistance.

MARCH 28. In the morning, celebration of the Festival of the Air and presentation of the medals for valour.

Then a general survey of Anglo-Italian relations with the Duce during our conversation at the Palazzo Venezia. He is satisfied with the progress of the negotiations and has waved the green flag for me to go ahead. In a short time we shall be able to clinch.

Ansaldo tells me that the anti-Anschluss agitation at Leghorn was originated and kept going by the Jews.

In Spain the Spaniards are going well and we more slowly—we have drawn the larger enemy concentration against our troops.

MARCH 29. The Duce has asked that the final conversation before the signing of the agreement with London shall take place at the Palazzo Venezia. That will serve to indicate that the conclusion is at hand.

Perth thanked me for the decision about the partial withdrawal of our forces from Libya. He asked that it should not be made public yet, as his Government wants to reserve it for the moment of the conclusion of the agreement, in order to produce the maximum effect. We reached agreement concerning Palestine, Arabia, the native troops, and other minor questions. Only three or four points are still unsettled. We may perhaps sign before April 10, which would be a good thing, as we don't want the signature to take place too near the Führer's visit.

Conversation with the Japanese Ambassador—general survey. He personally seems very pleased at the progress made in the talks with Perth.

APRIL 1.[2] Nothing worthy of note in Rome.

In Spain the victory of the legionaries takes on more and more of a strategic character. It is compromising, perhaps decisively, the Reds' chances of resistance.

APRIL 2. The question of the Marshals of the Empire[3] has had repercussions. It seems that there has been talk at the Palace of the

---

[1] Iglesias, in Sardinia. The aeroplane was in fact a French military machine which had lost its way in a fog while on a flight from Maison Blanche, in Algeria, to Bizerta.

[2] The leaf for March 30 and 31 is missing from the diary.

[3] On March 30, at a special sitting of the Chamber, a new rank, Marshal of the Empire, was created and conferred on the King and Mussolini.

thing being illegal. Mussolini got the Council of State to give an opinion—all perfectly legal. He passed this on to the King with a very curt letter. He said to me: 'I am fed up. I do the work and he does the signing. I am disappointed that what you did on Wednesday should turn out to be perfect from the legal point of view.' I replied that at the first opportunity we shall be able to go further. The opportunity will certainly come when the respectable signature of the King has to be replaced by the less respectable signature of the Prince. The Duce nodded and added quietly, 'When Spain is finished, we shall talk about that. . . .' And Spain will be finished one day. To-day the Red front has collapsed again. Gandesa has been occupied by the legionaries. Tortosa is the next objective. Once we get there, the Reds will be split in two and we shall have broken the back of their resistance.

I told Sparano, the Brazilian Commercial Attaché and a friend of Vargas, to inform his President, whom he will shortly see in Rio de Janeiro, that we should have liked to see more Fascist courage on the part of the new Government. A revolution does not consolidate itself by beginning to retreat.

Conversation with Perth. We have made striking progress. In principle we have agreed to sign on Thursday 14th or Monday 18th. I should like it to be Thursday 14th, which is Maundy Thursday. I signed the Belgrade Pact on Maundy Thursday and it has been a success.

APRIL 3. A long talk with the Duce about relations with Germany. In South Tyrol propaganda of a kind which we cannot tolerate is continuing. The 212,000 Germans there are getting too uppish and there is even talk of a frontier at Ala or Salorno. I advised the Duce to talk to the Führer about it. The anti-German current in Italy, fomented by the Catholics, the Masons, and the Jews, is strong and becoming steadily stronger. If the Germans behave imprudently in South Tyrol, the Axis may at any moment be blown sky high. We must give them a hint about the desirability of their reabsorbing their nationals. Geographically South Tyrol is Italian territory and, as we can't change the position of mountains or the course of rivers, the men will have to move.

The Duce has virtually told me to go ahead with the agreement with London on the basis settled with Perth. Public opinion will welcome it with immense enthusiasm, partly because it is seen as a possible way of disengaging ourselves from Berlin.

In Spain the offensive of the legionaries continues to sweep all before it.

APRIL 4. I put Teruzzi in the picture of the agreement with London, in so far as it concerns the Colonies.

Made arrangements with Jacomoni for my forthcoming visit to Tirana. I have asked that, if possible, the King should come and meet me when I arrive. We must gradually underline the protectorate element in our relations with Albania.

I gave my approval in principle to a plan for the new Ministry building in the Piazza Barberini. It must be worthy of the Mussolini era and of the role it will have to play—the Imperial Ministry.

The Turkish Ambassador and the Greek Minister announced to me their formal recognition of the Empire. I accepted the announcements calmly, without any profuse thanks. They have waited too long.

In a speech at Graz the Führer has hinted at the possibility that the new frontiers may not be regarded as military frontiers. The Duce noted this with pleasure. If this were so, it would be a highly politic gesture on the Führer's part, which would do much, in Italy, Yugoslavia, and Hungary, to win back the sympathy he has lost by the brusque effectuation of the Anschluss.

APRIL 5. Stayed at home in the morning with bad tonsillitis. Buffarini came to see me. He told me that yesterday the Queen, after severely criticizing Professor Bastianelli for his medical work, pronounced these words: 'Get rid of him. Make him a Marshal too, if you like, but get rid of him.' Which proves that the Duce's becoming a Marshal of the Empire has not yet been swallowed at the Palace. I was right in saying it is a question we have not heard the last of. There is more to come. Buffarini also told me that many shopkeepers are refusing to display the Führer's portrait. This is a symptom of a deeply rooted attitude.

Conversation with Perth. We are waiting for a reply from London on four points of minor importance, and then we shall have reached agreement. We shall be able to sign on Maundy Thursday or Easter Monday.

Bülow-Schnante[1] was very favourably impressed by the preparations for Hitler's visit.

In Spain we have met unexpected resistance before Tortosa. But we shall get through.

APRIL 6. An article in the *Journal des Nations* has made the Duce even more sceptical about the possibility of the League Council's accepting Chamberlain's formula that every state ought to be at liberty to recognize the Empire. He thinks that in fact the Council will take this opportunity to make a demonstration of the power of the League,

[1] Dankward Christian von Bülow-Schnante, First Secretary at the German Embassy. He was in trouble a few weeks later. Hitler was photographed, with ludicrous results, wearing evening dress and a top hat after a gala performance at the San Carlo Opera in Naples. Bülow-Schnante was held responsible and dismissed.

summon Tafari[1] to Geneva, and postpone any decision. This would
shake Chamberlain's position, if it didn't actually overthrow him. I
immediately conferred with Perth. He was not at all disturbed. He
said that every eventuality has been foreseen. The English Government
will not ask for a decision, for which unanimity is required, but simply
for a recommendation, which may be made by a majority. As for
Tafari, he will not be able to face the problem of the verification of his
credentials. Perth said that, even if they were likely to meet with a
refusal at Geneva, Chamberlain will not stop half-way. I reported to
the Duce, who told me to proceed with the negotiation.

Starace talked to me at length on the question of the Marshals. He
too is of the opinion that the crisis between the régime and the
Monarchy has now opened. We agreed on certain general principles.
He advised me to be careful with Buffarini, who talks rather too much,
with no evil intention, perhaps, but certainly imprudently.

Stiff Spanish resistance in the neighbourhood of Tortosa. The Duce
has telegraphed to the air force in the Balearic Islands for an attack in
force on the back areas of the Spanish troops. Franco doesn't want air
raids on cities, but in this case the game is worth the candle.

APRIL 7. I gave Gentizon[2] some information about the Pact with
London. Gentizon behaved well during the war, and always shows
understanding towards us.

The Duce informed me that the King wants to send a royal mission,
headed by the Duke of Spoleto,[3] to be present at Zog's marriage.
Evidently they are trying to dig their heels in. It is tiresome, because
it was unexpected and because Tirana is not London and to keep this
great, boozy Spoleto creature in order is not easy. But I saw that the
Duce wants to avoid a row, and I immediately gave the orders to
Jacomoni, who received them with reluctance. In any case the King's
representative will have a second-class reception by comparison with
the Duce's representative.

Long conversation with Antonescu,[4] Roumanian ex-Foreign Minis-
ter. He is something like Zacconi,[5] rather younger and rather thinner.
He said nothing which particularly struck me. He is pro-French, with
many reservations about the Jewish Blum Government. He is anti-
Russian, anti-Czech, and at heart also anti-Polish. He talks a lot about
Latinity—a theme which one often hears on the lips of those whose

[1] Ras Tafari was the name by which Haile Selassie was known before he became
Negus (King) in 1928.
[2] Paul Gentizon, Rome correspondent of *Le Temps*. Military correspondent during
the Abyssinian War.
[3] Aimone of Savoy, younger brother of the Duke of Aosta and cousin of the King of
Italy.
[4] Victor Antonescu, Foreign Minister, 1936-7.
[5] Ermete Zacconi, a well-known Italian actor.

own Latinity is open to question. He would like an understanding with us, particularly now, after the Anschluss. That is our intention also, but they must first get over the Hungarian hurdle by making an agreement about the minorities in Transylvania.

APRIL 8. Almost reached home to-day with Perth. Except for two or three details the whole complex of agreements is ready. Perth suggests that we sign on Easter Saturday. It seems that this will please Halifax, as it is his birthday. All very romantic. . . .

From Spain Gambara reports a disagreement between our command and the Spaniards. The *n*th disagreement. . . . The Spaniards may be partly responsible, but our men are not altogether blameless. So often they show a stubborn, provincial intolerance, which can only be explained by the ignorance of the world of most Italian officers. In any case I told the Duce that there is no need to be alarmed, because this is not our first experience of Colonel Gambara's telegraphic excesses. Although the march of the legionaries has been slowed down, on the whole things are going well in Spain.

APRIL 9. In fact there has been no sequel to Gambara's telegram. Berti telegraphs that the situation is unchanged. The Reds are clinging to their last line of resistance before being split in two. According to a telegram from Magistrati in Berlin, Franco has asked the Germans to withdraw their volunteers. No request of the kind has been made to us. On the contrary, Berti is asking for 300 new officers to replace losses, and in defiance of all agreements they will leave on Thursday.

Perth and I settled the last points in suspense. The final conversation will be to-morrow.

The new German Ambassador, von Mackensen, came to see me. I have known him for some time. Schooled by the experience of his predecessor, he said to me that the whole success of his mission will depend on the confidence which I shall place in him. At the moment I am prepared to trust him. If he behaves well, I shall trust him more. And naturally vice versa. I gave him a very friendly reception, and to enable him to start off by sending a 'good telegram'—a thing infinitely dear to the heart of the career official—I gave him some unpublished details of the Anglo-Italian agreement—

Villani is going to Budapest. I said to him that it is our intention that within a short time our relations with Hungary shall be defined, tightened, and harmonized with the rest of our policy.

APRIL 10. Another conversation with Perth—possibly the last. We may perhaps see each other once more for the final polishing of the agreement, but without giving any publicity to the meeting. The Pact is good—complete, solid, harmonious. I believe it really will be able to serve as the foundation for the new friendship between Italy and

Great Britain. Particularly important is the document concerning Arabia. It has been very hard work to obtain this kind of parity of position between us and the English.

Otherwise nothing worthy of note.

APRIL 11. Agreed with the Duce that Perth and I shall come to the Palazzo Venezia for the final conversation on Thursday next at 5 p.m. The Duce is pleased. I see this myself and even more is it confirmed by the King, who this morning at the signature congratulated me on the terms of the agreement, on the basis of the information given him by the Duce.

Berti telegraphs that to-day our troops are preparing bases for a new attack. Let us hope this one will reach the sea. .

Saw Cobolli[1] about the plans for the new Ministry building. People are being very obstructive, but Cobolli and I hope to be able to build in the area Piazza Barberini-Via Veneto-Via Sistina.

Long conversation with Bocchini, who believes that the signature of the Pact with England will make a tremendous splash.

APRIL 12. Nothing worthy of note.

Conversations with Medici del Vascello and Buffarini.

APRIL 13. Completed the agreement with Perth. There were two or three points still unsettled. I gave him general assurances and in the evening, to get things finished, I went to the Palazzo Venezia. I found the Duce leaving. I drove with him to the Villa Torlonia and he approved of my views on the various points. Then I telephoned to Perth to give him confirmation. To-morrow we visit the Palazzo Venezia. On Saturday at 6.30 p.m. we sign at the Palazzo Chigi.

The scope of the agreement is vast—it is the beginning of a new era in our relations with Great Britain. Friendship on a footing of equality —the only kind of friendship we can accept, with London or with anybody else.

APRIL 14. The Duce greeted Lord Perth with a trace of ill humour. They have met occasionally at the theatre recently, but he had not received him at the Palazzo Venezia since the time of sanctions. Then he thawed. He read the texts of the agreements and gave his approval. Lord Perth, from a scruple of conscience, said that, when the question of recognition comes up at Geneva, Halifax will not repudiate the English policy of sanctions but will ask for a modified policy to meet the new situation. The Duce replied that that doesn't worry him in the least—he is only interested in the practical results. It would be boorish to expect England to put on sackcloth and ashes. On the contrary, he suggested burning incense to the memory of Eden. To his memory, be it noted. . . .

[1] Giuseppe Cobolli-Gigli, Minister of Public Works.

The Duce was pleased. With to-day's ceremony the Abyssinian enterprise is really concluded—concluded with an imperial agreement, due primarily to the iron tenacity of a man who believed and willed, alone, against the whole world, and often against many of his followers.

Amery,[1] a lively little English politician, talked to me about the situation. He is pleased at the agreement. He says that, if it had happened six months ago, it would have saved Austria. Now he regards the situation of Czechoslovakia too as desperate. He says that French intervention would have feeble results, like throwing stones at a lion engaged in eating a man—you annoy the lion and you don't save the man.

Signed an important commercial agreement with France. I kept out any note of exaggerated political optimism from the communiqué.

APRIL 15. I handed Mackensen the texts of the agreements with London. At the same time I underlined that there will be no change as regards the Axis. I also said that no particular importance should be attributed to the visit of Hore-Belisha.[2]

I have instructed Gayda[3] to write an article making it clear in becoming terms that the negotiations with London began before the Anschluss took place.

A long conversation with Cristich, back from Belgrade, on the situation resulting from recent events. I made a Minute of the conversation. The most important point is that Stoyadinovich intends to concert and harmonize his policy with ours, in so far as concerns the possibility of a German attack on Czechoslovakia with the support of Hungary and Poland. Quite rightly, he doesn't want to get mixed up in anything of the kind.

The Egyptians are asking for the same assurances as the English about the waters of Lake Tsana. The ministries are raising many objections. I believe we ought to consent. In the first place, because in practice it means nothing, and also because it is right to do a thing which helps to estrange Cairo from London.

9 p.m. I receive news that the Nationalists have reached the Mediterranean, and inform the Duce.

APRIL 16. The Duce agrees with me about the Tsana, and we have given our consent. The Pact is complete and ready for signature.

The French Chargé d'Affaires—France is the vanquished country of the moment—asked urgently for an interview. Very embarrassed, he read a long message from his Government asking for discussions with us before Geneva. There is just a touch of blackmail in this—an

---

[1] L. S. Amery, M.P. Secretary of State for India, 1940–5.
[2] Leslie Hore Belisha, Secretary of State for War, 1937–40.
[3] Virginio Gayda, editor of *Il Giornale d'Italia* and mouthpiece of the Fascist régime. Killed in an air raid on Rome in March 1944.

undeclared threat to oppose the British move in favour of recognition. I thanked Blondel for the communication and reserved my reply until I should confer with the Duce. France too has had a knock-out blow now.

I handed the Japanese Ambassador the text of the agreement and assured him of the solid nature of our sentiments for his country. Japan was our friend in difficult times. We shall not forget.

At 6.30 p.m. the Pact with England was signed. Lord Perth was moved. He said to me: 'You know how much I have wanted this moment to come.' It is true—Perth has been a friend. Witness dozens of his reports, which are in our hands. There was an atmosphere in the room of electric tension discharged. Many photographers and journalists. Then came the Egyptian Minister. The English treated him with great respect, because in the last phase of the negotiations Egypt has been rebelling against British tutelage and wanting to speak for herself. A crowd collected outside the Palazzo Chigi and shouted. Perth was cheered when he left. On the way to the Palazzo Venezia my car was surrounded and I was given an enthusiastic demonstration. The Duce was pleased. He praised me and said that he means to praise me in public. Meanwhile the crowd had arrived at the Piazza Venezia, so he showed himself on the balcony.

Then we got down to work. We examined the French request and decided to make a favourable reply.

APRIL 17. At 10 a.m. I received von Mackensen and informed him of the French move and of our decision. I handed him a copy of the memorandum left by Blondel and emphasized that we have consistently repulsed all overtures aimed at transforming the conversations with France into tripartite talks. With the Germans one always has to be laying the ghost of Stresa. They are so afraid of it that they are tempted to see it rise everywhere.

At the same time, things are not going well between us and our German friends in South Tyrol. Since the Anschluss the Germans there have been asserting themselves too much, with a steady increase of irredentist demonstrations which we cannot continue to tolerate. Prudence suggests prompt action, since certain agitations must be stifled at birth, in order that they may not be allowed to develop and require more drastic intervention. Only yesterday there was a more serious incident at Lasa, in which fire-arms were actually used. All this, on the eve of the Führer's visit, is serious.

I told the Duce that I should like on my own behalf to call Göring's attention to this situation. I have prepared a letter to Magistrati, which I shall show to the Chief to-morrow. If he agrees, I shall send it.

It is not enough for the German Government to disinterest itself in

the question and to repeat that our common frontiers are inviolable
—they must take action. They must repudiate the professional agitators. They must follow our example in Dalmatia. Propaganda ceased
and the Belgrade Pact flourished beyond all expectations.

APRIL 18. Aymard[1] expounded to me the programme for a review,
Audace, which he intends to launch as soon as possible, and asked me
for our financial assistance, to the extent of 200,000 lire for the first year.
The Duce approved of my letter to Magistrati. Meanwhile there
have been fresh incidents and we have evidence in our possession which
suggests that the authorities, possibly the minor authorities, know what
is going on. This danger to the Axis must be sterilized from the very
beginning. Otherwise we shall have serious complications. In his
presentation visit to the Duce, Mackensen said that the Führer had
decided to take radical measures against the agitators. Let him do so.
He must certainly know the names of the individuals at the head of the
irredentist activities in South Tyrol, just as we knew those of the leading
agitators in Dalmatia. A hint from him and the whole agitation will
cease. These Germans are indeed going too far—and not only in
Europe. I had a talk with the Brazilian Ambassador to-day, as I
wanted to put in a plea for our colonial institutions there. They are in
fact preparing a law against foreigners in Rio, simply as a result of the
excesses of the German community in Santa Caterina. As far as
concerns us, I was given ample assurances. But is it really a physical
necessity for these Teutons to exasperate the whole human race until
it forms a coalition against them? They must take care—that might
happen once again, and this time the retribution would be much more
serious than it was in 1919.

APRIL 19. I informed Blondel that we can begin conversations. On
our side there is no particular subject to be discussed except the recognition of the Empire. We are therefore waiting to hear the French
agenda, before making observations and proposals. Unofficially I told
Blondel that the French press should refrain from saying that all that
has happened and is happening has the object of weakening the Axis
—that is untrue and it only results in stiffening our position.
The Duce too is concerned about reactions in Germany and doesn't
want the *pourparlers* with France to be concluded before Hitler's visit.
It will be easy to arrange a little obstructionism—my visit to Albania,
slightly prolonged, will be useful for this purpose.
Czechoslovakia has recognized the Empire. So has Brazil, but with
a formula which is neither fish, flesh, nor fowl—I have already asked
for it to be modified.
Triumphal progress in Spain—by a bold move Gambara has taken

[1] Camille Aymard, a French journalist.

Tortosa in the rear and folded up the resistance of the Reds. The collapse should be not far off, and the initiation of conversations with France must help to discourage the Barcelona Government, abandoned by all to its inevitable fate. The Duce has telegraphed to Berti and to Franco.

APRIL 20. I told the Prince of Hesse to speak to Göring in my name about the situation in South Tyrol, which is becoming more and more unpleasant. Hesse was impressed by my exposition of the facts and said that he will intervene at once.

The Duce has been made furiously angry, and with reason, by the bad behaviour of some farmers from Bari who were being entertained in the Party House in Munich—they even relieved themselves on the stairs. A disgusting incident, likely to lower us to an unbelievable extent in the opinion of the Germans. The Chief said that our people must be imbued with a loftier national ideal, without which they cannot embark on the work of colonizing the Empire. He let fly at the 'sons of slaves', adding that if they had distinctive physical markings, he would exterminate them all, in the certainty of rendering a great service to Italy and to humanity. .

In the afternoon I took Amery to see the Chief. There was nothing particularly important in the conversation. Amery talked about Italy, England, and Czechoslovakia, and about economic questions. He would like the most favoured nation clause to be suppressed and a preferential arrangement between European countries to take its place.

Conversation with Piccio.[1] Flandin[2] intimates that he is prepared, if we wish, to be a candidate for the Rome Embassy.

Phillips was delighted with the agreement with London. I gave him some information about the talks with France.

APRIL 21. Monelli[3] gave me a report on the rapid change of public opinion in Paris. It seems that, with the exception of the Quai d'Orsay, which is as hostile as ever, the whole country is anxious for agreement with Italy.

The Duce talked to me about the state of the frontiers. He has prepared a memorandum, of which he is going to send me a copy. He intends, quite rightly, to seal the frontiers with Germany hermetically —and the frontiers with Yugoslavia semi-hermetically, because he believes in the possibility of a Slav-German alliance based on a common irredentism. I do not believe this. The Germans are hated, or at least feared, in Yugoslavia. But I agree about taking precautions in that direction too, as Yugoslavia might be invaded by the Germans. There

[1] General Piero Ruggero Piccio, Air Attaché at the Italian Embassy in Paris.
[2] Pierre Etienne Flandin, former French Prime Minister and Foreign Minister.
[3] Paolo Monelli, an Italian journalist.

must, however, be some plain speaking with Belgrade, and we must see if we can't arrange an understanding of a military nature straight away.

Conversation with Mackensen in the afternoon. I spoke to him about the restrictive measures taken by the Reich in Austria, particularly the abolition of the special tariff for Trieste and the order for the declaration by foreign residents of their foreign securities. All this, on the eve of the Führer's visit, cannot help but exacerbate people—the Germans must not forget that the Anschluss was a shock to many Italians. Mackensen saw the point and will do what he can. He also asked me about the situation in South Tyrol. I gave him only a brief explanation, as I do not want to deal with this question, which is of an internal nature, through diplomatic channels.

APRIL 22. Buffarini, Farinacci, Bottai.

Conversation with Blondel, who handed me the French proposals for discussion. I asked for time and reserved my reply until I should confer with the Duce. I observed, however, that there was one point on which we should find it difficult to agree: the French reservations on the section of the Anglo-Italian agreement dealing with the Red Sea.

It is clear that the Quai d'Orsay is alarmed at the idea of a *condominium* in the Red Sea and would like to be included in the arrangement.

Mussolini had just received Nicolas Franco when I saw him. He seemed displeased with the French proposals and said that the reply will have to be put off until my return from Tirana—which will be conveniently delayed. Nothing must be done until the Führer's visit is over.

I received the first Envoy Extraordinary of Manchukuo. He goes about with an interpreter, as he does not know a word of any foreign language.

APRIL 23. Council of Ministers.

The Duce showed me a very recent Leipzig publication, in which the question of South Tyrol is agitated again and offensive language is used about the Italian mountain population. He was indignant. 'These Germans,' he said, 'will compel me to swallow the bitterest pill of my life. I mean the French pill.'

Lunch with Hore-Belisha, followed by a conversation à *trois* at the Palazzo Venezia, chiefly on technical military matters. The Duce expounded his theories on the strength of the battalion, motorization, and the war of manœuvre. Hore-Belisha was full of praise for our military training and, like a good Jew, was as humble as could be about his own activities. He asked the Duce whether he thought there was any imminent danger of war. The Duce said No. Hore-Belisha thinks there is.

Conversation with Tatarescu.[1] A big man, who speaks perfect
French and has a more subtle intellect than his appearance suggests.
Like all Roumanians, he fears the consequences of the Anschluss, all
the more as he thinks it possible that Hungary may become a satellite
the Greater Reich. I was very reserved, as I always am with loquacious
types.
Received the Yugoslav Naval Mission.

APRIL 24. Another long talk with the Duce about the South Tyrol
question. Göring's reply has arrived, by way of Magistrati, but it does
not seem to me very explicit.
Later the Duce telephoned to me. 'I have clarified my ideas on the
subject,' he said. 'If the Germans behave well and are obedient Italian
subjects, I shall be able to encourage their culture and their language.
If, on the other hand, they hope to move the frontier post one single
yard, they must learn that it can't be done without the most bitter war,
in which I shall combine the whole world into a coalition against
Germanism. And we shall crush Germany for at least two centuries.'
The Brazilian Ambassador announced to me the official recognition
of the Empire. He was anxious to connect this step with the new laws
against the activities of foreigners in Brazil, in order to prove that these
laws are not directed against us.
Von Mackensen assured me of Germany's perfect goodwill for a
discussion and settlement of our problems with regard to the Anschluss.
Mussolini's opinion of Hore-Belisha is definitely unfavourable.

APRIL 25. Journey to Tirana. The usual popular demonstration
—double-barrelled, for me and for the Duke of Bergamo.[2] Reception
at Court. I met the Queen,[3] who is charming and has already learnt
to smile as a sovereign should, and also the royal princesses.

APRIL 26. Conversation with the King and a reception. It is
important that the King should have come in person to pay me a visit
at Libohova's house. The significance of this breach of etiquette must
be obvious to all.

APRIL 27. The wedding—the ceremony passed off with more
dignity than one might have expected. The Queen was radiant, the
King actually appeared moved, the courtiers were on their toes. The
populace remained indifferent and even seemed, by contrast, more
ragged than usual.

APRIL 28. Visited Italian interests.
Conversation with the King at Durazzo in the afternoon. Of this

[1] G. Tatarescu, Roumanian Prime Minister, 1934 to December 1937
[2] Adalberto of Savoy-Genoa, a cousin of the King of Italy.
[3] Countess Geraldine Apponyi, a Hungarian.

and of my other conversations, and also of my impressions and intentions, I shall draft a memorandum for the Duce. I leave Albania more firmly convinced than ever of the need for a radical solution.

APRIL 29. Came back on the *Bande Nere*. All the way from Bari to Rome the local inhabitants greeted me enthusiastically at the stations.

APRIL 30. I gave the Duce an account of my visit to Albania. I shall sum up my impressions in a report. But he agreed at once about the necessity for a radical solution and said that, so long as we get Albania, he is prepared even to have a war. I handed him a magnificent specimen of copper ore from the mines at Alessio, with the words 'Here are the Carthaginian figs.'

Berti has sent a report on the situation in Spain. The Duce, after summing things up, gave this directive: the corps of volunteers is to remain in Spain as a proof of Italian solidarity, but it will not be employed in any more operations on a large scale. Only in exceptional cases may permission be given for the employment of a particular detachment. The volunteers will leave Spain at the end of the war, or if and when 'non-intervention' makes some decision.

I resumed the negotiations with Blondel and found him very conciliatory. He agrees on the impossibility of reaching a conclusion before the Führer's visit and has accepted almost all my remarks.

I had a short talk with Perth, in connexion with the visit of the French Ministers to London. The results have been communicated to Grandi by Halifax.

Another long conversation with the Duce, in which I gave him an account of my activities of to-day. We laid the foundations for a pact of mutual respect to be proposed to the Germans during the forthcoming visit, a pact which would give some actuality to the Axis, now that the questions specified in the Protocols of October 1936 may be regarded as exhausted.

PART III

MAY 1, 1938 – SEPTEMBER 30, 1938

THE CRISIS OVER CZECHOSLOVAKIA

MAY I, 1938–SEPTEMBER 30, 1938

THE CRISIS OVER CZECHOSLOVAKIA

Ciano outlines a German-Italian treaty—The Führer in Italy (May 3–9)—Duce and King—Plans for Albania—France and the Red Sea—Mussolini makes a strong speech in Genoa (May 14)—Italy disinterests herself in Czechoslovakia—Negotiations with France at a standstill—Perth protests—Incidents in the Sudetenland—Perth on England's attitude to the Czech problem—Settimelli—Anti-French feeling—Ciano speaks in Milan—Air raids on Barcelona—Ciano meets Stoyadinovich in Venice (June 16–18)—Plans for reclamation in Albania—Germany offers a military alliance—Chamberlain in difficulties—England and the Italian troops in Spain—Implementation of the Pact postponed—Mussolini's 'third wave'—Offensive in Spain (July 13)—'Not persecution but discrimination'—Hungarian leaders in Rome—Red resistance in Spain—Opposition from the Church over the racial question—Progress in Albania—Germany prepares for action in Czechoslovakia—Pessimism over Spain—Anti-Jewish measures (September 1)—Germany's unknown plans—The Führer proposes a meeting with Mussolini—Plans for a partial withdrawal from Spain—Chamberlain at Berchtesgaden (September 15)—Mussolini tours northern Italy—Chamberlain at Godesberg (September 21)—Hesse in Venice with a message—Mussolini orders partial mobilization—Chamberlain appeals to Mussolini—Mussolini proposes a Conference of Four—Munich (September 29)—Ribbentrop proposes a Tripartite Alliance.

MAY 1. I presented an outline of the possible treaty with Germany to the Chief. He agreed. I shall propose the treaty to Ribbentrop, and point out to him that it is in our common interest to sign. We have made a Pact with London; we shall shortly be making one with the French: unless we define our relations with Berlin as well, everybody will say that the Axis has been liquidated and we are going back to Stresa.

In the afternoon I worked at writing my report and plan for Albania. It is preserved in the volume of my writings.

MAY 2. Nothing particular.

I went to see the Führer's apartment at the Palace. They have taken the opportunity to redecorate the house at our expense. The Princess and the Prince used to have most unsuitable bathrooms. Their new ones will be what is called princely.

Initialled the payments agreement with Spain.

Blondel sent me proposals for various articles of the agreement.

MAY 3. Arrival of the Führer.

MAY 4. I shall not record a chronicle of the Führer's stay, as it is amply reported in the press. I shall confine myself to a few unpublished incidents and conversations and impressions.

The first thing is of a domestic nature. The Court has absolutely declined to retire into the background and has shown itself to be a useless encumbrance.

When the Führer arrived, the populace was greatly disappointed to see that the founder of Italy's political power was not by his side in the triumphal progress through the imperial streets, which owe their conception and their realization to him. The Germans probably felt it as much as we did. At Naples too there was some sort of unpleasant incident, due to the incompetence of those in charge of the ceremony. The whole atmosphere is moth-eaten—a dynasty a thousand years old does not like the manner of self-expression of a revolutionary régime. To a Hitler, who to them is nothing but a *parvenu*, they prefer any paltry little king, of Greece or Denmark even, with a crown on his head and some indeterminate number of quarterings.

When Ribbentrop told me of the incidents, I made him speak to the Duce. The Duce said: 'Tell the Führer to exercise patience. I have been exercising patience for sixteen years. . . .' Ribbentrop replied that the one good thing the Social Democrats did in Germany was to liquidate the monarchy for ever.

The military parades have been magnificent. The Germans, who may have been a little sceptical on this point, will leave with a very different impression.

MAY 5. Ribbentrop has offered us a pact of military assistance, public or secret, whichever we prefer. I did not hesitate to tell the Duce I was against this, just as I have tried to delay the conclusion of a pact for political consultation and assistance.

The Duce intends to make the pact. We shall make it because he has a thousand and one reasons for not trusting the western democracies. I myself thought it was better to postpone it, in order not to create difficulties for Chamberlain just before the meeting of the League Council, at which he is to launch the recognition of the Empire. The signature of a pact, which might be susceptible of various interpretations, including that of a secret alliance, would make his task more difficult and put a weapon in the hands of the opposition at Geneva.

MAY 6. The Führer has been restrained in his conversations with the Duce. With me Hitler has not talked politics. Ribbentrop, on the other hand, is exuberant and occasionally frivolous. The Duce says he belongs to the category of Germans who are a disaster to their country. He talks about making war right and left, without naming an enemy or defining an objective. Sometimes he wants, in collaboration with Japan, to destroy Russia. Sometimes he wants to hurl his thunderbolts against France and England. Occasionally he threatens the United States. This leads me always to take his projects with a grain of salt. About specific and actual problems he is calmer. He declares that the Czechoslovakian question is not urgent and that a system of regional autonomy might perhaps delay the solution for several years. He adds, however, that, should it ever be necessary to liquidate the affair by force of arms, it would be done in a matter of days, before anyone had time to react.

The Polish corridor is accepted for an indefinite period by Germany, which actually desires to see the power of Poland increased as a means of strengthening the anti-Bolshevik barrier.

He confirmed to me what Hore-Belisha had said on the subject of colonies. Hitler told Lord Halifax that the colonial problem will come up in its turn, that is in a few years. For the moment Germany does not intend to force the pace.

MAY 7. The Führer has had a greater personal success than I had expected. Considering that he arrived in the midst of general hostility and was only imposed by the will of Mussolini, he has succeeded pretty well in melting the ice round him. His speech of last night helped a lot. His personal contacts too have won him sympathy. Particularly among women.

The King remains as hostile towards him as ever and tries to make out that he is some kind of psycho-physiological degenerate. He told the Duce and me that the first night of his stay at the Palace, at about one in the morning, Hitler asked for a woman. This caused a great commotion. Then it was explained—apparently he can't get to sleep, unless with his own eyes he sees a woman remake his bed. It was difficult to find one, but at last a hotel chambermaid arrived and the problem was solved. Supposing it to be true, it would be interesting and mysterious. But is it true? Or is it rather malice on the part of the King, who also insinuated that Hitler injects himself with stimulants and narcotics?

MAY 8. Mussolini believes that Hitler puts rouge on his cheeks in order to hide his pallor.

Hess and Himmler said to Anfuso that at the Palazzo Venezia there is an atmosphere of revolution, while at the Quirinal you get the impression of living in the world of an old-fashioned film.

The spectacle at the Stadium was superb. Even more than the military organization, which was perfect, the Germans must have appreciated the civil organization of the country, which is a thing more complicated and difficult to achieve. When the civil organization is perfect and the spirit of heroism is awake in a people, military organization is easily arrived at.

MAY 9. Florence welcomed the Führer with heart and head. It is a sensitive city, which understands everything. Hitler's speech on Saturday completely transformed the situation—even more perhaps than the declarations of respect for our frontiers the Italians loved the lyrical impetus with which they were made.

The farewell between Hitler and Mussolini at the station was very affectionate. Both men were moved. The Duce said: 'Henceforth no force will be able to separate us.' The Führer's eyes were full of tears.

When Goebbels was going through the rooms of the Quirinal, he said, as he passed the throne: 'Keep that gold and velvet object. But put the Duce on it. That chap'—indicating the King—'is too small. . . .'

MAY 10. In the train the Duce discussed my memorandum on Albania with me. He agrees with my decisions and believes that the month to act will be next May. That means we shall have a year for preparations on the spot and also in the international sphere. Since a diplomatic crisis will be precipitated and France and England will inevitably be against us, it is important to secure the pact with Germany. The pact will also serve to recommend a policy of moderation to Yugoslavia. Separated from her eastern and western friends and squeezed between Germany and Italy, Yugoslavia will have no choice but to adopt the attitude which we adopted towards the Anschluss.

I spoke to Jacomoni and told him to prepare for me a plan for local action—public works, charities, economic, sporting, and if possible political organizations.

Otherwise nothing new, except that at Geneva an anti-Italian charade is in preparation for Tafari's arrival. Halifax and Bonnet[1] may manage to suppress it, but they are putting up a poor show.

MAY 11. Conversation with Blondel. On all points it is easy to reach agreement, except Spain and the Red Sea. On Spain, he says that no French Government could father a Franco-Italian pact which did not mention the Spanish problem. And Mussolini does not want to mention it. For the Red Sea they would like to be associated with the Anglo-Italian agreement. The usual French mania for transforming the bilateral into the collective. As he left, Blondel said to me: 'I leave with a heavy heart.' I reassured him, not because I am optimistic, but because I did not want to weaken Bonnet's action at Geneva to-morrow.

The Spanish Ambassador is not opposed to our repeating to the

French the assurances given to London, provided that we ask for similar assurances from Paris and the closing of the Pyrenees.

MAY 12. The Duce was quite uncompromising towards the French requests. He rejects the idea of their adherence to the agreement for the Red Sea, which he means to regard as an Anglo-Italian *condominium*, and he refuses to talk about Spain with Paris. When I said that in that case we shall fail to reach an agreement, he replied that he will reach one with Berlin on the lines of Ribbentrop's proposals. And when I added that the agreement with London might also be damaged or even ruined, he talked about making an alliance with Tokyo. Once again the French will be to blame. God knows how hard I have worked to prevent the alliance with Berlin, which is burdensome for the present and worrying for the future. But I have come to think that French pettiness will render my efforts vain and that before long a new document will be signed in the halls of the Wilhelmstrasse. Mussolini has made up his mind.

I gave the Swiss Minister a dressing down for the arrest of some irredentists in the Ticino—with such effect that Ruegger turned pale. Switzerland must be prudent and not annoy us—her future is not rosy.

Stoyadinovich has let me know that he hopes to see me at Venice in June. Good. I will talk to the Duce and fix a date.

The American Ambassador expressed fears about the realization of a pact of military assistance with Berlin. I reassured him.

At Geneva the Abyssinian question has been buried.

MAY 13. I informed Perth of the difficulties we are meeting in the negotiations with Paris. I also told him that it would be most undesirable for England to associate France with the arrangement for the Red Sea and Arabia. It may actually not be possible, owing to article 3, which obliges Italy and Great Britain to resist every attempt on the part of a third power to establish itself in Arabia. We have virtually established a *condominium* of two powers—why turn it into one of three? And then there is the question of Spain—and here Mussolini is not prepared to compromise. Perth tried to facilitate an understanding, but he had to admit in the end that the French are bad negotiators.

On board the *Cavour* I told the Duce of my conversation with Perth. He is more and more anti-French. He says they are a nation ruined by alcohol, syphilis, and journalism. In his speech at Genoa he will not mention France. Nor Switzerland, whose attitude he finds unsatisfactory.

Talking of Spain, he said that he intends our troops to take part in a new offensive. To get them ready for action again he is prepared to send some officer reinforcements, as it is the officers who are most tired.

If, however, the London Committee reaches a decision about evacuation, he is ready to comply with it as far as we are concerned.

MAY 14. We arrive at Genoa at 8 a.m. The city looks beautiful, casting off the mist and clothing itself in the sun. Flags, sirens, salvoes. The crowd. The Chief speaks. It is a very strong, anti-French speech. The crowd hisses France, laughs, ironically, at the agreement with London. I have compared the speech as he delivered it with the draft he had prepared, in Sebastiani's possession. The draft was entirely different—the attack on France was lacking, he was more polite towards the English and less definite in promises towards Berlin. He was carried away by the crowd. Good. Now we must await reactions from Paris and London. Then we shall see what the tone of the negotiations can be, if indeed they are going to continue.

In the afternoon the Duce spoke again at the Fascist Headquarters. 'Genoa is, after Rome, one of the four imperial cities—Pisa, Ravenna, Venice, and Genoa. We too are now imperial and carry our flag beyond the seas, not as a Signoria or a Commune or a Republic, but as a united nation. Once Italy is united, it cannot but be an Empire. Once it is an Empire, it cannot but dominate other Empires. The enthusiasm I have seen to-day convinces me that the Italian people are not weary, but ready for a new assault.'

After spending the evening at the Medicis' house, I left for Rome.

MAY 15. Reactions to the speech are, for the moment, less strong than one might have expected. But I believe they will increase. Nothing new at the office. Peru has recognized the Empire.

MAY 16. I caught up with my interviews, receiving a series of more or less interesting personages.

All tne envoys, particularly those of the Danubian and Balkan states, have their heads full of the division of Balkan Europe into an Italian and a German sphere of influence. I gave the lie to this rumour put about by the French press.

I told the Czechoslovak Minister that we hope for a peaceful solution of the Czech problem, but that we are not directly interested in the question, and therefore cannot do more than preserve an attitude of neutrality. We did not move for Austria; can we be expected to move for Prague?

Villani brought me a secret pact for consultation, including a clause for military assistance in the event of unprovoked aggression on the part of Yugoslavia. I am rather sceptical about the advisability of these documents which are theoretically secret but become public just when they are likely to cause trouble. I shall speak to the Duce on these lines.

Grandi has sent me a letter for the Duce, asking to be appointed Minister of State. Here is a man who serves the régime disinterestedly.

MAY 17. Met the Duce at the station. In the car I informed him of Villani's *démarche*. He too is rather sceptical about the usefulness of a document of this kind. Stoyadinovich has declared to us that under no circumstances would he attack Hungary. Meanwhile the Duce wants Budapest to leave Geneva—after that we shall be ready to talk.

The Chief is working steadily to weaken Geneva, with a view to our action in Albania.

I had a long talk with Jacomoni about Albania and gave the Chief a list of a series of measures to be taken in order to prepare the ground. I also discussed the question with Pariani. He read my memorandum of May 2 and agrees completely on every point. He thinks that, with good preparatory work, the *coup* may be effected with comparative ease.

The Duce is still very worked up against France. He told me to postpone all communication with Blondel until the end of the week. I informed the Duce that in the present situation, and after his speech at Genoa, I consider it useless for me to make my report to the Senate. He agrees. I have telephoned to Federzoni to cancel the debate.

The Norwegian Minister made a statement to me about recognition, in such ambiguous and hesitating terms that I refused to accept it. He will telegraph to his Government to clarify the situation.

MAY 18. Lord Perth made a *démarche* concerning the consequences of the Genoa speech. I made a Minute of the conversation. In my reply I tried to draw a distinction between our relations with France and those with England—I don't know how far I was successful. However, Perth made his announcement very politely and with a certain bitterness—he was sincere in desiring the agreement and he is sincere in deprecating every possible cause of disturbance.

I received the Japanese Ambassador, who thanked me, as he always does, for a multitude of little things and then got down to the serious business: relations with England. He was pleased when I told him that the agreement with London has not weakened our feelings for Tokyo, and still more pleased when I did not deny that Anglo-Italian relations have, if only indirectly, felt the consequences of our difficulties with Paris.

The Belgian Ambassador. Petty affairs and great pomposity.

Cini—a clumsy physique, clumsy thinking, clumsy laughter. He tried hard to make me forget his Germanophobia of a few weeks ago and praised everything that he had abused—even Starace.

MAY 19. I found Mussolini more exasperated than ever with France. On the basis of my Minute he approved of the way in which

I had spoken to Perth. In consequence of a report from Tirana about the exaggerated activity of the German Minister, he told me to let Ribbentrop know that we regard the Albanian question as a 'family matter'. That is the phrase they used for Austria and the Sudeten Germans. It means 'hands off'.[1] The Duce declares that he is ready to go into Albania at once, even at the cost of setting fire to the European powder barrel. He is already making the necessary military preparations.

In the afternoon I saw Zanfirescu, the new Roumanian Minister. Like many of his countrymen, he is verbose, empty, and pompous. He can't open his mouth without talking about the Latin origin of his people, and he does it in such a way that every time I am left less convinced of the truth of his assertions. He does all the talking himself, which is a good thing, because I have read many of his telegrams and they show that you only have to say one word and he attributes the most fantastic statements to you. The Roumanians are the most untruthful of all diplomats. Zanfirescu entertained me with an account of the negotiations between Roumania and Hungary. He says that progress is slow because of Magyar obstructionism. It is quite possible, because I know what Kanya thinks on the subject. However, I expressed no opinion.

MAY 20. I saw the Duce twice. In the morning I found him in an easier mood than that of the last few days. He confirmed that he does not intend to begin discussions with the French and is waiting for the results of the economic negotiations in Berlin. He laid down certain principles for our policy towards Budapest: in the event of Hungarian action against Czechoslovakia, with German connivance, we remain disinterested; in the event of an unprovoked attack by Yugoslavia (an absurd supposition, which may be ruled out) we would help Hungary. In return Budapest must leave Geneva. Tirana too will have to leave Geneva, as I suggested in my memorandum on Albania.

Afternoon—the Duce was slightly worried about Chamberlain's position. He is being attacked in the press and Eden is being talked of again. I have telegraphed to Grandi to find out how things stand and whether we can make any move to strengthen the Prime Minister's position. When I hinted at the possibility of Eden's return to power, Mussolini shrugged hiss houlders and said: 'We shall see. One way or the other it will suit us well enough.' He is relying on the support of Germany on the continent.

Serious incidents in the Sudetenland, with a threat of complications with Germany. Slowly and inexorably the question is ripening.

[1] In English in the original.

MAY 21. Norway has recognized the Empire.

I went to see the Duce again in the afternoon, with Wysocki, who was making his farewell visit, and remained behind alone with him. He is pleased at the commercial agreement which Guarneri has reached with Germany. He had been given to understand by Guarneri that things were going badly, and I told him what Guarneri said when Hitler arrived—'the funeral of the Axis'. The Ministry for Trade and Currency is a centre of masonry—the Duce too is convinced of this.

He talked to me about the incidents occasioned by Sem Benelli's[1] play, *Orchidea*. He says there are still three kinds of anti-Fascist demonstration in Italy—funerals, the theatre, and witticisms. He criticized Sem Benelli's writing, which he regards as a public display of the worst side of human nature. 'Every house has a lavatory and we all know it is there. But that doesn't mean we show it to the guests who come to visit us.'

I reported on the Czechoslovak situation, which is growing more tense as a result of yesterday's incidents. Mussolini confirmed that he is not interested in Czechoslovakia's fate. In any case, he does not think that France will mobilize. I have been told that Paul Boncour,[2] asked whether he would mobilize in the event of German aggression against Prague, replied 'presque'. In that 'presque' lies the whole of democracy—it shows that the greatness of France is no more.

Conversation with Perth (Minute made). He told me what Great Britain has done in Prague and Berlin, and said that he regards the situation to-day as extremely dangerous—more dangerous than at any time since 1918. I confirmed Italian neutrality on the Czech question. According to Perth, France may mobilize at any moment.

MAY 22. The Duce believes that the Czech situation is not so alarming as many people think. He abused elections, saying that they have always brought misfortune to humanity. The French Revolution, the Spanish war, the Austrian crisis, and now the tension in Czechoslovakia have all followed or preceded agitations connected with elections. You cannot allow decisions of far-reaching importance to depend on that gelatinous mass, by definition irresponsible, which is the people. 'The people never knows what it wants, except to work little and earn much.' And yet to-day the peace of the world may depend on some drunken cretin, who provokes an incident in order to exercise his 'right' to vote. And all this simply in order to elect local officials for the Sudetens!

Lord Perth asked very urgently for an interview and I received him at 7 p.m. In a state of great alarm, he informed me of the communication made to von Ribbentrop yesterday. I made a Minute of the

---

[1] Sem Benelli, Italian poet and dramatist.

[2] Paul Boncour, French Foreign Minister, March to April 1938, and previously from 1932 to 1934.

conversation. Briefly: fresh counsels of moderation and a confirmation that in the event of war London will be by the side of Paris. I reassured Perth, telling him that, unless new and unexpected collisions have taken place to-day, Germany will not move. I displayed perfect serenity and told him that the Duce too is quite calm. That seemed to encourage him.

MAY 23. In Berlin too, according to what Magistrati said on the telephone, it is the English who are ringing the tocsin. They have gone so far as to put about a rumour that the Embassy is ready to ask for its passports. That is exaggerated—the elections have passed off without too many clashes and the situation is beginning to settle down. Meanwhile recent events have proved two things: that Germany is not ready for a collision, as some (particularly Ribbentrop) would like it to be believed, and that England is terrified at the idea of a war. Mussolini says that that is natural in a people which has a comfortable life and has made a religion of eating and games. Fundamentally, the Germans too have this tendency to hedonism, he thinks, but they are restrained by their heroic philosophy and by lack of space and wealth.

Conversation with Villani. I again explained our attitude towards the pact offered us and, following the Duce's instructions, I told him we will discuss it when Kanya comes to Italy. I hinted at the possibility of their leaving Geneva, but I saw that Villani blushed and began to drag in the topic of the minorities.

I informed von Mackensen of the state of the conversations with Blondel and the results of my meetings with Perth. Then I bluntly raised the question of Albania and said that we regard it as a 'family matter'.

Viola is optimistic about the situation in Spain. He says that Franco means to attack in Catalonia soon and that he expects this action to be the end of the rubber.

MAY 24. Opening of the *Dopolavoro*[1] Exhibition—very successful.

The Duce has told me to go to Milan and given me a few directives for the brief speech I am to make there.[2] I am to burn incense to Chamberlain. As far as the English are concerned, he wants to spread a little balm on the wounds he made at Genoa—or if not wounds, at least scratches. Perth recommends a policy of goodwill from Italy at the forthcoming meeting of the Non-Intervention Committee. I assured him I have already sent Grandi his instructions.

Bonnet has sent for Prunas and again given him general assurances in the sense of understanding and agreement with us. The Duce too

[1] *Dopolavoro* (After Work), the Fascist organization concerned with athletic, cultural, and other leisure activities.
[2] At the opening on June 2 of the second National Congress for the Study of Foreign Questions, organized by the Milan Institute for International Politics.

found the conversation very inconclusive—it took place in the Minister's private house, as the move did not meet with the approval of the bureaucrats of the Quai d'Orsay. With men of this kind at the helm of France it is not easy to come to an understanding.

MAY 25. Nothing very important. The French press, by all this shaking of the fist at Germany over the Czech question, seems likely to aggravate the situation. After an agreement reached on the telephone by Alfieri and Goebbels, our press will enter the lists to-morrow against the Parisian papers.

I have prepared an outline of my speech at Milan on June 2, but I shall have to await developments. At the moment days count like months, and the situation changes with the speed of the cinema.

MAY 26. The Franco-British press and certain rather untrustworthy quarters in Germany have raised doubts about the real attitude of Italy over the Czechoslovak problem. This led me to summon Ambassador Mackensen and repeat to him that our point of view is exactly that expressed to the Führer and to Ribbentrop—we are not interested in the fate of Prague and we are absolutely solid behind Germany. I also offered, if Berlin likes the idea, to confirm this line of conduct by a note in the *Informazione Diplomatica*. Although nothing new has happened, the Duce was more pessimistic to-day and foresees war. He declared that he will immediately enter the struggle by the side of the Germans.

Graziani talked to me about the Empire. He is not very convinced of the possibilities of the Duke of Aosta as Viceroy. He is weak and too much in the hands of his subordinates. This was to be expected, for royal princes are used to respect but not to command. Senator Gasparini[1] has expressed to me a rather similar opinion. He is, however, more hopeful than Graziani about the possibility of pacifying the Empire within a relatively brief period.

MAY 27. Berlin has not yet replied to our offer. They will, however, have to let us know their real intentions—do they want to proceed to the disintegration of Czechoslovakia or are they satisfied with a system of regional autonomy? From what Ribbentrop said in Rome, it seems to me that in the first instance they incline to the second alternative. It is now proved that it was Henderson who was responsible for ringing the tocsin at the wrong moment. He lost his head and made London believe that war was imminent and inevitable. And this panic of his easily communicated itself to the hysterical pacifism of the British.

At the 'Non-Intervention' Committee a little advance has been made towards the solution of the Spanish conflict. Following an incident in which one of our observers was arrested by the Reds, Grandi has sent one of his familiar 'Austerlitz bulletins' and has tried the usual whipping

[1] Jacopo Gasparini, former Governor of Eritrea.

up of the press. That happens every time the Committee meets. My own reflection is this: a man can save his country once, but there are very few instances of the same man doing it twice. Why does Comrade Count Grandi try to persuade himself that he saves his country four times a month?

The Duce told me about a letter he has had from Settimelli,[1] who is at the moment in Monaco. Having received a passport, he is immediately preparing to turn traitor. It was to be expected.

MAY 28. Council of Ministers. Nothing particularly important.

Apropos of Settimelli, the Duce told me that he is going to try to get him brought back to the Italian frontier, making use of the services of a British police official. He has given me Settimelli's letter.

At the Senate the Foreign Ministry budget was approved by acclamation, after a little speech read by Senator Crespi[2] and prepared by me and Federzoni.

Conversation with von Mackensen. The Germans will be delighted if we lay down our line of policy in an *Informazione Diplomatica*. But in order to do this, we must know precisely what their real intentions are. In Rome they gave us to understand that the regionalization of Czechoslovakia might be enough for the moment. But do they still hold to this opinion? Or do they rather want a disruption of the country? In any case, we must know. They must reveal their intimate thoughts to us. The Ambassador thinks that the acceptance of Henlein's[3] requests might satisfy Berlin. But he is not certain and, before giving a binding reply, he would prefer to make certain by telephoning Ribbentrop.

The commercial agreements have been signed in Berlin. The forecasts of the experts were pessimistic. Actually all has gone well. Politics have prevailed.

MAY 29. Spanish ceremony in the morning. The Adriano Theatre was packed. I was greeted with a loud demonstration. The two orators, Milan Astray[4] and the poet Pemán,[5] spoke with enthusiasm and colour, though their rhetoric strikes our public as rather baroque.

Fascist review in the afternoon.

Finished my speech for Milan.

MAY 30. The Duce has approved the draft of my speech, and says that he is going to give instructions to the Party to set in motion a great wave of anti-French feeling throughout the country. He authorized me

[1] Emilio Settimelli, a journalist. In 1929 he had published a volume of adulatory essays on Mussolini, *Mussolini visto da Settimelli*.
[2] Silvio Crespi, an industrialist.
[3] Konrad Henlein, leader of the S.D.P. (Sudeténdeutsche Partei).
[4] General Milan Astray, commander of the Spanish Foreign Legion.
[5] José Maria Pemán y Pemartín, a Spanish Catholic poet.

to tell Perth that the negotiations with France may be considered broken off, particularly as with its usual idiocy the Paris press, which is really to blame for the crisis, is trying to give an anti-German flavour to the agreement between Italy and France. I shall also recommend Perth to expedite the implementation of the Anglo-Italian Pact.

The Duce added that he will make the agreement with France eventually—on the eve of the occupation of Albania, so that the blow may be struck in an atmosphere of general euphory.

In the afternoon I took the Spanish air force officers to the Duce. Afterwards I received them at the Palazzo Chigi. I said a few words, telling them how the Italian decision to intervene was made and assuring them that, notwithstanding all committees, we shall not abandon them until the Nationalist flag is flying from the loftiest towers of Barcelona, Valencia, and Madrid.

Del Croix has cooled considerably in his enthusiasm for France, after being thoroughly badly treated in London by the delegation of the country whose praises he has assiduously sung for so many years. He is getting to know the French now—better late than never.

MAY 31. A great hullabaloo is being made in Germany over the people's car—seven million are to be built and almost every family will have its own little car. Mussolini's comment, on reading a report on the subject to Attolico, was that this will promote the spirit of hedonism already innate in the Germans and make the people less warlike. If you turn your people into bourgeois, you also turn them into pacifists.

De Bono mentioned to me rumours of a ministerial reshuffle, and asked me what truth there is in them. It is astonishing that a man of seventy-two, who from the first days of the régime has been sitting more or less in the front row of the stalls, should still be ingenuous enough to believe in rumours. . . .

Bulgaria has recognized the Empire. They had already made a gesture in that direction—now it is a full and formal recognition.

The Japanese Naval Attaché has shown me a report about a supposed military agreement between France and England. They have also spoken to our Attaché in Tokyo. They would like to make a secret pact with us. I am not opposed to the idea. One sees, from the historical point of view, that Italy and Japan will have to march side by side for a long time.

Von Mackensen has confirmed that Germany's intentions towards Czechoslovakia are pacific and has declined the offer of an *Informazione Diplomatica*. The press has already done good work. I in my turn have declined Ribbentrop's proposal to send a commission to South Tyrol in order to remove the last hopes of the German-speaking population. We will look after this problem by ourselves.

JUNE 1. Nothing particularly important.

I telegraphed to Berti to move our troops from Saragossa and send a battalion or so to the front. They have now been resting for more than forty days, and it seems from reports we have had that a bad impression is being created by the sight of Italian troops filling the cabarets and brothels in the back areas, while the Spaniards are fighting a grim battle. It is true that our soldiers worked hard for two months, broke through the Red lines, and opened a path to the sea. Nevertheless, the soldiers of Fascism must not, at any moment or for any reason, set an example of indifference to the struggle.

Japan continues to press for the strengthening of her military ties with us. The Duce too is in favour of the idea.

JUNE 2. My speech went well. Though it wasn't easy to warm up this collection of old vegetables. Retired ambassadors, retired generals, retired admirals, and other retired brains made up the greater part of the audience—all people who would have been more inclined to applaud a conservative speech leading Italy back to the path of pacifism or even collective security.

Pirelli told me at the station, without concealing his satisfaction, that during the discussion in the afternoon on politics in the Balkans an anti-German atmosphere was generated. I immediately told Starace to put all the speakers under observation and, if necessary, take disciplinary measures. This terrified Pirelli, who tried to produce some sort of excuse but only succeeded in making the situation worse.

I don't like these meetings. You immediately get a parliamentary atmosphere. These old men find themselves together again and they think nostalgically of the Chamber of the good old days, of eternal principles, of Masonic lodges. And in these suggestive surroundings they forget that they have at least hidden their green aprons under black shirts.

JUNE 3. I gave the Duce some impressions of the meeting. He thinks as I do and says it will be the last. As for my speech, he was pleased with it—the international press too, with the natural exception of the French press, has given it a good reception. The Duce confirmed that he has given the Party orders to produce a 'wave of Gallophobia in order to liberate the Italians from their last remaining slavery: servility towards Paris'. The Chief has also ordered me to resume the dispatch of volunteers to Spain, in small groups and in mufti. Two thousand to start with.

The Prince of Hesse confirmed to me that the Führer does not intend to force the situation in Czechoslovakia. He will do so, however, if provocations on the part of the Czechs continue. Hesse also told me, as a family secret, that the King of Greece shows signs of mental unbalance. He is in the hands of two spiritualists, whom he consults before taking any decision. He claims to be protected by the 'Red Cloud' and to be in direct communication with it!

I assured Plessen that there had been no official negotiations for the delivery of Caproni aircraft to the English. There were simply private commercial conversations. I also told him that we should be against a proposal for mediation in Spain and that we regard the conversations with France as broken off.

I had a long talk with Perth. Taking advantage of the euphory produced by my Milan speech, I asked for the implementation of the articles of the Pact of April 16. I made a Minute of the conversation. Perth seemed to me very reasonable. He too is convinced that you cannot remain engaged all your life—the moment comes when you have to get married.

JUNE 4. I received the new Polish Ambassador.[1] I had already met him when he came here as head of the Military Mission. He is a man with a fine presence, pretty frank and a little too self-possessed. He claims to be animated by the best intentions towards us.

Giro, the head of the *Dopolavoro* in Albania, reported to me. He is now in control of considerable elements in the country. Public opinion is steadily rising against the King and his brigands. Italian intervention in the event of disturbances would meet with no opposition, and after three days of quiet we could impose ourselves in such a way as to destroy every trace of the desire to resist. The common people, who are suffering, are far removed from politics and would welcome with joy any improvement in material conditions. I told him to be ready for everything but not to act without orders from me. Meanwhile he is to carry on propaganda among the masses by means of the *Dopolavoro*, relief work and sport.

The Duce is angry with Farinacci, the leader of the anti-Semitic movement, for himself having a Jewish secretary, Jole Foà. This is the kind of thing which foreigners see as proof of a lack of seriousness in many Italians.

JUNE 5. Nothing new. The Duce went off to Romagna. Sunday at the sea.

JUNE 6. Ajello[2] tells me that there is violent hatred of France in Leghorn. Apart from the memory of the so-called Vespers of 1917,[3] the problem of Corsica is felt there more than anywhere else in the country. On a fine winter day it seems as though you could hold out your hand

[1] General Boleslaw Wieniawa-Dglugoszowski.
[2] Umberto Ajello, *Federale* of Leghorn.
[3] The incident alluded to in fact took place in November 1918. French troops awaiting repatriation in Leghorn aroused the hostility of the inhabitants, and riots broke out. As in the Sicilian Vespers in 1282, an insult offered by a French soldier to an Italian woman is said to have been the immediate cause of the trouble.

and touch Corsica. Ours it is, one of the group of our islands, inhabited by our people. They can't understand in Leghorn why it has to belong to foreigners. And at night they go furtively and let down their nets in Corsican waters. When Corsica is ours, it will give a formidable impetus to Leghorn.

Agreed with Cavagnari to send Admiral De Courten to Japan. As the political agreement with Tokyo is to be buttressed by a military agreement, it is desirable to have the man for the job on the spot straight away.

General Gambara thinks it possible for our troops in Spain to be used again while we are waiting for the evacuation. We still have about 20,000 Italian combatants, plus 18,000 of the Arrow division[1], plus a Spanish division. With this force he thinks we can mass for a breakthrough in the direction of Valencia. I told him to go ahead. He is a soldier with great qualities, a little temperamental sometimes, but intelligent and courageous.

JUNE 7. Nothing new.

JUNE 8. A short talk at the sea with Stein and Helfand. They were particularly interested to know what truth there is in the rumours of forthcoming ministerial changes. I contradicted all the gossip. Stein said that he for his part hopes I will stay at the Palazzo Chigi and not go to the Party and the Ministry of the Interior. Helfand added that worse things could happen. . . .

I received Mr. McAneny,[2] President of the New York Fair. The Ambassador was with him. He is said to be an important man, but he doesn't look it. He is a wizened, dim little old man, bundled up in an old-fashioned morning-coat. He said just what all Americans say, playing in a suitable manner the old gramophone record of pacifism and collaboration. With emphasis, but without conviction. Phillips was delighted.

The international press is very excited about Franco's air raids. It appears from a French intercept that in Barcelona all the dumps of fuel are on fire—65,000 tons of petrol. The fire is expected to last four days, and all ships have had to leave the harbour, because the blazing oil floats and was being carried towards them by the current.

JUNE 9. Franco-British excitement over Franco's air raids continues, but I don't believe it will lead to anything positive. Meanwhile the Duce has decided to increase the reinforcements we are sending to Spain. This month and July two thousand are to go instead of one thousand—four thousand in all. And this figure might be exceeded.

[1] A mixed division of Spanish and Italian troops.
[2] George McAneny, a banker prominent in New York municipal affairs.

JUNE 10. Nothing new.

Colonel Piéche,[1] of the Carabiniers in Spain, is pessimistic about the duration of the war and the possibility of Franco reorganizing the country. Many parts of it, he thinks, are still irreconcilably red.

JUNE 11. In the evening Bocchini and Buffarini came to see me, in great alarm over the reports of the activity which Settimelli is planning in France. He is going to start by publishing a sensational book. This would not have happened if I had been able to act, through Emanuele, while Settimelli was in Monte Carlo. The Duce approved. But then Bocchini suggested the possibility of a legal solution and the Duce preferred it. But the legal solution failed, and now the operation looks more difficult. However, we have agreed upon a plan—Settimelli will have to return to Monte Carlo, and we shall then have a better chance of success. I hope it may be possible to abduct him by motor-boat. If not, we shall see. Emanuele is skilful, unscrupulous, and always ready to act. A traitor like Settimelli deserves no respect.

Otherwise nothing new. The question of the air raids in Spain is beginning to subside.

JUNE 12. Nothing new. Sunday at Capri—went by seaplane with Ciccino. Dined with the old *habitués* of the Aragno Café.[2] The passage of the years has left a deep mark alike on faces and on minds.

JUNE 13. Report from Talamo[3] on the situation in Bulgaria. There are fears of a union with Yugoslavia, and many circles are working to discredit Yugoslavia. Overwhelming influence, economic and therefore also political, of Germany. Not much scope for us. We shall try to get hold of the aeronautical market, which is still partially free.

Jacomoni brought me some reports on Albania and formulated various proposals. He is by nature a moderate man and inclines to a half-way solution, which would allow the King to remain but subject him more and more to us. But he agrees on the advantages of getting rid of him, when the moment comes to opt for the radical solution of annexation. Among the various requests of the King the most important is that for a yacht. We must give him one and man it with an Italian crew. That will guarantee the impossibility of his escaping in any eventuality.

Berti telegraphs that Franco intends to push on towards Valencia on Saturday. But on the strength of his fourteen divisions he has declined our offer to send the Volunteer Corps into action. He reserves the right to employ it for the capture of Madrid, which ought to follow shortly after that of Valencia.

[1] Colonel Giuseppe Piéche, commander of the Italian Carabiniers in Spain.
[2] A celebrated literary café in Rome.
[3] Marchese Giuseppe Talamo Stenolfi di Castelnuovo, Italian Minister in Sofia.

JUNE 14. I made the final arrangements with Cristich for Stoyadinovich's stay in Venice.

I have ordered 500 tons of maize to be sent to Albania, which is now suffering from a severe famine. This is the kind of gift of which the people are most sensible.

I have authorized Berti to arrange for the repatriation of some of the most fatigued of our troops, whom he will be able to replace by the 4,000 reinforcements we are sending.

JUNE 15. To Romagna. A brief talk with the Duce, during which I informed him of recent diplomatic developments, of which he approves. He gave orders for Senator Prampolini[1] to be sent to Albania to study the reclamation of land there. Dined at Anfuso's house at Stra. Arrived at Venice late in the evening.

JUNE 16. Nothing much, except the arrival of Stoyadinovich. Very friendly.

JUNE 17. At the Lido, where we had a long conversation. Minute made. On the whole all is going very well. The two countries are still more closely united as a result of the Anschluss. We confirmed the policy of close collaboration.

JUNE 18. Stoyadinovich left. A very friendly farewell. The crowd cheered Yugoslavia enthusiastically.

A brief talk with Balbo. Sour and hostile to everything. He spoke ill of the Germans, defended the Jews, attacked Starace, criticized *voi*[2] and the business of the Roman salute.

With the Duce at Riccione. He is satisfied with the results of my conversation with Stoyadinovich. He ordered me to send a further 1,000 tons of maize to Albania. He confirmed his intention to act and occupy Albania before the end of 1939. I told him about my talk with Balbo, which made him very angry. 'That man,' he said, 'will end like Arpinati or even worse. If he attempts to move a finger, I shall put him under arrest.' He told me not to act against Settimelli for the present. 'He will pay for it later. My enemies have always ended up in jail—and sometimes under the surgeon's knife.' He confirmed his policy of uncompromising autarky and spoke again of the need for a severe discipline. 'Italy will never be sufficiently prussianized. I shall not leave the Italians in peace, until I have six feet of earth over my head.' He attacked the monarchy, describing it as 'the brake on the régime'. He thinks of doing some liquidation here too after the end of

---

[1] Natale Prampolini, a landowner and industrialist, who had played a leading part in reclamation schemes in Italy.

[2] The Fascists were trying, without much success, to replace *lei*, the polite form of address in the third person, by the less formal *voi* (equivalent to *vous*).

the war in Spain. Morally and physically he is in tremendous form. I returned to Rome by car.

JUNE 19. Nothing worthy of note. At the sea.

JUNE 20. My conversation with Perth (Minute made) was not very fruitful from the point of view of Anglo-Italian friendship. It is not possible for us to accede to the request that we should promote an armistice now, just when Franco is winning. In civil war there can be no compromise. I reported to the Duce. I consider that this deferment of the implementation of the agreement to the Greek Calends is very dangerous. France is at her old game of troubling the waters. Herriot[1] told Tamburini[2] that he regards war between Italy and France as inevitable.

Volpi. I chilled his enthusiasm for France and England. He guesses that we have designs on Albania and is pleased. He insists also on a subsequent operation in Anatolia.[3]

The Princess of Piedmont was fishing for news of the monarchy question. She said that, if she were not what she is, she would be against dynastic rule. She is going to teach her son several trades, as she believes that one day the boy will have to work and live by his work. The Savoy family believes in divine right. She does not. The only merit she recognizes in dynasties is that they don't try to make money—an obvious dig at the Fascists. She distrusts Starace and feels he is an enemy. I denied this and tried to soothe her apprehensions by telling her there is no need to worry.

JUNE 21. I instructed Prampolini to go to Albania to study the plans for reclamation. Naturally I did not conceal from him the political purpose of his mission. This excited him, and he accepted with delight. He will do well there. Jacomoni, who was present at the conversation, will present him to the King.

Opening of the Italo-German Congress of Law, with a good speech by Frank.[4] Even the anti-Axis Bottai and De Francisci[5] applauded warmly. They see which way the wind is blowing. . . .

The Mission just back from Japan confirms the warmth of Japanese sentiments towards us and the remarkable military strength of the country. Contrary to what masonic-Jewish propaganda would like us to believe, Japan has committed only a very small proportion of her forces in China. The war potential is intact.

I delivered our note about Swiss neutrality.

[1] Edouard Herriot, former French Prime Minister. Mayor of Lyons.
[2] Antonio Tamburini, Italian Consul-General at Lyons.
[3] Volpi had large financial interests in the Levant.
[4] Hans Frank, German Minister for Justice.
[5] Baron Pietro De Francisci, former Italian Minister for Justice.

JUNE 22. I informed von Mackensen of my conversation with Perth, of my reply and of the Duce's decisions. He is very pleased. Every now and then these Germans require an injection of confidence where we are concerned. And yet they ought to understand by now that the Italy of Mussolini follows a straight line and is true to her word. But it will take us a long time to undo the platitudes produced by a still longer tradition of servility, intrigue, and pandering. We shall succeed.

The Duce is back. I met him at the airport. I informed him that the Volunteer Corps will go into action again in Spain very soon. He is pleased. He approved of my replies to Perth and absolutely refuses to compromise—we shall not modify our policy towards Franco in the smallest degree and the agreement with London will come into force when God pleases. If indeed it ever will. He is in a good mood, because the crops, particularly the corn, have recovered after all the bad forecasts and promise pretty well.

I assured Conde, who was slightly anxious, of our intentions. I told him that the best way to give the lie to the gossip is to send the Italian legionaries into battle on the road to Valencia straight away.

Talked to Pariani about Albania and decided on the building of the road from Shiak to Mare.

JUNE 23. The Duce talked about economic questions. He says he means to introduce monopolies for sugar, alcohol, and electricity. Fascist Italy cannot be less courageous than Giolitti, who in 1906 made the railways a monopoly. He criticized generals who go in for oratory. He says you must never talk to soldiers about death—on the contrary you should persuade them that they will kill and themselves always remain unhurt.

I saw the Duke of Aosta at the sea. He appears to be well, but his wound is still unhealed. Three months after the operation this is an ugly symptom. He means to go back to East Africa and is very keen on plans and programmes. On the whole he is optimistic about the situation in the Empire. He thinks we shall be able to reduce expenditure, and obtain just as good results if we are not in too much of a hurry. He does not speak well of the colonial officials—50 per cent incompetent and 25 per cent thieves.

Balbo came with me to the Ministry, where we had a long conversation. In the car he uttered literally these very revealing words: 'There no longer exists a taste for sincerity in Italy.' He is depressed. He thinks of staying in Libya, as he realizes that that is still the best solution. Fundamentally he is a man easily dominated and also easily outmanœuvred.

Conversation with the Turkish Ambassador. Minute made. I declined the offer of a pact for the eastern Mediterranean and encouraged the Turks to make a *coup de main* on the Sanjak of Alexandretta. France will not be able to react, without committing herself in such a way as to weaken herself still further on the Continent.

JUNE 24. I took the Duce the notes about Swiss neutrality. We only sent them because the Germans had done the same. We saw no need for them ourselves. The Duce commented: 'When I say that Switzerland is the only country which can be democratic, they take it as a compliment and it is in fact a frightful insult. It is like telling a man that he alone can be a hunchback or a eunuch. Only a base, vile, insignificant country can be democratic. A strong and heroic people tends to aristocracy.'

I telegraphed to Grandi and Prunas to inform them that if, as is rumoured, there should be a Red 'raid'[1] on an Italian port, we should immediately proceed to acts of war. I have also informed Berlin.

I assured Villani that Yugoslavia has friendly intentions towards Hungary. She is even thinking of a pact, without simultaneous action on the part of her allies of the Little Entente. Hungary must not, however, take the initiative in an attack on Prague, but wait for the fruits of German action. I emphasized the advantages of an understanding between Budapest and Bucharest, with the object of further isolating Prague and France. Imredy[2] and Kanya want to come to Rome, in July. It might be better to postpone it a little. Nothing is decided about Geneva. I repeated that we are waiting for Hungary to leave the League.

JUNE 27.[3] Attolico has sent a long report describing some conversations with Ribbentrop. Briefly what it amounts to is a renewal of the offer of a military alliance.

The situation has changed since the beginning of May. Relations with Great Britain have not developed as we might have hoped. The offer assumes a new value. Mussolini is in favour. He has told me to telegraph accepting a visit of Ribbentrop to Como, during which 'the matter will be discussed in all seriousness'. Meanwhile he wants to prepare public opinion. 'We shall have to explain to the Germans,' he added, 'that I shall make the alliance when it ceases to be unpopular. I am working in this direction.' At the same time we are endeavouring to ascertain the precise relations between Berlin and Tokyo.

Received a visit from Lutze,[4] full of admiration for the organization

---

[1] In English in the original.
[2] Bela Imredy, Hungarian Prime Minister, 1938–9 and 1944–5.
[3] The leaf for June 25 and 26 is missing from the diary.
[4] Viktor Lutze, leader of the S.A. (*Sturmabteilungen*) since the death of Röhm in 1934.

of the Militia—it is indeed making miraculous progress under the guidance of Russo.

Conversation with Cristich—general survey. Another with the Czech, to whom I repeated the usual formula: come to terms with Berlin. Another with the Brazilian about a question of the right of asylum.

Grandi told me on the telephone that things are looking blacker in London. The news of fresh attacks on British ships has roused public opinion. There will be seventeen questions in the Commons to-morrow. Chamberlain's position is more and more shaken. I have informed the Duce.

JUNE 28. The situation in London is becoming steadily more difficult for Chamberlain. Grandi, enigmatic and anxious not to compromise himself, describes the situation as very sombre. Mussolini is calm. Very calm. He does not intend to force Franco into stopping the air raids, and he has no desire to make any declaration of this kind. He awaits events with his usual statuesque imperturbability. I saw Perth, who is very alarmed. I made a Minute of the conversation. He fears that Chamberlain may fall. The Duce, on the other hand, does not believe that this can happen before the visit of the English King and Queen to Paris, i.e. before July 19. 'If Chamberlain falls,' he added, 'we shall see who takes his place. I shall base my decisions on the positive and concrete factors of the situation which then arises. For the moment I am waiting.'

Prampolini has received his final instructions for his mission to Albania. He is as enthusiastic and dynamic as a boy of twenty.

Report from Admiral Riccardi[1] on his mission to Malta. Nothing particularly important. His reception was apparently very friendly.

JUNE 29. I found the Duce very irritated at the rumours in the international press about my conversation with Perth. He is afraid people will try to give it the significance of a threatening pressure on the part of London. I suggested we should get Gayda to write an article on the basis of my Minute of the conversation. He accepted, but added that, if the press continues to make a fuss about every interview with Perth, he will forbid me to receive the British Ambassador, as he did some years ago in the case of de Beaumarchais,[2] who for a long time was refused access to the Palazzo Chigi. The Duce is angry with Grandi for his anxiety in the last few days. 'When are you going to make up your mind to put him in the corner?' he said.

We are in for an incident with Brazil, because Lojacono gave asylum to Captain Foumier, who led the revolt against Vargas a month ago.

[1] Admiral Arturo Riccardi, Under-Secretary for the Navy and Chief of Naval Staff, 1940.
[2] Maurice Caron de Beaumarchais, French Ambassador in Rome, 1927–33.

Lojacono had in fact no right to do this. Asylum may be given at most in flagrant cases. We shall see how the situation develops. It is difficult to judge from here, so I am leaving Lojacono to get himself out of his own mess. But I have no great confidence in his abilities, and I fear he may already have compromised himself unnecessarily.

Massimo tells me that the Germans were much alarmed by the rumours of my being transferred to the Party and Ministry of the Interior.

JUNE 30. The Duce gave me a minute of the note I am to hand to Perth on Saturday in reply to his communication to me in our conversation of the 20th. Briefly, he rejects in sharp terms the suggestion of an armistice and unilateral evacuation. He confirms that he will only resume conversations with France after the implementation of the Anglo-Italian agreement. This note will stir up the situation again—to-day it is beginning to settle down. But these lulls are temporary and sporadic—the general picture remains black. In the scheme for the evacuation of the volunteers I have found several details of procedure of which we had not been informed and which seem to me quite unacceptable. To search the volunteers, keep them under observation in special camps policed by international guards armed with hoses and tear gas, and subject them to other tyrannical measures of this ridiculous nature, is neither possible nor honourable. I telephoned Grandi. Octopus-like, after fouling the water he has withdrawn from the discussion. I will talk to the Duce to-morrow. I am certain that he will refuse to expose the Black Shirts of Malaga, Santander, Guadalajara and the Ebro to such humiliations.

Received von Mackensen, who brought me a photograph of von Ribbentrop with a most friendly dedication. I gave him mine in return.

JULY I. A few modifications have been made in the note I am to give Perth to-morrow evening. At my suggestion the Duce removed the word 'absurd', used more than once to describe the English proposals for an amnesty and evacuation, and substituted a less offensive epithet. In addition, I am to tell Perth that, until the Pact comes into force, we resume liberty of action, that we request the publication of the documents, and that we are waiting for a definite reply. It is a strong note—a crisis in our relations with London is almost inevitable.

Grandi reports that he has obtained the removal from the evacuation scheme of the unacceptable points about the disarmament and the rest of the petty persecution of the volunteers. This is just as well, for the Duce, after I had discussed the matter with him, was determined to defend the pride and the honour of the Black Shirts, even at the cost of shattering the whole scheme.

Berti has communicated the plan of attack. It is to begin on the 6th, and the line of advance for the Corps of Volunteers is Teruel–Valencia. We shall get through. We always have got through. Meanwhile the dispatch of reinforcements continues. It has been decided that about 600 artillerymen are to go.

JULY 2. I am not well. However, I stayed in the office to see Perth. I made a Minute of the conversation. Perth was overwhelmed, literally overwhelmed, by the reading of Mussolini's note and by my declarations. Usually he is witty and quick in argument, but to-day he was bewildered and vague in his replies and had little to say for himself. To use a boxing term, I might describe him as 'groggy'.[1]

Mackensen was very satisfied—immediately afterwards I handed him the note and gave him an account of the conversation.

I came home with a raging fever.

JULY 3. At home—still feverish and uncomfortable.

JULY 4. I am better, but very weak and exhausted by my illness. I listened to the Duce's speech at Aprilia on the wireless. When I heard his voice, I started to cry like a small child.

JULY 5. Back to work.

I found the Duce still quivering with excitement from yesterday. More and more decidedly and openly anti-French. He says that the Paris press is simply strengthening the Axis with its talk of Mussolini's desertion of Hitler. 'If the day should ever come for that to happen, I would tell him so frankly. That is my style. I am not a traitor.' He attacked Catholic Action sharply. He says that the priests are deceiving themselves, if they think they are a positive force in Italy. A priest of Verona, which is a Catholic province, only had to prohibit dancing for all the young people to desert the churches and flock to the dance halls. In Romagna on the other hand the priests are too shrewd to prohibit dancing. In any case, even Mary danced round the ark.

Pirelli, with his disingenuous candour, came begging on behalf of the Institute of Foreign Politics. I spoke to him about the Congress, and he pretended it was news to him. He is just back from London, where he says he found a very tense situation. He now puts on a no compromise act, though it makes his flesh creep, and even grits his teeth and talks like a Germanophile.

Agostini[2]—about Göring's chamois.

Buffarini—we made a survey of the internal situation.

JULY 10.[3] The Duce has made me ask Berti whether he requires reinforcements and on what scale. He is ready to grant anything Berti

---

[1] In English in the original.
[2] A. Agostini, head of the Forest Militia.
[3] The leaves for July 6 to 9 are missing from the diary.

asks, over and above the figure of almost 5,000 men already sent in the last few weeks. The position with London is getting more and more complicated. This—in the Duce's opinion—serves to divert towards the Axis the sympathies of the enervated and defeatist bourgeois class, which, after the agreement of April 16, hoped for peace through an understanding with the western democracies. Mussolini is very angry with this section of the bourgeoisie, always ready to let its trousers down. He talks of a third wave, to be set in motion in October, with the support above all of the masses, workers and peasants. He intends to introduce the concentration camp, with more severe methods than those used in the present form of police detention. A first hint of the turn of the screw will be given by a bonfire of Jewish, Masonic, and pro-French literature. Jewish writers and journalists will be banned from all activity. All this, in any case, was foretold in the Duce's preface to the Acts of the Grand Council. Henceforth the revolution must impinge upon the habits of the Italians. They must learn to be less 'sympathetic', in order to become hard, relentless, and hateful—in fact, masters.

JULY 11. Gave Blondel a reply about the frontier incident. There was really nothing in the reply, but the tone was fairly conciliatory. However, I did not omit to point out more than once that the tourist who crossed the frontier was a lieutenant of the artillery. Neither Blondel nor I alluded to politics.

Conversation with Hesse, sent here by Ribbentrop. Purpose: the pact of military assistance. Ribbentrop insists that this pact should be made. I replied that the Duce and I share his ideas, but that we want to see how relations with London develop and prepare a broad foundation of popularity for the agreement. In any case, Ribbentrop, who says that Japan too is prepared to participate in the pact, appears to have renounced the idea of a visit to Como, which would open the door to rumour prematurely. He wants the preliminary negotiations to be conducted secretly through Hesse, without the knowledge even of the Embassy.

Perth communicated to me London's reply to our conversation of July 2. Minute made. Nothing to be done. Our point of view is not accepted—for the settlement of the Spanish affair they demand effective evacuation. There is no alternative but to wait. With all the dangers which waiting involves.

JULY 12. The Duce too is dissatisfied with the British reply. On our part there is nothing more to be said. We shall await the development of events in Spain. As for my conversation with Hesse, the Duce, while taking a keen interest in the affair, says we should postpone the commencement of the preliminary conversations for the present. The

Japanese Ambassador has been put in the picture of the situation, as we see it. I have also informed Mackensen of the result of the conversation with Perth.

Baldur von Schirach[1] came to see me. I was very polite to him and decorated him with the Grand Cordon of San Maurizio. It seems that some time ago he took offence because he only had a ribbon regarded by him as inadequate. That explains some of his slightly unorthodox behaviour towards us and his futile flirtations with France. When I spoke to the Duce about it, he replied: 'Certainly. You can give him my decorations too, if you like.' The Duce's contempt for decorations is such that he doesn't even trouble to refuse them.

JULY 13. The offensive in Spain has begun. Final goal Valencia. First objective Segorbe. Berti has issued a laconic announcement. Gambara has sent a telegram like himself, full of fire. Reading it, the Duce commented: 'Gambara is a general I am keeping my eye on. I like him. He is not one of those soldiers—there are plenty of them—who wander into the barracks by mistake, when the right door for them is that of the convent. He is a soldier who loves war. I'm sure *he* doesn't put cotton-wool in his ears when the guns are firing.' No news during the day. At midnight an official dispatch informs us that it is 'going well'.

Sereggi brought me a project of King Zog for a revolution in Turkey. As rumours have already begun to circulate in Tirana to the effect that we are planning an action in Albania, I don't want any attempts at a diversion. However, I shall examine the project. I told Sereggi that, in view of my heavy commitments in the West, I have no aims in the Adriatic beyond the *status quo*. I promised assistance and interest in Albania. Particularly in the sphere of land reclamation. I conferred with Prampolini, who seems to have been fired with enthusiasm by his first visit to the country. He goes back soon to continue his investigations. But he is already talking of the reclamation at Durazzo as easily practicable. He assures me that we shall be able to plough in December 1939, and that in five years we shall have full-scale harvests. It is excellent land and the expenses, for the Durazzo region, are very small—20 million lire for 3,500 hectares.

JULY 14. The offensive in Spain is making good progress.

The Duce announced to me that the *Giornale d'Italia* is to publish a 'statement'[2] on the racial question. It purports to be written by a group of scholars under the aegis of Popular Culture. But he tells me that in fact he drafted almost the whole thing himself.

JULY 15. Pariani's report on Germany is very optimistic. He finds that the army has made giant strides. Moreover, the idea of military

---

[1] Baldur von Schirach, leader of the *Hitlerjugend*.   [2] In English in the original.

collaboration with us has been popularized in officer circles, which up to last September were lukewarm and full of reservations. The slogan *Credere, ubbidire, combattere,*[1] in Italian, has been adopted in the barracks. The Duce is justifiably proud of this. In Italy too the Duce intends to give serious attention to the character of the officers. It is useless to stuff a lot of culture into a lieutenant or a captain. The leaders must be scientists and artists, but subalterns and commanders of small units require courage and the spirit of initiative. 'All the great retreats have been started by the failure of a second lieutenant to hold his ground.'

On the racial question the Duce said that he is going to get the Secretary of the Party to summon the 'scholars' and announce to them the official attitude of the régime towards the problem. An attitude which signifies, not persecution, but discrimination.

Civilian officials are to be put into uniform. I am much in favour of this measure, which strengthens the discipline and the decorum of the bureaucracy.

JULY 16. Operations in Spain are progressing very well. Apart from the communiqués, Gambara's dispatches are very significant and permit the highest hopes. Pariani suggests preparing a fast motorized brigade and sending it in, as soon as Valencia is occupied, to give the final blow.

Nothing else important.

JULY 17. Good news in Spain. The action is developing swiftly and surely. Gambara's dispatches confirm that he is preparing to carry out an encircling movement on Valencia—a bold move, but it may give practical results.

The Duce is pleased. Taking his cue from the question of the double salute in the army, he let fly at the monarchy, which is apparently opposing the adoption of the Roman salute. 'It has needed all my patience,' he said, 'to tow this wretched monarchy along. It has never done anything which would commit it to the régime. I am still waiting, because the King is seventy and I hope that nature will come to my help.' He is more and more determined to get rid of the Savoy family at the earliest opportunity. He also talked about the revolution in manners, particularly in relation to racial problems. He is studying a measure which will forbid the marriage of Italians with persons of other races, including Jews. 'All this,' he said, 'will increase the hatred of foreigners for Italy. Good. I will do anything I can to sever relations with France and England—nothing can come from that quarter except *pourriture.*'

We have refused an invitation from Roumania to a conference relating to the Danube, from which Germany is excluded. 'I will not

[1] Believe, obey, fight.

even go to the technical conference,' declared the Duce. 'My conduct towards Germany must be so correct as to give *me* the right to call them "bereter",[1] if the occasion ever arises.'

The Hungarians have met with a refusal our request that they should leave Geneva.

JULY 18. The whole day was spent on the Hungarians. I had a first conversation with them at the Palazzo Chigi. As I foresaw, Kanya made his tirade against the Yugoslavs, whom, with the old Ballplatz mentality, he insists on calling Serbs. He would like us to get wrong with Belgrade, and is asking for a kind of military guarantee in the event of attack by Yugoslavia. Not a hope. We have not the slightest intention of impairing our good relations with Stoyadinovich in order to procure a success for the more or less democratic government of Mr. Imredy. Yugoslavia would automatically rush to the arms of France, and the politico-military advantages which the Axis has won in the Danubian basin and the Balkans would be at an end. We may perhaps blow the Belgrade Protocols sky high by occupying Albania. But in that case there will be a positive advantage. For the sake of hoisting the Italian flag over this country which belongs to us, it is worth facing even a crisis of that kind. But certainly not now, to assist the political game of these arrogant and petulant Hungarians.

Then there was a conversation at the Palazzo Venezia, with the Duce. Minute made. They sang more or less the same tune. But there was no change to be got from the Duce either. Kanya, who is far from pleased, said to me in the evening: 'Hungary's misfortune is that Ciano and Göring are in love with Stoyadinovich.'

JULY 19. At the sea, where I read to Kanya, so far as it concerns him, the Minute of my Venice conversations with Stoyadinovich. He had to admit that Stoyadinovich was quite explicit in ruling out an attack on Hungary, so long as Hungary does not take the initiative in a conflict with Prague but follows in the wake of Germany.

We talked about Austria. He told me that Schmidt no longer has a political post but is making 200,000 marks a year. I reminded him of our conversation in Budapest, when I refused to negotiate with Guido Schmidt, because I regarded him as a traitor. Schuschnigg—the Hungarians too would like to do something to get him out of the prison in which he is virtually confined. I spoke of my approach to Ribbentrop and the meagre results it achieved. 'The Germans have many qualities,' said Kanya, 'but they are always destitute of political tact.'

JULY 20. Talked about Hungary with the Duce. His faith in the country's future has been much shaken since he made the acquaintance of Imredy. He describes him as a man of bogus energy—that is to say,

---

[1] i.e. *Verräter* (traitors).

a dangerous man and typical of the kind of ruler produced by a moribund régime. His verdict on Kanya is also severe: an old Hapsburg relic. Only a frankly nationalist party will be able to come to grips with Hungary's serious problems—the agrarian question, anti-Semitism, treaty revision. The visit to Rome has completely fizzled out. The attempt to disturb Yugoslav-Italian relations was a failure. Last night, while we were waiting at the Baths of Caracalla, the Duce authorized me to wait until I meet Stoyadinovich, before making the requests we have agreed upon. This is a good idea. Made through diplomatic channels, the *démarche* would have taken on a disagreeably inquisitorial character. The Duce was very proud to display the splendid spectacle at the Baths. He took a personal interest in arranging the details, even fixing the prices of the seats. He wanted them to be very cheap for the common people—two lire. At the end of the performance he said to me, indicating Imredy: 'A man who cannot make a better response than that to the applause of the people is not a leader.'

Portugal has recognized the Empire.

The advance has been resumed in Spain.

JULY 21. A telegram from Berti announces that the new attack on the Red defensive positions along the River Palancia will begin at 4 p.m. to-day. Once we are through this line we should be able to march on Valencia. The Spaniards have put another division under our command, in addition to the Arrows. A good sign.

The Duce is annoyed about Captain Wiedemann's[1] futile visit to London. It is probably just another case of press hysteria. But it ought to have been avoided. We are still almost completely in the dark, and the Auswärtiges Amt may well be in the same position. 'I should like to see the German comments,' said the Duce, 'if I took it into my head to send Sebastiani to see Georges Bonnet.'

The visit of the British King and Queen to Paris is not, so far as political results go, exceeding the modest forecasts made for it. It has taken on a democratic character—something quite different from the Führer's visit to Italy. The French press gives more space to the interminable menus of the banquets offered by the Popular Front than to anything else. *On y mange bien en France.* The King, like everyone else, will come away with this slogan in his mind. And it may not occur to him to think that, when a people eats as well as all that, it is inevitably less keen on dying.

JULY 22. The offensive in Spain continues with pretty favourable prospects. But resistance is still stiff.

Conversation with Guarneri. As usual, he is pessimistic. Very anti-German. He is also worried about the racial question, which he thinks

---

[1] Fritz Wiedemann, Hitler's personal adjutant.

will have damaging repercussions in the economic and financial sphere.

JULY 23. We are held up in Spain for the moment. Resistance is tenacious. Gambara intends to make a strategic manœuvre.

At Alessi's[1] request I am interesting myself in the change of owner-ship of the *Piccolo*. The Mayers—Jews—want to get rid of it.

Nothing else worthy of note.

The Duce is in Romagna.

JULY 24. To Abetone. Then to Leghorn, where the *Federale* told me that there is much sympathy for the anticipated anti-Jewish measures. But the problem does not appear to be as serious in Leghorn as it once was. The Jews were the leaders of anti-Fascism and have been liquidated together with it.

JULY 25. In Spain the Reds have crossed the Ebro at two points. I don't believe their offensive strength is any greater than it was in other similar attempts. But it is disagreeable that the Whites should have allowed themselves to be surprised, with the first immediate result that our offensive on Valencia has been checked.

Lord Perth came to ask for lenient treatment of the journalist Cremona,[2] who has been expelled. The reason for his expulsion was that Cremona, in conversation with other journalists, said that Musso-lini cannot press his anti-Semitic campaign too far, because in the past he received money from the Jews and even from a Jewess, the Sarfatti. *Inde ira* . . . Perth asked to have another conversation with me to-morrow, I think to discuss the Czechoslovakian problem.

Dindina has had an operation on her ear for otitis. She did not suffer at all. But I felt so sorry for her under the anæsthetic. Then suddenly she was all right.

JULY 26. A second conversation with Perth. Minute made, though there was nothing important.

In Spain the situation is on the way to being restored on the Ebro front.

Commotion over Starace's communiqué (actually written by the Duce) on the Jewish question.

JULY 27. Nothing worthy of note.

JULY 28. Since the shorthand report of a speech of Chamberlain's did not make it clear whether he regards the evacuation of the volun-teers from Spain as not only a necessary, but also a sufficient condition for the implementation of the Pact, I have given Crolla instructions to inquire precisely into the Prime Minister's intentions.

---

[1] Rino Alessi, editor of the Trieste paper *Il Piccolo*.
[2] Paul Cremona, Rome correspondent of the *Christian Science Monitor*.

Gambara has sent a nervous dispatch. It is the pessimistic influence of Berti, who would like to come to Italy to discuss . . . politics. Politics—too often the unhappy mania of soldiers.

JULY 29. Nothing worthy of note.

JULY 30. Following the Pope's speech, violently critical of racialism, I summoned the Nuncio and gave him a warning—if the Vatican continues on this path, a clash is inevitable because since the conquest of the Empire the Duce regards the racial question as fundamental. It is the lack of racial preparedness of the Italians which caused the Amhara insurrection. I spoke quite plainly to Borgongini, explaining the premises and the aims of our racial policy. He seemed pretty convinced, and I may add that he showed himself personally very anti-Semitic. He will confer with the Holy Father to-morrow. I think it is right to take steps to avoid a crisis, but if the Church wants one, we shall not be the losers.

The news from Spain is pretty static. We are waiting for Berti to arrive here.

JULY 31. Ill with tonsillitis. I am to stay in bed until August 7.

AUGUST 8. Back at work. General Berti gave me an account of the condition of our troops. Curiously enough, he is for once less pessimistic than usual. He is full of praise for the heroism of the legionaries. He thinks, however, that unless we decide to send further reinforcements on a large scale, we shall have to evacuate the infantry, even if it means unilateral action. He is waiting for a decision.

The Duce is very worked up about the racial question and very angry with Catholic Action. He has ordered that all Jews are to be struck off our diplomatic list. I am to begin by recalling them to Rome. He attacked the Pope violently. 'I do not underestimate his strength,' he said, 'but he must not underestimate mine either. 1931 should have taught him. A sign from me would be enough to unleash all the anti-clericalism of the Italian people, which has found it hard work to swallow a Jewish God.' He repeated his theory about the paganization of Christianity through Catholicism. 'That is the reason why I am both Catholic and anti-Christian.' He refused to receive Grandi, who was left crestfallen in the ante-room.

I received the Nuncio. We discussed the question of Catholic Action. As for the race problem, the Pope, now that he understands what it is really about, shows signs of disarming.

The Japanese Ambassador told me that his Government intends to make a frontier agreement with Russia, that for this reason their counter-measures have hitherto been restrained, but that if the U.S.S.R. should intensify its provocations there might be no limit to the consequences. I indicated our understanding and sympathy.

AUGUST 9. I had a talk with Father Tacchi-Venturi.[1] We agreed
about the advisability of taking steps to avoid a conflict between the
Holy See and Fascism. There is no real issue to fight about. The
friction with Catholic Action is unimportant and may easily be kept
within bounds, if there is goodwill on both sides. Tacchi-Venturi
distrusts Starace. 'If a man has once been a mason,' he said, 'he is
a mason for the rest of his life.'

I received Blondel, who brought me a vague expression of France's
goodwill to arrive at an understanding. Apart from that we talked
about routine administrative questions.

AUGUST 10. I discussed with the Duce the draft reply which Franco
has prepared for the Non-Intervention Committee. Although many
things in it don't seem perfect, we decided not to raise objections,
particularly as the Germans are in fundamental agreement and Franco
is in a hurry to reply.

At the sea I saw the Ambassador of the U.S.S.R., who came to talk
to me about the commercial *pourparlers*, which are not making progress.
I gave him an appointment for to-morrow evening. I took him to task
about an article full of personal insults, which has appeared in the
Journal de Moscou. I asked him whether he was the author and said
that, as he was using his imagination, he might have done better.
He was very embarrassed, but denied that he had written it. Then,
to extricate himself from a tricky position, he said: 'I promise I shall
write against you when I am no longer Ambassador.' To which I
replied: 'When you are no longer Ambassador, I promise I shall never
write a word about you again.' The Russian Counsellor, who is
intelligent, saw that I had scored a hit.

Jacomoni reported to me on the situation in Albania and the progress
of our preparations. All is going very well. The alarms about imminent
Italian action have died down since my conversation with General
Sereggi.

AUGUST 11. I told our Military Attaché in Greece to keep a close
watch on military preparations in the direction of the Albanian frontier.
I don't want the Greeks to be prepared, with the possibility of an ugly
incident when we occupy Albania. They may already have got wind
of our plans. I know they are setting up artillery in the Janina
district.

Conversation with the Russian Ambassador about the commercial
negotiations, which have reached a deadlock over the minimum quantities requested by us before we will agree to their demands for aircraft
supplies.

[1] Father Pietro Tacchi-Venturi, a Jesuit attached to the Congregation of Rites. He
played a large part in the negotiation of the Concordat of 1929.

Pater[1] and Jacomoni showed me the plans for the Sporting Club Theatre in Tirana, which I approved in principle. I want to create an absolutely first-class Italian centre, which will consolidate our nationals and gather foreigners and Albanians round us. It will be opened at Christmas.

AUGUST 12. Berti was with the Duce. He had a talk with him during my illness, in which he explained the situation. To-day it was a question of tying up the loose ends. By way of a most lucid exposition and some rigorous logic the Duce arrived at the following conclusion. There must be plain speaking with Franco and we must find out what his intentions are. If he is really prepared to renounce the assistance of the foreign volunteers, then, without obliging us to submit to the humiliating formalities required by the 'Non-Intervention' Committee, he must send away our infantry with every honour. If, on the other hand, he is still anxious to have us, then, in view of the fact that with our present forces operations are impossible and the further fact that we are not disposed to remain in Spain as spectators, we shall send 10,000 men as replacements. If, lastly, a crisis occurs in the 'Non-Intervention' Committee and France reopens the frontier, we can send one or more divisions to bring the war to a rapid end. Berti will see Franco and give us a reply before the 20th.

Report from Piccio on the state of feeling in France. Much anxiety. A Minister in office has told him that in the event of conflict with the Axis the defeat of France is already regarded as inevitable by the French leaders.

Gave Fransoni[2] instructions for his mission to Prague.

AUGUST 13. Nothing worthy of note.

AUGUST 14. To Venice by air.

AUGUST 15. At Venice, with the family.

AUGUST 16. Back to Rome by air. A good flight. Nothing very important at the office. The Duce, as always, is calm. He talked about Balbo's visit to Germany and the war in Spain. As Balbo seems to be worrying about the hidden reasons for his mission, the Duce authorized me to tell him that he wanted to have him as the most competent— 'which is not true', he immediately added—observer of German air power, now that things are moving towards a showdown. Balbo was delighted when I told him this. In any case he was enchanted with the visit, the Germans, their aeroplanes, everything. Now that his vanity has been flattered, he talks like the most convinced supporter of the Axis. I gather one thing from his account—the German air force is very powerful and technically much more advanced than ours.

[1] Pater, an Italian architect. A friend of the Mussolini family.
[2] Francesco Fransoni, recently appointed Italian Minister in Prague.

It was a long conversation with Balbo. Still in a state of euphory from his journey, he had abandoned his attitude of criticizing everything and everybody, except where Aosta and the Empire was concerned. Balbo is just a great boy, spoilt, restless, lively, ignorant, and at times potentially tiresome. Not, I think, dangerous, because he has no means of being dangerous.

I received the Polish Ambassador. He brought me a message from Beck about Geneva, a message without any importance except as a proof of the Polish desire to keep their contacts with us alive.

AUGUST 17. I described my conversation with Balbo to the Duce. I confirmed that he is not aware of the manœuvre but is actually delighted with what he regards as a success. Mussolini replied: 'One is always happy when one does not understand.'

I advised the Duce to have an important street in Rome named after d'Annunzio, instead of an avenue on the Pincio, which is what the Governor has done. If Rome can honour so many more or less negligible dead men with a main street, that wonderful Italian, Gabriele d'Annunzio, deserves something more.

At the sea I introduced Balbo to the Russian Counsellor. Balbo, who adores talking, started a more or less futile discussion. 'Balbo is sympathetic and also intelligent,' said Helfand afterwards. 'But I am convinced that all this talk about anti-Mussolini aspirations is nonsense. Balbo doesn't come up to Mussolini's waist.'

AUGUST 18. Nothing important, except that the Duce flew to Pantelleria. In the present situation of extreme tension this will make a great noise in the world. He telephoned me when he got back. He is enthusiastic about the military preparations of the island, which have reached a very high degree of efficiency.

At the sea the English Chargé d'Affaires[1] asked me again, formally, whether or no it is true that we have given arms to Franco recently. Inevitably, I reserved my reply.

AUGUST 19. The Duce and I settled the reply to be given to the English: As we have an expeditionary force in Spain, as this force is fighting, as the wastage of munitions proceeds at the same rate as, or faster than, that of men, and as we cannot send our soldiers into battle armed with olive branches, we have sent what is necessary to prevent their being massacred by the arms infiltrating—as the English well know—in large quantities over the Pyrenees. This is what I am to say to Sir Noel Charles to-morrow. The consequences of this reply are not difficult to foresee. Particularly as Franco's note to the 'Non-Intervention' Committee will also cause a little commotion.

[1] Sir Noel Charles, Counsellor at the British Embassy in Rome. Chargé d'Affaires in the absence of Lord Perth. High Commissioner in Italy, 1944-7.

According to a report from the Assistant Military Attaché in Berlin, German officers regard action in Czechoslovakia as inevitable and imminent—end of September. Everything is said to be ready down to the last detail. The air force is to play the principal role. Through political channels not a word has been said to us yet. We ought therefore to stick to the position as it was in May, when we were assured that a recourse to force could be ruled out, at least for some years.

AUGUST 20. I spoke to Sir Noel Charles in the form anticipated. Minute made of the conversation. He personally did not boggle at our reply, but I doubt whether its reception in London will be as friendly....

I gave Attolico written instructions to see Ribbentrop and ask for precise information on what the Government of the Reich intends to do in Czechoslovakia, with the object of 'enabling us to take measures in time on our western frontier'. This communication will have a considerable effect on the Germans, as it demonstrates just how far we are prepared to go. Actually the news from berlin suggests more and more that the crisis of the Czech question is at hand. Will the conflict be localized or will France set fire to the powder barrel? In that eventuality there is no alternative for us but to fall in beside Germany immediately, with all our resources. The Duce is decided on action. Hence the need to know things completely and in time.

AUGUST 21. Berti's account of his conversation with Franco has arrived. Franco turns down the idea that we should send new divisions —the most he will accept is that we send 10,000 replacements to maintain our present forces in a state of efficiency. In these circumstances the Duce, after a long discussion, has come round to the idea of reducing rather than increasing our forces in Spain. The Littorio and March 23 divisions would be concentrated into a single division, the rest, between ten and fifteen thousand men, would be repatriated, their repatriation to be negotiated with the English, whom we could confront with the dilemma of either implementing the agreements of April 16 or allowing them to lapse. If they choose the latter alternative, our path is clear for a military alliance with Germany.

It seems to me an excellent plan. Above all it serves to set in motion again a machine which has been stationary for too long and to extricate us from an unpleasant impasse. Franco, I think, will be satisfied with a solution of this kind. And the Germans, it seems to me, cannot help but approve.

In the afternoon I went to Venice.

AUGUST 22. The Duce has himself drafted a telegram for Berti on the lines of what was settled yesterday. As is usual on occasions of exceptional importance, he has ordered me to give a copy of the telegram to the King.

It seems that the Pope made another disagreeable speech yesterday about exaggerated nationalism and racial ideology. The Duce has summoned Father Tacchi-Venturi for this evening and proposes to deliver an ultimatum to him. 'Contrary to what is believed,' he said to me, 'I am a patient man. But I must not be made to lose my patience, or I react by making a desert. If the Pope continues to talk, I will tickle up the Italians and in less than no time I will turn them into anti-clericals again. The men in the Vatican are insensible, mummified. There is a slump in religious belief—no one believes in a God who bothers about our petty troubles. I should despise a God who bothered about the personal affairs of the policeman standing at the corner of the Corso.'

Nevertheless, it would be a good thing if this friction came to an end. In the present difficult international situation a conflict with the Church would help nobody. I have always acted on this principle with Borgongini.

Buffarini came to talk to me about his quarrel with Starace. He feels that he is suspected and is uneasy. Starace really does distrust him. I shall try to bring them together—this is not the moment to annoy the Duce with palace squabbles.

AUGUST 23. Nothing worthy of note.

AUGUST 24. Some reports from Barzini[1] have made the Duce worried about the situation in Spain. He used violent language about Franco, for letting the victory slip when he already has it in his grasp. The Duce believes that a return to the offensive and to victory by the Reds is not impossible. He is indignant with the French press—a libellous rag, *Aux Écoutes*, has published idiotic reports about an imaginary liver disease of his. 'This Europe,' he said to me, 'is destined to perish because it suffers from a mortal corruption—it tells lies.'

The news from Bled[2] is good—parity of armaments for Hungary is in itself a notable improvement. If Kanya does not let himself be governed, as he usually does, by his absurd prejudices against the Roumanians and the Serbs, there is a chance of an agreement being reached about minorities too. In any case, the Bled meeting has marked a new phase in the crumbling of the Little Entente. Czechoslovakia is isolated. The French system of friendships is completely upset.

I said good-bye to Admiral Somigli, who is setting off with two cruisers on a voyage round the world. I spoke to him about the general situation and, as I had already explained to Cavagnari, I added that

---

[1] Luigi Barzini senior, special correspondent of the *Popolo d'Italia* in Spain.

[2] At Bled, in Slovenia, on August 23, Hungary and the states of the Little Entente signed an agreement by which Hungary's right to parity of armaments was recognized and the four states renounced the use of force in their mutual relations.

his mission of peace may, in the event of a general conflict, be transformed into a task of war. With great composure he described his plan for that eventuality—piracy and a high price for his skin. Somigli is a man who will keep his word.

AUGUST 25. Villani came to see me on his return from a holiday. He is pleased with the results of Bled. He confirmed that pacts with Roumania and Yugoslavia about the minorities are now ready, but are being held up because of Czechoslovakia. He had to admit that I was right when I told him in March 1937, on my return from Belgrade, that I had put a charge of dynamite under the Little Entente. We also talked about the possibility of war in the near future. In Budapest too nothing precise is known about the intentions of Germany. They believe, however, as we do, that, whatever the solution turns out to be, the crisis will probably be precipitated soon after the departure of Runciman[1] from Prague.

I have sent a telegram of congratulations to Stoyadinovich and another to Kanya, partly to underline the part we have played in the affair.

Suvich, on the subject of America, repeats what we more or less know already. He adds, however, that, in his opinion, in the event of a war America will enter the struggle earlier than is generally believed.

AUGUST 26. Attolico has spoken to Ribbentrop in the sense of my instructions of the 20th. The reply is not altogether clear. There is a great desire for action and everything is now ready or very nearly —but the final decision does not seem to have been made yet.

The Duce is indignant with Franco for the 'serene optimism' with which he conducts the war. 'Serene optimists,' he said, 'find themselves under a tram as soon as they leave home in the morning.'

Borgongini-Duca came, by order of the Pope, to talk to me about the announcement which is to put an end, for the present at least, to the friction between the Party and Catholic Action. I prodded him and he let himself go on the subject of the Pope. He says he has a thoroughly bad character, authoritarian and almost insolent. Everybody is terrified of him in the Vatican. Borgongini himself trembles when he has to enter His Holiness's room. He treats everybody with arrogance, even the most illustrious cardinals. When Cardinal Pacelli, for instance, goes to report, he has to write down all his instructions at the Pope's dictation, like any little secretary. The Pope's health is now good again. He eats little meat, a good deal of cooked fruit. He drinks a limited amount of red wine. He takes a good deal of exercise in the garden. In spite of his eighty-two years he continues to govern the Church even in

---

[1] Lord Runciman was in Prague from August 3 to September 16, as an unofficial mediator between the Czech Government and the Sudeten Germans.

the smallest details. 'I shall govern until there is a Conclave,' he is always saying.

I had a visit from a lunatic called Hilda de Toledano. With a great air of mystery she declared that she was the King of Portugal and offered to include her kingdom in the Roman Empire.

AUGUST 27. Conversation with Charles, in consequence of the expulsion of Mrs. Bastienille, of the *Daily Telegraph*. I was able to get the order cancelled—her offence was, in any case, venial.

Nothing else worthy of note.

AUGUST 28. Asked Berti for a reply to the Duce's telegram.

Nothing worthy of note.

AUGUST 29. The Duce is angrier than ever with Franco for his flabby conduct of the war. He is afraid there may be some very serious surprises. 'Put on record in your book,' he said to me, 'that to-day, August 29, I prophecy the defeat of Franco. Either the man doesn't know how to make war or he doesn't want to. The Reds are fighters —Franco is not.'

Our Ambassador Rosso reaffirms his conviction that, in the event of a Czech-German conflict, the Soviets will confine themselves to assistance in the air and will not make a total intervention. The same thing was intimated to me yesterday, in veiled terms, by Helfand.

The Czech question is more burning than ever. The Duce anticipates that the Germans will make the Sudetens act and an insurrection will break out inside the country. If Benes reacts violently, it will be possible for Hitler to bring off an intervention which will have a plausible justification in the eyes of the world. It will be difficult for France to move. She is not ready for war of any kind, still less for an aggressive war. The English will do everything to avert a conflict, which they fear more than any other country in the world.

AUGUST 30. The American Ambassador, who was to have left on Thursday, has had to postpone his leave. He is very worried about the situation and asked me what our attitude is. I put on the usual record, pro-German and anti-Czech—the whole responsibility must be borne by Prague. I in my turn asked what America will do. He replied that it is the most emotional country in the world. It is therefore difficult to make any prophecy. At the moment the United States are pacifist, but some event in the course of the war may alter the situation from one hour to another.

The Duce has given orders to cancel the round-the-world voyage of the 7th Division. This is not the moment to scatter our forces. He also announced to me a project he has for turning Migiurtinia[1] into a concession for international Jewry. He says the country has important

[1] Migiurtinia, the northernmost portion of Italian Somaliland.

natural resources, which the Jews could exploit. Among others there is
the shark fishery, 'which has the great advantage that, to begin with,
many Jews would get eaten'. He is anxious for more thorough knowledge of the Führer's intentions and programme for the Czech crisis.
I have written a letter in my own hand to Attolico for this purpose.

The English Chargé d'Affaires returned to the question of the new
supplies of aircraft sent by us to Franco. I replied rather dryly, more or
less in the terms of my reply of August 20 to a similar question.

AUGUST 31. I accompanied Muti to the Duce. His exposition of
the situation in Spain, made at the behest of Ambassador Viola, is
pretty pessimistic. We ought not to be surprised if in the course of the
next month or two things take a turn for the worse for Franco. The
country is full of distrust and scepticism, the troops are weary, the other
generals are restive. The reputations of Jague and Vigon are increasing
in Nationalist circles, while Franco's star does not shine as brightly as
it once did. The Reds have recovered the initiative on almost all
sectors of the front and won considerable successes. The action of the
crossing of the Ebro has raised their morale and lowered that of the
Nationalists, who in their initial disorderly flight got as far as
Saragossa. The Italians too are tired. Viola proposes that not one,
but both our divisions should be withdrawn from Spain, leaving and
possibly reinforcing our air force, tanks, and artillery. Gambara will
be here to-morrow with Berti's proposals. We are waiting for them
and then we shall decide.

The Roumanian Minister has asked for the adherence of Italy to the
Danube agreement. He said to me that under no circumstances will
Roumania allow Russian troops to pass through her territory, without
first fighting with all her resources.

SEPTEMBER 1. Council of Ministers. Measure against foreign Jews
resident in Italy.

Flew to Venice.

SEPTEMBER 2. Flew back in the morning. The Duce is disturbed
by the fact that the Germans are letting us know almost nothing of
their programme with regard to Czechoslovakia. He ordered me to
talk to Hesse. He wants to know how far Germany intends to push
things, and to what extent and how she expects to be helped by us.
Attolico's reports do not, at the moment, provide decisive evidence—he
personally is against our committing ourselves too far.

Hesse agrees with us on the need for closer contacts. He says he has
recommended action in this sense to Göring. Hesse did not unbutton
himself, but he says that he knows important things which he cannot
reveal without the authorization of his chiefs. Under seal of secrecy he
told me that no German initiative will be made before October—the

defence lines are not yet ready. He will leave to-morrow morning for a conference with the Führer—Ribbentrop is far from well informed.

The new Argentine Ambassador paid me his duty visit. He is not particularly striking.

Gambara reported on the situation in Spain. He will confer with the Duce to-morrow. The soldiers (Berti has not yet spoken to Franco in accordance with the instructions of August 22) have some idea which does not coincide with those of the Duce, but they do not dare to express it clearly. We shall see to-morrow.

Prunas has sent a telegram about a conversation between Bonnet and the German Ambassador in Paris. The terms were quite precise— France, England, and Russia would intervene at once, with American support. Will such language have a useful effect on Germany, or has Hitler perhaps already gone too far to draw back?

SEPTEMBER 3. Conference at the Palazzo Venezia with Gambara, who put forward the views of the commanders of the Volunteer Corps on the advantages and disadvantages of leaving troops in Spain. The Duce's idea of leaving a single division was ruled out as equally compromising and more dangerous. Either withdraw all the infantry, or send reinforcements to strengthen the two present divisions, take over command of the Arrows, get the Spaniards to give us two divisions, and attack Barcelona with this combined force. The Duce ruled out this proposal and agreed to the total withdrawal of the infantry. He drafted a telegram for Berti, with orders to communicate it to Franco. If Franco agrees, good. If not, we shall find another solution, but the Duce will impose his own conditions about the method of conducting the war. The Duce is convinced that Franco has lost his best chances of bringing the game to a speedy end. Now the situation has changed, and time, as always, is working against the side which wastes it.

Attolico has had a talk with Ribbentrop. Nothing new. If there is provocation the Germans will attack. Apparently nothing else has been decided by the Führer. It is entirely in our interest not to press for further replies. It is clear that the Germans do not want to let us into the game. That leaves us the most complete liberty of action in any eventuality.

According to reports from Budapest the Hungarian soldiers foresee a clash as inevitable and imminent. Kanya on the other hand regards it as inevitable but not imminent—next spring.

SEPTEMBER 4. The Duce was very worked up about the Jews. He hinted at measures which he intends to get the next Grand Council to adopt, and which will, taken together, constitute the Charter of the Race. Actually the Charter has already been drawn up by the hand of the Duce. The Grand Council will do no more than sanction it with its deliberations. As for the Jewish concentration colony, the Duce talks now not of Migiurtinia, but of Jubaland, which offers better conditions for life and work.

The Duce went on to say: 'I am familiarizing the Italians with the idea that there is something else they can do without—the Vatican. Materially, the contribution which the Vatican makes to us is negligible—there is no money coming in from it. In a Rome of eighty or a hundred thousand inhabitants it counted for something. In the flourishing and industrious Rome which will soon pass the million and a half mark it has no weight at all. Pilgrimages are becoming rarer, worse attended, and poorer. The fight against these powerful forces, as many consider them to be, serves to give the Italians a backbone. It also serves to show that certain mountains are no more than blisters.'

To Lucca, for the races.

SEPTEMBER 5. Borelli[1] tells me that there is an oppressive atmosphere in Milan. The anti-Semitic measures and the demographic measures have hit too many people to be popular. But the Duce, when he believes it to be necessary, has the courage to be unpopular. And in the end he turns out to be right.

Sola, giving his opinion on the present situation, says that the attitude of Roumania is linked with that of Britain. If London embarks upon a war, Bucharest will follow. In that case the Russian troops will have an unopposed passage through Bessarabia. If this is true, many calculations will have to be rapidly revised. Roumania is of little account as a military force, but she may be a decisive factor owing to her position.

Contradictory reports from Berlin—Ribbentrop hints at a resumption of negotiations with Prague, while his Under-Secretary tells Attolico that the crisis will be precipitated about the 20th. Meanwhile we still have not had a clear and decisive statement. Why?

Pariani was relating to me a conversation he has had with Canaris, the head of the German Intelligence Service, when I was told about a *démarche* made by the French Military Attaché, informing us of the mobilization of reservists on the Rhine frontier. He added that nothing of the kind has been done on the Alpine frontier. I telephoned the news to the Duce, who instructed me to inform Berlin, saying that the thing leaves us indifferent so long as we do not know the decisions of the Reich. 'This is a dirty trick on the part of France,' he said. 'It will have bad consequences.'

Pariani gave me a report on the condition of the army—reassuring.

SEPTEMBER 6. Starace talked to me last night about the internal situation. According to him the country has been slightly shaken by the recent measures. 'I am sorry to have to use the word,' he said, 'but

[1] Aldo Borelli, editor of the *Corriere della Sera.*

there is an atmosphere reminiscent of Quartarella.[1] The Party is solid
and in good shape. So are the people. The unrest is in the bourgeoisie.'

Cavallero[2] is optimistic about the military operations in the Empire.
He expects to be able to liquidate the last centres of rebellion before
Christmas. In the event of a general war, he is not afraid of a large-
scale rising of the inhabitants. At present, while our military preparations are not yet complete, he thinks that offensive action might take
the form of an operation with a small radius in the Sudan. In two
years he expects to have the resources to occupy Egypt, and he is also
studying a surprise action against Aden, in order to deprive the English
of this base.

The Prince of Piedmont came up to me at the sea and asked for
news of the situation. I gave him a report on Czechoslovakia and
Spain. His attitude is very correct and calm. In the course of the
conversation Sforza[3] was mentioned. The Prince is indignant that he
is still a Senator and has the Collar of the Annunziata. 'We must get
him out of the Senate,' he said. 'Then we can take away the collar
as well.'

Hesse is back from Berlin with a message from Hitler to the Duce.
We shall see it to-morrow. In the way of concrete news from the
German-Czech front there is nothing.

SEPTEMBER 7. This morning's press reports seemed optimistic on
the subject of Czechoslovakia, on the grounds that Prague was likely
to accept or nearly accept the German demands. Later in the day,
however, there were more sceptical reports from a German source—it
seems that the wave of euphory was deliberately created by London
and Paris.

I went with Hesse to the Duce. He has had two conferences with
the Führer and he read us a long memorandum dictated by him. I am
preserving it among my documents. The conclusion is: he will attack
if Czechoslovakia provokes him—at the moment he is not in a position
to fix a precise programme.

Franco, unwillingly it seems, has accepted the withdrawal of our
infantry. The Duce has returned to his original proposal and offered,
through Berti, to leave one division. He is afraid that a complete
evacuation might be regarded as a betrayal of Franco by us and he
prefers to march with his comrade all the way to the end.

I received Countess Castelbarco Toscanini, full of woe about the
withdrawal of her father's passport and worried about the reactions in

---

[1] Quartarella, the wood near where the body of Matteotti (see note on p. 83). was
discovered on August 15, 1924, two months after his disappearance.
[2] Count Ugo Cavallero, Commander-in-Chief in East Africa. Chief of General
Staff, 1940–3. Committed suicide in September 1943.
[3] Count Carlo Sforza, Foreign Minister, 1920–1 and again 1947–51.

America, where he was to have conducted some concerts in the near future. The Duce is irritated that so many Italians, among them the Princess of Piedmont, should have gone to Lucerne for the Wagner concert. But the withdrawal of the passport was the result of a telephonic interception, from which it transpired that Toscanini had attacked the Duce for his anti-Semitic policy, which he described as 'medieval stuff'.

SEPTEMBER 8. Thanks to the incidents at Moravska Ostrava the Czech ship of state is back in mid-ocean again.

I received the mission from Manchukuo at the Palazzo Chigi. The leader is a timid Chinaman and at his heels are two Japanese, a soldier and a civilian, who don't even allow him to breathe without their permission. The scene was repeated at the Palazzo Venezia in the presence of the Duce.

Received Blondel. He wanted information on our attitude. I expressed myself more or less in the language of *Informazione Diplomatica* No. 19, which will come out this evening and which has been written entirely by the hand of the Duce. Blondel would like to know what are the mutual commitments of the Führer and the Duce. I put on an air of mystery. The truth is that there is nothing precise. But it is clear that in any eventuality the Duce intends to march on the Axis line.

SEPTEMBER 9. I authorized Casertano[1] to subsidize Mizzi's party in the Maltese elections to the extent of 150,000 Italian lire.

The Duce has given Berti instructions to bring the conversations with Franco to a conclusion: if he prefers, we leave one division of nine battalions—otherwise we withdraw the whole of the infantry. According to the Duce the evacuation of the troops will not be able to take place before the second half of October.

Sparano confirmed to me what he had already told the Duce—Lojacono has got himself into an untenable position in Brazil. He will have to be replaced. I am recalling him for discussions—we shall proceed by degrees.

I watched a rehearsal of to-morrow's demonstration by the youths of the G.I.L.[2] They are getting on better than I expected. One must remember that their training has been done in a few weeks and that most of these boys come from villages where there is absolutely no sense of discipline. Some of them don't even speak Italian.

SEPTEMBER 10. The G.I.L. demonstration went well. The Duce was pleased.

Conversation with Hesse. Nothing worthy of note. He talked about

[1] Raffaello Casertano, member of the secretariat of the Fascist Party. Head of the Press Office in East Africa during the Abyssinian War.
[2] *Gioventù Italiana del Littorio*, the general organization which included the various Fascist youth organizations, for both sexes and all ages up to 21.

the Military Pact again. He says he has mentioned it to the Duce.
I reserved my reply. Then, in some confusion, he said that he had to
speak to me about a private matter. The Queen has commissioned
him to approach the Duce or me on behalf of her Jewish doctor
Stukjold. Apparently the Queen is very indignant about his expulsion,
and so is the King, who had great confidence in this doctor. But he
doesn't dare to talk to the Duce about it. And they are both counting
on a friendly mediation from me . . . I did not commit myself, but
pointed out with a smile to the Prince of Hesse that the Führer would
hardly approve of missions of this nature being entrusted to him, a
German and a Nazi. He turned pale.

SEPTEMBER II. To Ponte a Moriano and to Bagni di Lucca for
the 'Poetry Prize'.

Franco has opted for the retention of one legionary division in Spain,
on the lines of our latest proposals.

SEPTEMBER 12. Many communications from Berlin. The most
important is one proposing a secret meeting between the Duce and the
Führer at the Brenner, on any day, *but not later than September 25*. The
proposal was made by Göring to Magistrati and then confirmed in
Hitler's name. I told the Duce about it on the telephone (at Rocca
delle Caminate) and he replied: 'It is an idea which I do not reject.
We will talk about it.'

Nervous reports are coming in from the various capitals. Switzerland
and Belgium are putting their frontiers in a state of defence. In Paris
there is talk of six classes being called up. Grandi has telegraphed to
ask in the name of Chamberlain that the Duce should intervene to
restrain Hitler, who according to the English has not been informed
by those round him of recent British moves. We are not taking the idea
up. 'An absurdity of this kind,' said Mussolini, 'proves that the English
are suffering from a displaced uterus.' And he instructed me to let the
Germans know that, if at this juncture they require a gesture in their
favour, he 'is ready to go a step further than the last *Informazione
Diplomatica*'. I passed this on to Attolico, who is assailed every now and
then by a spasm of fear of war and would like to go into reverse. He
will, therefore, carry out this order in a very lukewarm way. The
Führer's speech. It seems to me very strong and certainly not of a kind
to produce a clearing of the atmosphere. He talks of war with an
unprecedented note of decision. And it is this that sets the tone of the
speech. The Duce too, according to a telephone message from Alfieri,
regards the Nuremberg speech as serious.

Suvich is leaving Washington for the Adriatica di Sicurtà.[1] He is
not pleased at this, and he has, very delicately, protested.

[1] Riunione Adriatica di Sicurtà, an insurance company.

Volpi talked to me about some personal questions of an intimate nature.

SEPTEMBER 13. The Germans have accepted our offer. Attolico telephoned to me from Nuremberg, after a conversation with Ribbentrop, and asked that an *Informazione Diplomatica* should be published saying that the Carlsbad eight points have now been superseded and only a radical solution, on the principle of self-determination, can put an end to the Czechoslovakian crisis. I informed the Duce, and he rapidly drafted *Informazione Diplomatica* No. 20, dictating it to Anfuso. Then I conferred with him about his meeting with Hitler. He does not reject the idea but asks that it should be postponed until the beginning of October, as until then he is occupied with visits to the provinces. I informed Attolico.

I delivered instructions to Alfieri on the degree of emphasis to be given to the *Informazione Diplomatica* and on the tone of the press in general—actually on this occasion it has been good.

I telegraphed to Berti to form the single division and commence the operation of concentrating the men to be repatriated. I also asked for the exact figures of those who are coming home, as they will be useful to me in my talks with the English.

Conversation with the American Ambassador. He wants to go on leave and is trying to adapt the European situation to his personal requirements, so that he may leave with his conscience at peace. His conscience, if nothing else!

Conversation with Cristich. Important, and I have made a Minute. He confirms that Stoyadinovich intends to bring his attitude into line with that of Italy.

8 p.m. Telegraphic reports from Prague about the ultimatum delivered to Benes by Henlein after yesterday's incidents. I speak to the Duce. He agrees that the situation is very serious, but thinks that Benes will end by accepting the ultimatum. 'Swallowing bitter pills is what democracies are made for.'

SEPTEMBER 14. The first reports of the rupture of negotiations between Prague and Henlein arrived last night. To-day has passed in an alternation between optimism and pessimism as different reports come in. There is talk of serious incidents between the Sudetens and the police, with scores of dead. From Berlin our Military Attaché[1] telegraphs that the mobilization of the air force has begun, with the calling up of two thousand pilots and the concentration of squadrons on the airfields near the frontier. Diplomats have been flocking to the Ministry. In general, they take a gloomy view. They all ask to be enlightened on the subject of the *Informazione Diplomatica*, and want to

[1] General Efisio Marras. A partisan leader in 1944. Army Chief of Staff, 1948.

know whether Italian solidarity will go to the length of standing beside
Germany in the event of war. Without giving a precise reply, I have
allowed it to be understood that the answer is Yes. The British Chargé
asked whether self-determination means a plebiscite. Yes. In that case,
he said, it will be difficult to get it accepted by Benes. The Belgian
Ambassador said: 'You are asking Czechoslovakia to commit suicide.'
    8 p.m. *Coup de théâtre.* Attolico telephones that Chamberlain has
asked for an interview with Hitler and will be received at Berchtesgaden
to-morrow. I telephone the news to the Duce, who is astonished.
'There will not be war,' he exclaims. 'But this is the liquidation of
English prestige. In two years England has twice been floored.'

    SEPTEMBER 15. The wave of optimism produced by the news of
Chamberlain's journey has been checked as a result of the reports piling
up in confusion, from Prague and from Berlin, about civil war in the
Sudetenland. It seems that Benes is allowing his men to shoot at will.
And the dead are numbered in tens—some papers say in hundreds.
Attolico, usually an optimist, telephones that 'if Chamberlain were not
on German soil, the forces of the Reich would already have come to the
help of the Sudetens'. I received von Mackensen, who came to thank
me for the Duce's article 'A Letter to Runciman'. He described it as
a historic document. The Ambassador is rather pessimistic. He says
that, unless Chamberlain has in his brief-case decisive and rapid proposals, it will be impossible for the Führer not to give help to the Sudetens.
We examined together the Balkan situation in the event of war, now
that Yugoslav neutrality is assured. In our opinion Greece and Turkey
will not move.
    The Duce has rung me up frequently from Rocca. He is calm.
Resolute and imperturbable, he awaits the developments of events. But
he is less optimistic to-day than yesterday. At 8.30 p.m. Attolico
telephones that in Berlin an intervention in Czechoslovakia is not
considered imminent, although there are reports of more and more
serious incidents. Nothing is yet known of the Hitler-Chamberlain
conversation which began at 5 p.m. and is taking place in the presence
of a single interpreter. Late in the evening Attolico gives me the first
reports of the conversation and the communiqué.

    SEPTEMBER 16. Interpretations of the Hitler-Chamberlain conver-
sation vary—so therefore do tendencies towards optimism or pessimism.
In general there is a feeling that the atmosphere has been cleared. The
project for a further conversation in the near future is interpreted in
a favourable sense. The Duce is worried about the attitude of Benes.
He is afraid that he wants to force the Führer's hand by persisting in
violent anti-German repression. He still hopes to provoke a conflict,
which may perhaps for him be the only way out.

I have seen many diplomats. The Roumanian categorically denied the report of French origin concerning free transit for the Russians through Bessarabia. The Frenchman and the Russian, at the sea, asked for news, which I did not give them. Blondel is pessimistic. He recalled the days of 1914, when he was at the Embassy in London. Then too nobody wanted to die for the Serbs, and yet the war happened. And the world then was much happier than it is now, and there were so many reasons for preserving peace. The Pole and the Hungarian came to thank me for the action taken by the Duce, and formally announced that they intend to raise the question of their minorities. The Jap wanted news. The Englishman brought me a message from Chamberlain of goodwill with respect to the implementation of the Anglo-Italian Pact.

I asked Attolico to give me precise news—partly for the purpose of the speech the Duce is to make in Trieste—and he telephoned that he will do so late in the evening.

Reports from Prague are better—but the intransigence of the Benes Government is confirmed (8.30 p.m.).

SEPTEMBER 17. Attolico told me last night the points which Hitler would like to be emphasized in the Duce's speech: the solution must be speedy and it must be integral, i.e. it must free all the minorities from servitude to the Czechs.

This morning, after a little routine administration, I flew to Lucca, stopped there for a few hours, and then went on to Forlì, where with Starace and Alfieri I joined the presidential train. I gave the Duce the latest news. 'I have made my decisions,' he concluded. 'If war breaks out in Germany, Prague, Paris, and Moscow, I shall remain neutral. If Great Britain intervenes, generalizing the struggle and giving it an ideological character, then we shall throw ourselves into the flames. Italy and Fascism could not be neutral.'

Personally the Duce is inclined to think that the dispute will end by having a military solution. This conviction was strengthened when he learnt at Bologna the latest news about the formation of a volunteer corps by Henlein and the fresh incidents in the Sudetenland. He is as calm as ever. He got his man to tell us that he does not want to be disturbed during the night, even if important news arrives, 'unless war breaks out'. From Abano, where the train stopped for the night, I telephoned to Rome and to Berlin. The press reports are somewhat exaggerated.

SEPTEMBER 18. From Venice to Trieste on board the *Camicia Nera*. A wonderful day. The sea was a mirror and the sky the purest blue. Trieste welcomed the Duce in a riot of sun, flags, and devotion. It was said that the city was depressed as a result of the Anschluss and the racial policy. But I have never seen a more fervid reception, nor a more explosive fervour than here in Trieste. The Duce spoke. A great, calm speech. Rarely do words have the weight of deeds—but for once this is so. Even if nothing happens, the Duce has written to-day a page of history made up of courage, loyalty, and honour. There is at once a feeling that the European political horizon has grown clearer. Confirmation of this comes from every capital. Meanwhile reports from London on the Chamberlain-Daladier meeting, though not precise, indicate an unequivocal withdrawal. The only negative element in to-day's news is Hodza's[1] speech. He declared that Prague does not want plebiscites and is prepared for resistance. But for how long, if London and Paris let them down?

SEPTEMBER 19. I accompanied the Duce on to Yugoslav territory. Very warm welcomes. Speeches exchanged were very friendly and very significant at this moment. Here is a result which few would have expected when I went to Belgrade in March 1937.

The news of the Czech situation is on the whole more hopeful. The Duce too is beginning to incline for a peaceful solution.

Flew to Rome.

I received a hundred Yugoslav workers and spoke to them in a cordial and comradely tone. Afterwards I had a talk with Cristich. He wanted news, but I hadn't much to give him. Charles wanted to see me and left me a little note with general expressions of goodwill over the Czech crisis. Without making any mystery, he added that the object of these frequent visits is to let it be seen that contacts between Rome and London are cordially maintained.

Meanwhile there comes confirmation of a Hitler-Chamberlain meeting next Wednesday. And to-morrow the Führer is to receive a Hungarian representative (Horthy[2] or Imredy?) and a Pole. Attolico attaches much importance to this meeting. I tried—unsuccessfully—to find the diplomatic representatives of the two countries in Rome. I shall talk to them in the morning. I shall tell them to reinforce their action—Germany must not be the only one to profit from this situation.

SEPTEMBER 20. Villani and Wieniewa were very satisfied with what I told them. And I believe an injection from us was needed, because the attitude of London and Paris towards the demands of Hungary and Poland seemed pretty discouraging. Even Berlin doesn't seem very anxious to associate the fate of the Sudetens with that of the minorities of other countries.

The day has passed mostly in waiting for Prague's reply—we learnt this evening that it is negative. Hence new waves of pessimism.

[1] Dr. Milan Hodza, Prime Minister of Czechoslovakia.
[2] Admiral Miklos Horthy de Nagybanya, Regent of Hungary.

The Duce spoke at Udine. I listened to the speech at the Ministry. Berti informs us that he is preparing the division to be repatriated in the Seville area, in three regiments. But the whole thing has had to be postponed, as our divisions are still being used to stem a Red offensive. I have confirmation from a reliable source that our troops are tired. Very tired. And that the idea of leaving a division in Spain has not had at all a favourable reception. Anonymous and even signed letters asking for repatriation are numerous. Signs of restlessness are increasing. I should be sorry if this meagre division of discouraged veterans were to let us in for serious trouble one day.

SEPTEMBER 21. Still no decisive news from Prague to-night. It seems, however, that Benes is capitulating. The delay in announcing the news is due, according to reports from our Minister, to the fear of disturbances.

From Spain, Nulli[1] confirms that the repatriates will amount to about 10,000, ready to embark by the end of September. Meanwhile, Negrin[2] has announced at Geneva that the Red Government is, as a unilateral action, dismissing all its volunteers. Why are they doing this? Do they feel themselves so strong? Or is it merely a demonstration of a platonic nature? So far as we are concerned, I think this robs our partial evacuation of some of its flavour. But it has the advantage that the initiative is not made to appear ours—this would certainly have lent itself to disagreeable comments about Italian weariness, betrayal of Franco, etc.

SEPTEMBER 22. The Duce has returned to Rome. I conferred with him on the Spanish problem and of course on the Czech situation. The Chief is sceptical about Spain. He believes that Franco, who has now lost his chance of victory, will come to a compromise with the other side. We shall lose our four milliards of credits, and for this reason we must pull out what we can while we can. On the Czech problem he insists on the necessity for a solution of the Hungarian and Polish problems as well.

Received the German Ambassador. Made a Minute of the conversation. In the name of the Führer he thanked me for all that the Duce and Italy have done. He told me to expect a message from the Führer, of which as usual the Prince of Hesse will be the bearer.

In the afternoon I received Perth and Villani. Minutes of both conversations. Perth was particularly anxious to impress upon me that there is no truth in what is said about England not making war at any price. Untrue. England does not want war, but she will fight if

[1] Colonel G. B. Nulli-Augusti, attached to the 'S' (Spain) office in the Foreign Ministry.
[2] Dr. Juan Negrin, Spanish Republican Prime Minister.

Germany does not know how to stop at the point where moderation counsels.

Vague reports from Prague. Resignation of Hodza. Military Cabinet. Red flags and demonstrations in the streets. At the same time it appears that the Germans are occupying the frontier towns and posts. Can all this happen without a clash?

In Spain the March 23 Division has performed prodigies of valour. Wonderful legionaries, who protest and moan when they are resting and in the attack find once more the enthusiasm of the first battle. And they have been there twenty-two months!

No precise news of the Hitler-Chamberlain conversation.

SEPTEMBER 23. I got the impression from Attolico on the telephone last night that things are not going well at Godesberg. Confronted with the nebulosity of the English proposals, the Führer presents four precise demands. Meanwhile in the Sudetenland the guns are booming and the machine-guns emptying their belts. This morning there is a further complication—Chamberlain and the Führer do not meet, but Chamberlain writes a letter asking him to reconsider his demands and redraft them. I told the Duce. He regards this as extremely serious. 'When you start putting down points on paper,' he says, 'it means that you consider the situation to be desperate and are trying to justify yourself before history.' Ribbentrop telephones to Attolico that Hitler too will reply in writing and will not move from his position. Sure enough, up to 7 p.m. there has been no news of further conversations, except one between Henderson and Ribbentrop.

I received the Roumanian Minister. He made an important communication to the effect that Bucharest is beginning to appreciate the situation and understands the Hungarian claims, but asks that the Hungarians should not make any rash move and should confine themselves to reasonable ambitions. I did my best to encourage Roumania to betray the Little Entente. Not hard work, as there is nothing she wants to do more. The situation between Warsaw and Moscow is looking much blacker.

7 p.m. Pariani telephones to say that General Marras has informed him that 'to-morrow is the day'. Attolico confirms that 'the fatal issue of events' is now very near. I telephone the news to the Prefect of Florence, so that he can inform the Duce, who is on the way to Padua.

SEPTEMBER 24. Telephone messages, frequently contradictory, continued throughout the night. In the morning I learnt two precise pieces of news: general mobilization in Prague and the contents of the memorandum given by Hitler to Chamberlain, viz. a confirmation of his demands in their entirety, with the terminal dates of October 1 for the cession of the Sudetenland and November 25 for the organization of the plebiscites in the mixed areas. Ribbentrop assures us that until this date (October 1) German troops will not enter Czechoslovakia. The Duce, who after the first reports wanted to come back to Rome, has decided to continue his journey and I advised him to do so. He spoke at Belluno to-day, explaining the situation with precision. From Berlin we are told that the terms of the memorandum were to be kept secret. But now . . . News of mobilization in France. Also in England. The Yugoslav Minister confirms that his country's attitude is one of neutrality in any eventuality.

In the afternoon Berlin telephones that Hesse will arrive in Venice bearing a message for the Duce from the Führer. I set off on a night flight to meet him. A wonderful flight—the lights of Venice, on a calm September evening, look like a diadem of phosphorescent jewels.

SEPTEMBER 25. I receive Hesse at the Grand Hotel, and we leave at once by car for Schio, where the Duce is stopping for a few hours. He has no written message, perhaps no very precise mission. He is to thank the Chief for all that we have done and convey to him Hitler's promise that in any need, whether of defence or attack, all the forces of Germany will be at our disposal. He is also to give us the latest news of the situation. He repeats, as facts, what we more or less know about the conversations with Chamberlain and the German demands. The position is now clear: if by October 1 the Czechs have not accepted the terms of the ultimatum, Germany attacks. Naturally with the aim of totally destroying Czechoslovakia. (Hesse also hinted at the possibility of incorporating Czechs and Slovaks in the Reich, with a large measure of autonomy!) Hitler still believes that France and England will not march. But should they do so, he is ready for the conflict. He even adds that the military and political situation is so favourable to the Axis that it might be better to play now a game which will inevitably have to be played one day. Hesse adds that Ribbentrop is even more extremist in this direction. The Duce receives us in the presidential train. He is severe but serene. He listens in silence to Hesse's exposition. Then says a few words in reply. After thanking him for the communication, he puts forward his point of view: France will not march, because England will not fall in behind her. Should the conflict, however, become general, we will place ourselves by the side of Germany immediately after the entry of England into the war. Not before, in order not to give her justification for war. The Duce too reaffirmed his full conviction of our victory—force of arms and irresistible force of spirit.

We return to Venice. Hesse leaves for Berlin and I for Rome.

In effect, no new or decisive factor has resulted from the conversation. However, the Duce and I, though we did not incite Germany to war, have done nothing to restrain her.

During the flight I listen to the Duce's speech at Vicenza. Then he calls me to the telephone. He ventilates the possibility of a meeting between me and Ribbentrop, in order to clarify the conditions of Italian intervention. He also announces a small preliminary mobilization of 25,000 men.

Reports, very vague, from London and Paris, on the Cabinet meetings which have taken place. Daladier and Bonnet will be in Paris to-night. It seems that the Czech Minister[1] in London has already given a negative reply to Hitler's memorandum. People are kneeling and praying for peace in the streets in England. The Italians are waiting with calm and conscious strength.

In the afternoon I had a long conference with Pariani, who seemed pretty calm. More convinced than ever of the need for a lightning war. He thinks of using gas on a large scale, also against fortified positions.

SEPTEMBER 26. In the morning I went with Cavagnari to the Ministry of Marine and the Operations Office, where I examined the situation and the possibilities with the officers of the General Staff. Our Navy has a very hard task—in the initial stages at least it will have, alone or almost alone, to sustain the shock of two strong nations in coalition. The intervention of Japan is considered to be of supreme importance, even if it should result in the intervention of America.

Many diplomats—the Belgian, the Brazilian, and the Pole. There is now an atmosphere of war. The last hopes of all are attached to the message sent by Chamberlain to the Führer after the meeting which took place in London this morning. These hopes are of brief duration. At 7.15 p.m. Attolico telephones that the conversation has taken place. The proposal was for direct contact between the Prague and Berlin Governments, with perhaps the mediation of London. Proposal rejected—the Führer has brought forward the term of the ultimatum from October 1 to 2 p.m., Wednesday 28th. It is war. May God protect Italy and the Duce.

I received also the Yugoslav Minister, in order to clear up the ambiguity created by their representative in Tirana, who has spread rumours about an immediate occupation of Albania by us. Cristich repudiated his colleague.

Then I saw Mackensen, who informed me about a *démarche* made in Berlin by the Spanish Ambassador. Franco, worried by his position, is thinking of opening negotiations with London and Paris in order to make a declaration of neutrality. Nothing has yet been announced to

[1] Jan Masaryk, son of the first President of Czechoslovakia. Foreign Minister in the Czechoslovak Government in London, July 1940. Committed suicide in March 1948.

us by Conde. Disgusting! Enough to make our dead in Spain turn in
their graves. It raises the problem of the Volunteer Corps of Occupation. What will they do with them? I immediately gave Valle
instructions to start to study the evacuation of our air force.
I received the Duce at the station at 10.50 p.m. Meanwhile Hitler
has spoken—nothing more than we already knew. I inform the Duce
of the latest developments—he listens with great seriousness and concentration. His face and his gestures are grave—but he is also serene. He
reacts with disgust to the news about Spain. He ends by declaring that
to-morrow he will mobilize and begin to send troops to Libya. He
retired to his room as soon as we got to the Villa Torlonia.
The Spaniard has made the *démarche* about neutrality to Buti. But
in a modified form. He did not dare come to me about it. However,
upon reflection I see that neutrality is the only way in which Franco
can fight. Our men will stay there to continue a guerilla war against
the Reds. The Duce has sent a telegram to suspend the repatriation.

SEPTEMBER 27. The Duce received Valle, Pariani, and Cavagnari,
and gave orders for an initial mobilization sufficient to ensure armed
neutrality in the first phase. Then he had a long conference with me.
He is still perplexed about the attitude which the French and the
English will adopt and, in the event of their declaring war, about their
military tactics. An attack on the Siegfried line? Out of the question.
And as Germany, once Czechoslovakia has been liquidated, will not
attack in the west, one cannot rule out the possibility that the conflict
may be resolved without a clash between the giants. In any case, the
Duce wants to settle forthwith the basis of the political understanding
with Berlin and to create organs of military co-operation. With this
end in view he proposes a meeting between me and Ribbentrop. The
Germans accept and suggest bringing the soldiers too. Keitel[1] on their
side, Pariani and Valle on our side. We are to meet in Munich at
12 noon on Thursday.
No new moves on the diplomatic chess-board, except a confirmation
from Berlin that 'the day is to-morrow'. In the afternoon I received
Villani, to whom I repeated the usual recommendations of calm; the
Japanese Ambassador, who, unofficially, declared himself convinced
that Tokyo will intervene on our side; and Cristich, who came to
repudiate the conduct I have mentioned of their Minister in Tirana.
He told me that, according to the Czech Minister, Russian intervention
will take the concrete form of an air attack on Poland.
Chamberlain spoke on the wireless at 8 to-night—his tone was
depressed. It is that of a man who has abandoned all hope of peace.
In fact, short of a miracle. . . .

[1] General Wilhelm Keitel, Chief of General Staff of the *Wehrmacht*.

SETTEMBRE **28**

MERCOLEDI - s. Venceslao re - 271-94 SETTEMBRE

Ore 10. Mancano quattro ore allo scoppio delle ostilità, allorchè Perth telefona che chiede udienza. Lo ricevo subito. Dice, ed è molto commosso, che Chamberlain fa appello al Duce per un intervento amichevole in queste ore che considera le ultime ore utili per salvare la pace e la civiltà. Ripete la garanzia che Inghilterra e Francia hanno già offerta per la retrocessione dei Sudeti. Chiedo a Perth se devo considerare la démarche come un invito ufficiale al Duce di assumere il ruolo di mediatore. Sì. Allora non c'è tempo da perdere: l'offerta merita di esser presa in considerazione. Dico a Perth di attendermi a Palazzo Chigi. Vado dal Duce. Concorda subito sulla impossibilità di opporre un più del non ricevere alla domanda di Chamberlain. Telefona ad Attolico: "Andate dal Führer e ditegli, premesso ch'io in ogni evenienza sarò al suo fianco, che consiglio di dilazionare di 24 ore l'inizio delle ostilità. Nel frattempo mi riservo studiare quanto potrà esser fatto per risolvere il problema". Torno a Palazzo Chigi. Informo Perth che le ostilità dovevano aver inizio oggi e confermo che il nostro posto è con la Germania. Trema in volto ed ha gli occhi arrossati. Quando aggiungo che però il Duce ha accolto la richiesta di Chamberlain ed ha proposto 24 ore di rinvio scoppia in un riso pieno di singhiozzi e si precipita alla sua Ambasciata. Poco dopo chiede una nuova udienza. Reca un messaggio di Chamberlain al Duce e copia di quello diretto a Hitler: una concreta proposta di conferenza a 4 con l'impegno di arrivare alla soluzione radicale del problema sudetico entro sette giorni. Non si può rifiutare: se Hitler lo facesse si attirerebbe l'odio del mondo ed avrebbe tutta la responsabilità del conflitto. Palazzo Venezia: il Duce decide di appoggiare la domanda inglese, tanto più che ora il Führer. Aderendo al desiderio di Mussolini, ha

FACSIMILE OF THE PAGE IN CIANO'S DIARY
FOR SEPTEMBER 28, 1938

SEPTEMBER 28. 10 a.m. Four hours to go before the outbreak of hostilities, when Perth telephones to ask for an interview. I receive him at once. He says, with much emotion, that Chamberlain appeals to the Duce for his friendly intervention in these hours, which he considers the last in which something can be done to save peace and civilization. He repeats the guarantee already offered by England and France for the return of the Sudetenland. I ask Perth whether I am to regard his *démarche* as an official invitation to the Duce to assume the role of mediator. Yes. In that case there is no time to lose—the offer deserves to be given consideration. I tell Perth to wait for me at the Palazzo Chigi. I go to the Duce. He agrees at once on the impossibility of meeting Chamberlain's request with a flat refusal. He telephones Attolico: 'Go to the Führer and tell him, having first said that in any eventuality I shall be at his side, that I recommend that the commencement of hostilities should be delayed for 24 hours. Meanwhile I undertake to study what can be done to solve the problem.' I go back to the Palazzo Chigi. I inform Perth that hostilities are to begin to-day and confirm that our place is beside Germany. His face quivers and his eyes are red. When I add that nevertheless the Duce has accepted Chamberlain's request and has proposed a delay of 24 hours, he bursts into a sobbing laugh and rushes off to his Embassy. A little later he asks for another interview. He brings with him a message from Chamberlain to the Duce and a copy of another sent to Hitler: a concrete proposal for a Conference of Four with the task of reaching a radical solution of the Sudeten problem within seven days. It cannot be rejected—by rejecting it Hitler would draw the hatred of the world upon himself and have the sole responsibility for the conflict. Palazzo Venezia—the Duce decides to support the English request, particularly as the Führer has now, at Mussolini's desire, had a phonogram of instructions made. I telephone to Perth, to inform him, and to Attolico, to give him directions. Naturally I cancel the meeting with Ribbentrop and Keitel arranged yesterday.

Blondel too, it transpires from a telephone call, is preparing to make a '*démarche*'. Not a hope—it is not our intention that France shall interfere. The whole face of the question would be changed and the Germans would, rightly, smell a rat. I telephone to Perth: 'It transpires that France is preparing to put her oar in. I advise you that any *démarche* by Blondel would simply defeat its own ends. Find a way of preventing it. Our work would be imperilled.' He agrees and undertakes to comply with my request.

3 p.m. Attolico telephones that Hitler agrees in principle, making certain reservations of secondary importance. He lays down one condition, however: the presence of Mussolini, which he regards as the sole guarantee. The Duce accepts. We leave at 6 to-night, in order to be

in Munich, where the Conference is to take place, at 10.30 in the morning.

I return to the Duce with the American Ambassador, bearing a very tardy message from Roosevelt. I remain alone with the Duce. 'As you see,' he says, 'I am only moderately happy, because, though perhaps at a heavy price, we could have liquidated France and Great Britain for ever. We now have overwhelming proof of this.'

We leave at 6. The unanimous prayers of Italy are with us.

SEPTEMBER 29–30. In the train the Duce is in a very good humour. We dine together and he speaks with great vivacity on every subject. He criticizes Britain and British policy severely. 'In a country where animals are adored to the point of making cemeteries and hospitals and houses for them, and legacies are bequeathed to parrots, you can be sure that decadence has set in. Besides, other reasons apart, it is also a consequence of the composition of the English people. Four million surplus women. Four million sexually unsatisfied women, artificially creating a host of problems in order to excite or appease their senses. Not being able to embrace one man, they embrace humanity.'

At Kufstein we meet the Führer. We get into his carriage, where spread out on a table are all the maps of the Sudetenland and the western fortifications. He explains the situation: he intends to liquidate Czechoslovakia as she now is, because she immobilizes forty of his divisions and ties his hands vis-à-vis France. When Czechoslovakia has been, as she must be, deflated, ten divisions will be enough to immobilize her. The Duce listens with concentration. The programme is now fixed: either the Conference is successful in a short time or the solution will take place by force of arms. 'Besides,' adds the Führer, 'the time will come when we shall have to fight side by side against France and England. All the better that it should happen while the Duce and I are at the head of our countries, and still young and full of vigour.'

But all that seems superseded by the atmosphere which in fact has been created—an atmosphere of agreement. Even the people waving as the train passes make one realize their joy at the event which is in the air.

After a brief stop at the palace where the Duce and I are staying, we go to the Führerhaus, where the conference is to take place. The others have already arrived and are gathered round a table on which snacks and drinks are set out. The Führer comes half-way down the stairs to meet us and, with the rest of his suite, singles out us, the Italians, by a marked distinction of treatment. Brief, cold handshakes with Daladier and Chamberlain—then the Duce, alone, goes over to a corner of the room where the Nazi leaders surround him. There is a vague sense of embarrassment, particularly on the part of the French.

I talk to Daladier, and then to Francois-Poncet,[1] about trivial things. Then to Chamberlain, who says he wants to talk to the Duce. He thanks him for all that he has already done. But the Duce, coldly, does not take advantage of the opening, and the conversation peters out.

We enter the conference room. The four chiefs; Ribbentrop, Leger,[2] Wilson,[3] and I; and Schmidt, the interpreter. The Führer speaks—a few words of thanks and an exposition of the situation. He speaks calmly, but from time to time he gets excited and then he raises his voice and beats his fist against the palm of his other hand. Then Chamberlain. Then Daladier. Lastly the Duce, who affirms the necessity for a rapid and concrete decision, and with this end in view proposes to use as a basis for discussion a document which has in fact been telephoned to us by our Embassy the previous evening, as expressing the desires of the German Government.

The discussion develops formally and without very much animation. Chamberlain is inclined to linger over legal points; Daladier defends the cause of the Czechs without much conviction; the Duce prefers to remain silent and sum up and draw conclusions when the others have finished their dissertations.

We adjourn for lunch, which takes place in the Führer's private house—a modest apartment in a large building full of other residents. It has, however, many very valuable pictures.

The conference is continued in the afternoon and virtually breaks up into little groups which try to work out the various formulas. This permits us to talk with greater confidence, and the ice is broken.

Daladier, particularly, is loquacious in personal conversation. He says that what is happening to-day is due solely to the pig-headedness of Benes. In the last few months he has repeatedly suggested to Benes that the Sudetens should be given autonomy. That would at least have deferred the present crisis. He grumbles about the French war-mongers, who would have liked to push the country into an absurd and indeed impossible war—for France and England would never have been able to do anything really useful for Czechoslovakia, once she was attacked by the forces of the Reich.

The Duce, slightly annoyed by the vaguely parliamentary atmosphere which conferences always produce, moves round the room with his hands in his pockets and a rather distracted air. Every now and then he joins in the search for a formula. His great spirit, always ahead of events and men, has already absorbed the idea of agreement and, while the others are still wasting their breath over more or less formal

[1] André François-Poncet, French Ambassador in Berlin. Ambassador in Rome, November 1938. French High Commissioner in Germany, 1949.
[2] Aléxis Leger, Secretary-General of the French Foreign Office.
[3] Sir Horace Wilson, adviser to Chamberlain.

problems, he has almost ceased to take any interest. He has already passed on and is meditating other things.

However, he joins in the discussion again, when it turns to the question of including in the agenda the problem of the Polish and Hungarian minorities. The others, without exception, would gladly have said nothing about it. In fact they try to evade its discussion. But when there is a strong will, the strong will always predominates and others coalesce around it. The problem is discussed and solved by means of a formula which I do not hesitate to describe as very brilliant.

Meanwhile conversations à deux are taking place. There is a hint at the possibility of the Duce delaying his departure in order to permit a meeting between him and Chamberlain. But the idea is ruled out by the Duce, as he thinks that this might offend German susceptibilities. First I and then the Duce talk to Chamberlain. We tell him more or less the same things: we disinterest ourselves in Spain; withdrawal of 10,000 volunteers in the near future; goodwill for a speedy implementation of our Pact of April 16. Chamberlain hints at the possibility of a Conference of Four to solve the Spanish problem.

At last, at one in the morning, the document is completed. Everybody is satisfied, even the French—even the Czechs, according to what Daladier tells me. François-Poncet has a moment of shame while he is collating the document. 'Voilà comme la France traite les seuls alliés qui lui étaient restés fidèles,' he exclaims.

We sign, shake hands, and depart.

In Italy, from the Brenner to Rome, from the King down to the peasants, the Duce receives welcomes such as I have never seen. He says himself that this enthusiasm was only equalled on the evening when the Empire was proclaimed.

Ribbentrop has handed me a project for a tripartite alliance between Italy, Germany, and Japan. He says it is 'the biggest thing in the world'. He always exaggerates, Ribbentrop. No doubt we will study it quite calmly and, perhaps, put it aside for some time.

PART IV

AFTER MUNICH

AFTER MUNICH

Echoes of Munich—Progress towards the implementation of the Anglo-Italian Agreement—The Hungarians press their claims—Csaky in Rome—Assurances to Albania—Germany supports the Czechs —Axis arbitration proposed—Starace unpopular—Preparations in Albania—Ribbentrop in Rome (October 27–9)—Mussolini declines an immediate alliance—Ciano and Ribbentrop in Vienna (November 2–4)—The Belvedere Award—The racial campaign continues—A French Ambassador in Rome—Repatriation of Italians from abroad —Hungary still unsatisfied—Perth presents credentials to the King Emperor (November 16)—Hungary reprimanded—'Tunis, Corsica, Nice, Savoy'—Chamberlain to visit Rome—All ready for action in Albania—Duce and Pope—Ciano in Budapest (December 19–22) —Another disappointment in Spain.

OCTOBER 1. Still some excitement this morning, but of the second magnitude. News from Prague that Beck has sent an ultimatum, expiring at midday, for the cession of the territory demanded. The Czechs accept in principle, but would like a little time to prepare things in a seemly fashion. They cannot be blamed. There is no justification for this Polish impatience—they have waited twenty years, they can wait another day or two and avoid an incident which might make the situation difficult again. I telephoned in this sense to our Ambassador in Warsaw and instructed him to approach Beck. I spoke to the Polish representative in Rome myself.

France and England have acted too. Ribbentrop, on the other hand, who is actually not too pleased that everything has gone so smoothly, telephoned me to say that he will not make any *démarche* in Warsaw— he is almost inciting the Poles to attack. The ultimatum is extended for one hour, at the end of which Prague yields and this difficulty too is solved. The truth is that the Poles have become intransigent because they were not invited to Munich and because they fear a revival of the Four Power Pact.

In the afternoon, many diplomats. Among them Perth, to whom I gave a hint about a resumption of contact in the near future; Cristich, who read me a very friendly letter from Stoyadinovich; and Hotta, who brought with him Shigemitsu,[1] my old colleague in Shanghai, whom I

[1] Mamoru Shigemitsu. He was Japanese Minister to China in 1932, when Ciano, as Italian Consul-General, presided over a League of Nations Commission of Inquiry into the hostilities at Shanghai. Foreign Minister, 1943–5.

last saw many years ago in distinctly dramatic circumstances. He is now going to be Ambassador in London.

OCTOBER 2. The Prince of Hesse explained to me, at the Führer's behest, why the Munich meeting was followed by the codicil of an Anglo-German committee. Chamberlain asked the Führer for an interview and talked to him about the possibility of a conference on Spain and also about an extraordinary proposal to abolish the bomber aircraft of the Four Powers [sic!]. Finally he took a piece of paper out of his pocket and put before the Führer a draft of the communiqué, which he declared to be necessary to him for his parliamentary position. The Führer did not think he could refuse. And the Duce, to whom I related this story, said to me: 'Explanations are superfluous. You do not refuse a glass of lemonade to a thirsty man.'

The Duce and I examined the question of our relations with London. After what was said to Chamberlain at Munich there must be no delay in opening negotiations with Perth. I am to send for him to-morrow and officially communicate to him the withdrawal of the 10,000 volunteers. After which I shall bluntly ask him the question: are you now willing to implement the Pact of April 16? If they are, so much the better. If not, we must each play our own game. The Duce also tells me to indicate that the Grand Council might repudiate this agreement, which has been waiting too long for its consummation.

In the evening the Duce read to me over the telephone *Informazione Diplomatica* No. 21, on Hungary.

OCTOBER 3. Villani asked for our support in accelerating the implementation of the Munich decisions so far as Hungary is concerned. From what he said, and even more from what he did not say, it is clear that the Hungarians have designs on Slovakia. An error, a gross error, and I personally am against it. There would be reactions from Roumania, Yugoslavia, and Germany. Besides, the Slovaks don't want it. And there is no point in wiping out one injustice in order to commit another.

I had my conversation with Perth. I expressed myself on the lines agreed with the Duce. The arguments are so strong that Perth himself could not raise serious objections, though he tried to make a point about the question of our aeroplanes. I advised him not to create new difficulties and to stick to the terms of our former agreement. I confirmed that it is useless to talk of a Conference of Four or of further visits until relations have become normal—such things may follow, but they cannot precede, the implementation of the Pact. Lastly I added that a reply, at least in general terms, ought to be given before October 6, as the Grand Council will be in a position to review foreign policy and will want to crystallize situations which have hitherto not been defined in diplomatic documents.[1]

I received the Brazilian, the Roumanian, and the Portuguese. I telephoned to Prunas to say that, if a French Ambassador is to come, it is better it should not be Chambrun, as the newspapers prophesy. He was liquidated by the gossip about the non-existent friendship between the Fontanges[2] and the Duce and by the bullet which she planted in his backside.

OCTOBER 4. After a few applications of minor importance, I received Perth, at his request. He wanted elucidation of certain points in yesterday's conversation, viz.: does Italy intend not to send more troops after the withdrawal of the 10,000, and is she prepared to promise not to increase the number of the pilots and the aircraft on the Nationalist side? The reply to the first question is obvious and I gave it at once. On the second question I reserved the decision for the Duce. And I was right, because with good cause he rejected a promise which would do too much to weaken Franco's position.

Prunas telephoned the French decision about sending an Ambassador —it seems it is François-Poncet. The news leaves us more or less indifferent. It is good that the French have capitulated, but we don't want certain Italians to get excited and enthusiastic about it.

A certain Kworchak,[3] already known to me and now sent to me by the Duce, put before me the arguments in favour of the union of Slovakia with Hungary. I am suspicious of this idea. The Duce likes the Hungarians, in fact he says that they are the only people in Europe whom he finds sympathetic. I rather distrust them. After Slovakia it will be the turn of Croatia. And the Germans, who do not dare to make a direct attack on the problem of an outlet to the Adriatic, will hope to trace this path for themselves by means of the Magyars, who will eventually return to their inevitable, traditional policy of gravitating round Berlin. In the little map which was shown to me yesterday Fiume figured among the claims. That is significant. It won't do— our real friendship is with Belgrade.

OCTOBER 5. I informed Villani that in the event of a Czech attack —a thing which we in fact absolutely rule out—Hungary can count on our sending immediately 100 fighters, with the necessary pilots, to defend Budapest. We talked about Slovakia. Hungary's appetites are becoming more and more blatant. I recommended moderation. Afterwards I described to the Duce the conclusions I came to yesterday

[1] Ciano omitted one or more words from this sentence. The translation is conjectural.

[2] Magda de Fontanges, a journalist, shot and wounded the Comte de Chambrun at the Gare du Nord on March 17, 1937. She believed him to be responsible for separating her from the 'one love of her life', Mussolini.

[3] The spelling of this name is uncertain.

after my conversation with the Slovak propagandist (I have discovered that he is an ex-boxer in Magyar pay). The Duce agreed with me and ended by declaring that we must strengthen our ties with Belgrade.

I saw Perth and communicated the Chief's decisions to him.

Chvalkovsky has been appointed Foreign Minister and is preparing to leave for Prague. He has always been our friend and has had a clear understanding of the situation. His programme now is to settle the dispute with the three neighbouring states as rapidly as possible—afterwards he wants definitely to enter the orbit of the Axis. 'Friendship with the Axis—intimacy with Rome': that was my advice, and he accepted the whole of it. Henceforth Prague must enter the horizontal Axis, which will have to reach from Rome at one end to Warsaw at the other and which, if it is really strong, will make possible the existence of the vertical Axis. I accompanied the Minister to the Duce, who repeated to him the same advice. Chvalkovsky said that he has always been convinced of the impossibility of assistance from France and England. Bohemia is completely unknown in England. Once, when he was a student in London, he was given a violin to play at a party simply because it was known that he was a Czech. There was a confusion of thought between Bohemians and gypsies. He is thinking now of going to Berlin in order to present himself to the Führer.

OCTOBER 6. Perth brought the British reply. In principle they accept the implementation of the Pact after the withdrawal of the 10,000 men. But Chamberlain asks for a short breathing space. He does not want to present himself to the Cabinet, and subsequently to the House of Commons, with the words: 'Here you are. Take it or leave it. Mussolini has fixed the date.' At the moment, in spite of the vote of confidence, his position has been shaken, and in those circumstances it would become untenable. He asks for a delay until November 1. The Duce's first reaction to the English reply was unfavourable, but he ended by consenting to this. On the other hand, he naturally does not intend to give any assurances about the Air Force and its activities.

Grand Council. Problem of the Jews. Balbo, De Bono, and Federzoni spoke in their favour. The others against. Particularly Bottai, who surprised me by his intransigence. He is opposed to any mitigation of the measures. 'They will hate us because we have driven them out. They will despise us if we let them in again.' 'The discriminatory measures mean nothing,' said the Duce to me between the speeches. 'The important thing is to raise the problem. Anti-Semitism has now been inoculated into the blood of the Italians. It will continue to circulate and to develop of its own accord. So, even if I am conciliatory to-night, I shall be very stern when I prepare the laws.'

OCTOBER 7. I communicated our reply to Perth. No particular reaction. Barring surprises, I believe the Pact is now on the way to ratification in the course of the next few weeks.

Grand Council. The Chamber of the Fasces and the Corporations[1] was discussed. No particularly interesting contributions to the debate. The Duce made a veiled allusion to the Albanian project: 'I was born never to leave the Italians in peace. First Africa, now Spain, to-morrow something else.' The Grand Council applauded.

Fixed our position with respect to the Polish-Hungarian claims. They can't have Slovakia—the Slovaks must have full liberty to decide and may either stay with Prague or become autonomous. A common frontier between Hungary and Poland can be secured in Sub-Carpathian Russia. It seems, however, that Berlin is preparing to make difficulties about this solution too. This, from a German point of view, is logical. But I fail to understand the opposition of Roumania. Granted that henceforth Czechoslovakia is no more than an appendix of Germany, are the dear Roumanians really so keen to have a common frontier with the Germans? Surely they understand that contact between Poland and Hungary would in fact be a barricade protecting them. For us, situated as we are, this is a very delicate thing to tell them.

OCTOBER 8. Villani enumerated Hungary's territorial wishes: the Magyar areas, Sub-Carpathian Russia, and a plebiscite for the Slovaks. But reports from Berlin make it clear that Germany will stubbornly oppose the cession of any areas not touching the frontiers.

I made a long and successful speech at the Grand Council about the international situation. The Duce, who listened with the most profound attention, described as 'interesting, precise, and sometimes dramatic' the report of Comrade Ciano.

OCTOBER 9. The Duce telephoned to tell me that he 'found my report brilliant and that it was very much appreciated by the Grand Council.'

To Florence, and afterwards to Ponte a Moriano with Edda and Ciccino.

OCTOBER 10. The Hungarian Minister has been dramatizing the situation and even talking of general mobilization. I don't believe it. He told me in great secrecy that some groups inside Czechoslovakia are to be sent into action to-day. They have informed us and the Poles —as for the Germans, they don't trust them too much.

[1] A few weeks later the Council of Ministers approved a law abolishing the Chamber of Deputies, which had survived in a modified form from pre-Fascist days (the last contested election was in 1924). Its place was taken by a new Chamber of the Fasces and the Corporations, composed of the members of the National Council of Fascism and of the National Council of Corporations, all directly nominated by Mussolini or the Fascist Party.

I accompanied Grandi to the Duce—nothing striking in the conversation. Then the Duce talked to me about De Vecchi. 'My idea may seem to you Mehistophelean,' he said, 'but this is what we must do. Wherever I have put De Vecchi, he has always created a mass of trouble. He has never succeeded in anything. He is now doing very badly in Rhodes. Never mind. He must be encouraged to do even worse. He must be made to feel that his work is approved and his path must be greased until sooner or later he slips up so grossly, so unmistakably, that even without others passing judgment on him he will see for himself that he is liquidated. And then I shall have him off my hands for ever.'

OCTOBER 11. I received a long procession of people in the morning, but there were no important conversations, except an exchange of views with Pierre Lyautey,[1] whom I have known for a long time and to whom I can speak frankly. I told him of the sinister influence exerted by the French press on relations between the two countries—it has not yet begun to understand the Fascist psychology, still less that of Mussolini. It is always the one thing in a thousand likely to make the Duce furious which gets given the headlines. Even the atmosphere of Munich has been very rapidly spoilt by the French press.

I took Hesse to the Duce. He told us about a *démarche* of Poncet in Berlin for a Franco-German agreement on the lines of that concluded with London. He also talked about a possible pact for consultation between the four powers, to come into play if war threatens in Europe. We gave our approval on two conditions: that our relations with England are first regularized by the implementation of the Pact of April 16, and that Poland is also invited. We leave it to France and England, if they want to, to show her the door. They can incur the odium for it. Yugoslavia does not aspire to form part of the European directorate. Stoyadinovich described himself as *le coq qui chante sur son fumier*. And his *fumier* is the Balkans.

OCTOBER 12. The Duce told me over the telephone this evening to bring pressure to bear on Prague for the immediate cession to the Magyars of the areas with a clear Hungarian majority. He has been approached by the Military Attaché, who also informed him of Budapest's intention to mobilize to-morrow, if the Czechs persist in their obstructionist manœuvres. Meanwhile I have learnt that the new Foreign Minister, Chvalkovsky, has gone to Berlin and on to Berchtesgaden in order to place himself under the ample but not disinterested wings of Hitler.

OCTOBER 13. Sereggi brought me a personal message from King Zog and also left me a note about the declaration which he has been ordered to make. It amounts to this. Albania is now in Italy's hands,

---

[1] A French right-wing journalist. Son of Maréchal Lyautey.

for Italy controls every sector of the national activity. The King is devoted. The people are grateful. Why do you want anything more? This question was not asked, but it was the real reason for the conversation. I was kind and affable. This cheered him up. He was particularly appreciative when I told him, with emphasis on every word, that I have great sympathy for him and that in any eventuality I regard him as our man. We must hurry up with Albania. I received Prampolini, who brought me his magnificent report on the reclamation of the country as a whole. He is enthusiastic about what he has seen. He considers the coastal areas to be very superior to ours and, without exaggerated optimism, he believes that from the reclaimed districts alone we shall be able to import here 200,000 tons of corn.

Perth proposes to send his Military Attaché to Naples to be present at the disembarkation of the volunteers returning from Spain. No objection in principle on our part—so long as the thing is useful to Chamberlain for the parliamentary debates, which look like being severe.

Villani returned to the charge over the unspecified Hungarian demands. The truth is that they would like to have Slovakia, Ruthenia, everything—to create, in fact, mosaic state No. 3. They don't dare say so—because they are afraid of Germany. Villani told me that Mussolini advised Szabo[1] that they should mobilize. Is this true?

OCTOBER 14. Hesse has asked in the Führer's name whether Germany may make a declaration to France on the lines of that made to England. No objection on our part, especially as it will have the effect of giving us freedom of manœuvre with regard to Paris.

Growing tension between Budapest and Prague. Negotiations have been broken off. Hungary is in process of mobilizing. Count Csaky[2] has arrived here. He confers with me and the Duce. He wants our sanction for their mobilization and our support for the immediate summoning of a conference of the four powers. He is very excited, against the Germans particularly. He accuses the Reich of having permitted Prague to stiffen against Hungary. Czechoslovakia is now a German protectorate, which Berlin intends to use in order to increase German pressure on Roumania and on Hungary herself. He says that, since oil was discovered in Hungary, German policy has changed and is becoming insupportable. 'However,' he concludes, 'before we allow ourselves to be absorbed we shall die to the last man.'

In compliance with the Hungarian request we intervene in London, Paris, and Berlin in support of the proposal for a conference. I also speak to the Polish Ambassador and the Yugoslav Minister in order to ease two difficult situations. Then I am called to the telephone by

[1] Colonel L. Szabo, Hungarian Military Attaché in Rome.
[2] Count Istvan Csaky, *chef de cabinet* at the Hungarian Foreign Ministry. Foreign Minister, December 1938.

Ribbentrop. As was to be expected, the Germans are against a conference. They say that there will be opposition from France and
England, and that it is more advisable to act behind the scenes. As
I remain firm, Ribbentrop ends nevertheless by coming round to the
proposal. However, Csaky comes to see me again. Budapest is worried
by the attitude of Berlin. After all that they have solicited and obtained
they evidently feel embarrassed about us, but they now prefer not to
annoy the Germans and to abandon the idea of a conference and stick to
direct negotiations. For one thing Hitler has said that he has now
demobilized and that he does not intend to face another crisis. I go to
the Duce at the Villa Torlonia. We put a good face on it and give our
approval to the German idea. But this is the first time we have allowed
ourselves to be taken in tow and I am not at all pleased.

OCTOBER 15. The Duce, who has evidently found yesterday's
events hard to digest, telephones to me to propose to the Germans
making identical *démarches* in Prague and in Budapest, inviting the two
Governments to resume direct negotiations. This will explain, at least
in part, our change of front yesterday. Ribbentrop opposes the idea
—he says that a *démarche* of this kind might have the appearance of
pressure, which would be dangerous in the present phase. He asks us
instead to give our support in Prague to the Hungarian demands of
yesterday, which are simply the old demands, less Bratislava, which
the Germans are very keen on. The Duce consents.

Csaky comes to say good-bye and asks me to intervene in Prague
with a request for clemency for the forty Hungarian rebels who were
taken prisoner by the Czechs in Ruthenia. They all belong to the right.
If they were hanged, says Csaky, it would create so many martyrs of
the opposition parties and the position of Imredy, who has telephoned
about the matter, would be shaken to a very dangerous degree. I
telephone to Prague. In the afternoon Fransoni reports that the Czech
Government has received our *démarche* in the most friendly spirit and
that the Hungarian prisoners will be spared. Henceforth we can ask
for anything in Prague in the certainty of being listened to.

After having read reports from Poland, the Duce told me to inform
Berlin that we are not at all keen on a common frontier between
Poland and Hungary. He thinks that it would be quite valueless and
that any attempt at the encirclement of Germany is not just stupid,
but absolutely ridiculous.

I made the communication, but I confess that for my part I would
have been very glad to see Hungary and Poland knit together. Life is
long and may have many surprises in store for us. . . .

OCTOBER 16. Nothing worthy of note, except a brief conversation
with the Duce, in the course of which I handed him Prampolini's

report on reclamation in Albania and suggested making a start as soon as possible with the reclamation of Durazzo, the part of the scheme which is most economically valuable, most spectacular, and most useful for military purposes. It will also serve to soothe the not unjustified anxieties of King Zog.

OCTOBER 17. I announced to Blondel our *agrément* for François-Poncet. He asked me when we will appoint an Ambassador in Paris, but I gave him very little encouragement and dropped the subject.

I received Villani, who expounded Hungary's desires to me. Prague must make a concrete offer. Such an offer will be examined by Budapest, but fresh negotiations will not be commenced. If the offer appears satisfactory, it will be accepted. If not, the Axis powers can function as arbitrators.

I telephoned to Prague to express to Chvalkovsky our support of these Hungarian desires.

OCTOBER 18. Review of the Police—very successful. By comparison with those of previous years it shows further progress.

No new political developments.

Grand Council—a long report from Starace and a very brilliant summing-up from the Duce (he described the Vatican as anti-Catholic and the ghetto as Catholic, and said that all the Piuses have brought misfortune to the Church. He said of the present Pius that he 'will leave behind him a larger heap of ruins than any Pope before him'). A disconnected speech from De Vecchi, which filled the assembly with mirth. Instead of realizing what was happening, he thought he was having a great success and let himself go, talking nonsense and using language which can have no precedent in a political assembly.

OCTOBER 19. The Duce has gone to Romagna. There is nothing new. Fransoni has made the *démarche* in Prague. But he may have gone rather too far by mentioning straight away the possibility of Axis mediation. Chvalkovsky was apparently impressed. I indicated this to Villani and he thinks everything is going well.

Sereggi, on his departure for Albania, was given an assurance of our friendly collaboration and a promise that we will do something in the matter of reclamation. I have in fact proposed to the Duce, who still has Prampolini's project by him, that we should immediately set to work in the plain of Durazzo. 3,000 hectares can be reclaimed there at a cost of less than 20 million lire. This will serve to soothe Albanian anxieties. It will be a partial preparation for our work in the future. And it will also serve a military purpose, as any disembarkation in force will have to be based on Durazzo and its immediate vicinity. From the psychological point of view too it is a good thing that those who land in Albania, both soldiers and civilians, should feel that they have come to a healthy and fertile land and not to a desolate swamp. A better impression of this kind might have produced a different story in 1920 and we might have committed ourselves more whole-heartedly.

OCTOBER 20. I was called to the telephone by Ribbentrop last night. He told me a long story of how he had received the Slovak and Ruthenian representatives and settled with them a last plan to submit to Budapest. The German Minister will now receive orders to approach Kanya and recommend strongly the acceptance of the plan by the Hungarians. I smelt, though I had no proof of it, that the plan is bad from the Hungarian point of view. Ribbentrop was reticent and, when I mentioned the common frontier between Poland and Hungary, he wriggled out of the subject. The Duce does not intend to bring pressure to bear on Budapest. I said as much to Villani: 'If you accept the plan, which may be called a German plan, good—we are satisfied. If not, let us know what we can do for you.'

I went to Naples to receive the legionaries from Spain. They look very tough and not at all tired by their long campaign in a foreign country. The population received them well, but not with the warmth which I should have expected. The King, with whom I drove through the streets and with whom I also had a talk at the Palace, was almost indifferent and had not a word of human warmth for the legionaries. He regards to-day's event as part of the common run of ceremonies in which he is asked to take part. He talked mostly about Cora, whom he does not want to remain as Prefect of the Palace, and asked me to take it upon myself to liquidate him. Not much about politics. He simply reaffirmed his sceptical attitude to the Germans, whom he regards as treacherous and dangerous, and his sympathy for the English, who know how to stand by their agreements, just as the old Hapsburg Vienna did.

OCTOBER 21. Early in the morning Villani informed me of the disgust and indignation of the Hungarians over the Czech proposal. They are disgusted with Germany, because the Germans have made it clear that this proposal is to be the end of their efforts at mediation, and they are indignant with the Czechs for trying to strike the five towns out of the Magyar claims. Now while the Hungarians are prepared to compromise over Bratislava and Nitra, they are insistent about the towns in the eastern area, particularly Kassa, which they could not renounce without provoking a revolution in the country. Their plan is to ask for the arbitration of the Axis for the western area, and of the Axis plus Poland for the eastern area. I telephoned this to the Duce, and he agreed, but advised feeling the pulse of Germany before Poland is invited.

I saw Barzini junior,[1] and gave him some details to use in the Italian chapter of a book called *Four Days*, which describes the culminating days of the Czech crisis.

The Polish Ambassador, on receipt of information from Budapest, wanted to know what we think about the arbitration. I told him. Wieniawa is a cavalry general, not without brilliance, but an amateurish diplomat. He has, however, the great merit of being concise and prompt. When I praised him for this, he replied: 'You can lose everything else in life and get it back again, even a woman, but not time.' He also gave me news of the negative results of Beck's visit to Roumania.

Von Mackensen, on Ribbentrop's instructions, brought me a map showing the Czech proposals. It is clear that the Germans are acting on behalf of Prague. He didn't like it when I informed him exactly what the position is. He made a particularly wry face at the idea of bringing in Poland, which was entirely new to him.

Hotta is leaving Rome. I congratulated him on the victory at Canton. Hotta is a good sort but rather cold and timid and he does not belong to the new era. While we were working at the triangle policy, he went on talking to me about London. . . .

OCTOBER 22. Ribbentrop telephoned from Munich about the proposal for Axis arbitration. He is against it, but his arguments are simply dust in our eyes. The truth is that he intends to protect Czechoslovakia as far as he can and sacrifice the ambitions, even the legitimate ambitions, of Hungary. In his view arbitration is dangerous because it will end by satisfying neither Prague nor Budapest and by obliging us to have recourse to force in order to put our decisions into effect. This, I told him, may be ruled out, as arbitration implies the previous consent of the parties to accept its results. He had a lot to say against the Hungarians, whom he accuses of having changed their cards after the deal. But hostile as he is, he will never equal the hostility the Hungarians feel for him. He will telephone again after conferring with Hitler—he ventilated the possibility of a Conference of Four, though it was he who refused to consider it a week ago!

Conde presented me with a picture by Zuloaga as a gift from the Caudillo. A handsome and moving souvenir of the war in Spain: 'The Oldest Requete', with a landscape background full of war and flames.

Once again I learnt from the Roumanian Minister of the anxiety of his country, desperately seeking friendship with us, to escape or at least protect itself from the sombre threat of Germanism.

The Duce has given orders to go ahead with the reclamation of the Durazzo plain, on the left bank of the Arzen.

[1] Luigi Barzini junior, assistant editor of the *Corriere della Sera*.

OCTOBER 23. Villani was pleading his country's cause to me at an early hour. He wants us to insist about the arbitration with the Germans, because he is certain that without pressure from us they will put spokes in the wheels once more. Tension between Hungary and Germany is acute, though both parties are making efforts to conceal it. They both accuse each other of telling lies about the three eastern towns of Kassa, Ungvar, and Munkacs. In support of their thesis the Hungarians cite the testimony of no less a person than the German Minister in Budapest, though for obvious reasons it cannot be made public. Villani spoke very bitterly about Germany. He is worried about the fate of the Imredy Cabinet and fears it may be succeeded by Szalasi,[1] whom he describes as an agent in the pay of Berlin.

Ribbentrop telephoned in the evening. He repeated, as from the mouth of the Führer, what he had said himself last night. He does not want the arbitration, which would oblige him to show himself in his true colours to the Hungarians. He asked me if he may come to Rome at the end of the week to confer with the Duce and with me in person. I replied that he may. What is he up to? I distrust Ribbentrop's initiatives. He is vain, frivolous, and loquacious. The Duce says you only have to look at his head to see that he has a little brain. And he is very tactless. In these telephone calls of the last few days he has behaved in a manner which I find very offensive—always trying to impose his point of view. It has to be put up with at the moment. But sooner or later we shall have to call a halt to this tendency to a new political technique of *coups de téléphone*.

OCTOBER 24. A short talk with the Pole, who had nothing to tell me and nothing to ask.

I confirmed to General Berti that he is to be replaced in Spain, and he seemed more than a little upset. What vexes him more than his own removal is the appointment of Gambara, with whom he has had constant disagreements. And to think that it is just this friction which induced me to propose Gambara's appointment.

I saw the Duce after an interval of four days. He is annoyed by the chopping and changing of the Czechs and the Hungarians and has given me instructions to take up a position definitely against the claim on Ruthenia, as the French press has been giving an anti-German flavour to the attempt to create a common frontier between Poland and Hungary. He wants a legal opinion on whether the projected annexation of Libya can give the English a pretext to raise difficulties about the ratification of the agreement, to which, he says, 'I attribute no importance, but it is desired by the still existing half million of cowardly bourgeois, against whom I am going to set in motion my

[1] Ferenc Szalasi, leader of the pro-Nazi Hungarist or Arrow Cross Party. He was sentenced to three years' imprisonment in July 1938.

third wave.' He talked about some ideas of his for a Pact of Five with a reduction of armaments, which would bring war back to a more heroic level by eliminating everything that is too complex and mechanical. The practical result would be to limit those arms which are too expensive for us.

The Belgian Ambassador brought me a decoration and the Hungarian brought me his customary expressions of gratitude. But we are no further forward with the negotiations.

Long conversation with Buffarini, who raised a great hullabaloo about what he considers the dangerous hegemony of the Party over all sectors of the national life. He exaggerates, but there is something in what he says.

OCTOBER 25. Pirelli runs true to form—he came to me to break a lance about the immediate sending of an Ambassador to Paris, on the grounds that the French have made a 'fine gesture'. 'There you have the cowardly and disgusting bourgeoisie,' said the Duce, when I told him, 'against whom I am going to launch my third wave in my speech to the National Council of Fascism to-day.'

The Duce received the Spanish Ambassador, who presented him with a Grand Collar. He reaffirmed his uncompromising views about Spain. To bring the war to a victorious conclusion means paving the way for an imperial and heroic Spain—to end it by mediation means precipitating the country into the condition in which it was when Calvo Sotelo[1] was assassinated and the crisis began. He also pledged himself to give further assistance to Franco in the form of arms and supplies—but in future not in the form of men, in the first place because they are not useful and also because we are strictly watched and any dispatch of volunteers would place us in a difficult position with the English. However, the Duce concluded, the end is at hand: the Reds will yield, perhaps not at once, but before long, for the defeat of Prague makes inevitable the defeat of Barcelona too. And a military victory will give Franco the prestige necessary for governing, as in the case of Mustafa Kemal, who has lived for twenty years on the undisputed merit of having liberated his country by force of arms.

Buffarini came to finish his outburst against Starace. According to him, Starace is placing the country under a leaden cloak of personal and sectarian tyranny, and it is here that we must look for the principal cause of the restlessness and lack of enthusiasm in many sectors of the national life. I am not in a position to judge, but there is no doubt that everybody who gets the chance to do so says something of the kind. That Starace is much disliked is a fact. The Party is not in a healthy state and, on the pretext of depersonalization, it has become more personal than ever before. But Starace has also many qualities—he is

[1] Jose Calvo Sotelo, a former right-wing Minister of Finance, was murdered on July 13, 1936, five days before the military revolt broke out in Spanish Morocco.

a good organizer, he gets things done, and he is, probably, loyal. In any case there is nothing to be done at the moment. The Duce protects him with drawn sword. In due course we shall see.

OCTOBER 26. At the Grand Council last night there was a lively debate on Balbo's proposal to grant full citizenship to the Arabs. It is easy to recognize here a flat contradiction of our racial policy. The real Party men, like Farinacci, Starace, and Alfieri, did not hesitate to oppose the proposal. Nor did I. The project has been shelved and will be presented again in a very different garb. It is interesting to observe how anti-Balbo the Grand Council is. The mere fact that the measure had assumed a Balbian character was enough to produce a solid phalanx of opposition.

I gave Senator Prampolini confirmation of his instructions to start work on the reclamation of the Durazzo plain, on the left and later on the right bank of the River Arzen. Apart from the advantages I have enumerated earlier, the plan has the very important one that it permits us to concentrate two legions of labourers, who can form the bridge-head of the landing.

Received Berger-Waldenegg, whom I had not seen since the Anschluss. He is serene and dignified and very much a gentleman. He has no recriminations or regrets. He sees the situation with clarity: there are still certain unpleasantnesses in Austria, but it will all settle down in the end. The younger generation will be Nazi. The most serious obstacle is to be found in the fight against religion. He is going to stay in Italy. He wants, and indeed needs, to work. I promised to help him, and I will as soon as I can.

OCTOBER 27. Conversation with Jacomoni.[1] Our preparations in Albania are going ahead rapidly, so rapidly that we may have to advance our time-table, as the alarm may have reached the circles round the King. The operation is beginning to take shape clearly: assassination of the King (it seems that —— will undertake this for a reward of ten millions), riots in the streets, descent from the mountains of the bands we can trust (practically all the Chiefs except the Chief of the Kmia tribe), appeal to Italy to intervene politically and if necessary militarily, offer of the throne to the King Emperor, and a

---

[1] Note by the publishers of the Italian edition: With regard to the references in the present volume, in this and the following entries, to the idea of suppressing King Zog of Albania, Ambassador Jacomoni, after seeing certain extracts from the diary which appeared in the daily press, conveyed to us a communication in which he points out that, from the legal proceedings before the High Court of Justice relating to the foreign policy of the régime, it transpired clearly that the project of eliminating King Zog by violence, a project opposed by Jacomoni himself, died as soon as it was born, inasmuch as, not only did Ciano fail to cultivate the idea subsequently, but with respect to King Zog a policy was carried out which aimed until the end at the realization of new and better agreements, with the most absolute respect for his person, which was safeguarded until the moment when he crossed the Albanian frontier.

little later annexation. Jacomoni guarantees that all this can take place without trouble at a month's notice.

The Duce promises himself he will talk to Ribbentrop about the fight against Catholicism. 'It is useless and idiotic,' he said to me, 'and it makes the Axis unpopular with the Catholic Italian masses.' De Vecchi gave a long exposition at the Palazzo Venezia of the military situation in the Dodecanese. It may be summed up as follows: the Navy is admirable, the Army is all right, the Air Force is hell. And I believe this goes for the rest of the country too.

The Japanese Military and Naval Attachés brought me a pact of triple alliance, identical with that which Ribbentrop handed me in Munich. I am still inclined to put it into cold storage, particularly as Perth has secretly informed me of the British decision to implement the April Pact as from the middle of November. We must keep both doors open. An alliance now would close, perhaps for ever, one of the two, and that not the least important. I touched lightly on the subject with the Duce, and he seems to think as I do.

OCTOBER 28. Ribbentrop has in fact come about the triple military alliance. We discussed it straight away last night at the Grand Hotel. He repeated the speeches he made here in May—he has got the idea of war fixed in his head; he wants war, his war. As for precise marching orders, either he has not received them or he does not tell us what they are. He does not name the enemy or indicate the objectives. But he wants war in the course of the next three or four years. I was extremely reserved, but I gave him to understand that we still have other problems to solve and perhaps other conceptions of the future organization of international life. Recent events have proved the great solidarity between the totalitarian states. The alliance exists in practice. Why open the door to rumour by a pact the only consequence of which would be to draw upon us the odium of aggression?

Czech-Magyar question. He had not appreciated the political importance of Axis arbitration. As I told him, it sets the seal upon the fact that all Franco-British influence has collapsed for ever in Danubian and Balkan Europe. A gigantic event, as significant as Munich itself. I may have convinced him. But he is hostile to the Hungarians and defends the cause of the Czechs with a zeal which can only be called shameless.

A second conversation this morning. He reaffirmed the ideas he expressed last night and in addition agreed about the advisability of helping Franco until final victory.

I reported to the Duce. He agrees upon the necessity for postponing to a future date the commitment of an alliance, which would be most unpopular in Italy, not least on account of the resentment against Germany felt by the great Catholic masses. The Duce talked about

France. He explains French military heroism as produced by the instinct to defend individual property—*la ferme, la cave, l'argent*. For the Italians war is a phenomenon of the defence of the frontiers—for the French, rich and miserly hoarders, it means the preservation of their own goods. That explains why the French are such good soldiers on the defensive.

The Hungarian Minister is awaiting with anxiety the results of the conversations with Ribbentrop. I received him for a moment at the Palazzo Chigi. I did not tell him all, as it would worry him beyond measure, but I gave him to understand that German resistance to the solution desired by the Hungarians is strong and that I shall have hard work to remove it. Ribbentrop now speaks with hostility, not only about the Magyar leaders, but about the whole people. An ugly sign. Very ugly. But perhaps instructive. After fostering the friendship and the illusions of the Hungarians for twenty years, they abandon them and even oppose them, when to help them means making a small sacrifice. I have fought very strenuously. If the arbitration takes place, I think it will succeed in snatching the three eastern towns from the Germans. But it will be a very hard struggle.

The conversation *à trois* took place at the Palazzo Venezia in the afternoon. Minute made. Ribbentrop, who was perhaps expecting a pure and simple acceptance of the offer of an alliance, was taken aback, so much so that the Duce instructed me to speak to him again after dinner, in order to emphazise that postponement does not mean refusal and that solidarity between the Axis powers is total even without a written document.

I also had a talk with Hesse. It was a nasty shock to Ribbentrop when I alluded to the pact of consultation between the great powers proposed to us by Hesse in Hitler's name on October 11. Hesse now confirms the thing and has given me details—he says he received instructions from Göring, in the Führer's carriage and in his presence, during their first visit to the Sudetenland. It is extraordinary that the Foreign Minister should know nothing about it, but this is not the first time that has happened in Germany. It is yet another proof that there are two antagonistic trends in existence—Göring wanting to organize peace, and Ribbentrop intending to prepare for war.

After dinner I asked Villani to come and see me at home, in order to give him a few suggestions which I think may be useful to the Hungarian cause. Unofficially, he hinted at the possibility of placing Aosta on the Hungarian throne. It would be interesting to ascertain whether there is anything serious behind this hint.

OCTOBER 29. The Duce wrote a brief note at the Villa Torlonia, replying to Germany on the question of the alliance. The note accepts in principle, though the date is postponed, and establishes the principle of an offensive as well as defensive alliance. He read it to Ribbentrop this afternoon and gave him a copy. To-day's conversation produced nothing new. Afterwards Ribbentrop came to the Palazzo Chigi and we fixed a few points about the Vienna arbitration. He defended the Czech cause sword in hand and contested the Hungarian claims of territory with the same zeal with which the Germans made claims from Prague at Munich. However, I get the impression that, if we insist, we shall have our own way over the three eastern towns.

OCTOBER 30. A visit from the Hungarians to brief me for my discussions with Ribbentrop over the arbitration. The deputation was headed by Count Esterhazy, whom I have met several times in Budapest and also in Tirana, where he distinguished himself as a dancer of the csarda. I did not know that the leader of the Magyar minority in Czechoslovakia was the same Esterhazy whom I had admired for his prowess as a dancer, and I found it strange to be discussing frontiers and weighty problems with him. My admiration, however, is reserved for the *danseur*! And this nobleman at the head of the movement gives me the key to all the vacillations, uncertainties, and fears of which the Hungarians have given proof in recent weeks.

Moral of the conversation: they would be content if they could have Kassa, Ungvar, and Munkacs. I shall also try to do something about Nitra—the town itself must be regarded as lost, but we ought to save the country round it.

Mackensen came in the evening to inform me on behalf of Ribbentrop that he agrees upon the advisability of giving the Magyars the three disputed towns.

OCTOBER 31. The Duce approved my plan for the Vienna negotiations. He is pleased at the way things are turning out. It deserves to be recorded that he was the first to speak of arbitration and that, as always, his vision was clear. He foresees a period of *détente* in Europe. He does not, however, mean to make concessions to the French—an insurmountable abyss must be dug between us and them. This will be rendered easier for us if, as it seems, they are going to go in for being Celtic.

Lord Perth communicated to me a few details of the parliamentary debates on the implementation of the April Pact.

I left for Bolzano. Many comrades came to the station, notably Starace and the whole National Directorate of the Party.

NOVEMBER 1. At Bolzano I visited the industrial area, now very important and being rapidly developed. The appearance of the city is changing from northern to Mediterranean. The hand of Mastromattei[1]

---

[1] Giuseppe Mastromattei, Prefect of Bolzano.

is perhaps a little heavy, but very efficacious. In ten years or even less it will be difficult to recognize in Bolzano the Bozen of the old days.

Marriage ceremony in the villa of the Duke[1] and Duchess of Pistoia. Not interesting, except for the contrast between the rather old-fashioned dress and ceremonial of the royal family and the pure twentieth-century setting of the building. Some uniforms and genuflexions clash with modern furniture.

Demonstration at the station. I found Ansaldo in the train and had a long talk with him. He is the most cultivated and intelligent journalist that the régime possesses.

Innsbruck. I made a brief tour of the city. It was cold. Few people in the streets.

Romano, the Consul, says that Innsbruck has suffered much from the Anschluss—it lived principally on foreign tourism, which has now completely stopped. However, the régime is taking root among the popular classes—there are no longer any unemployed. The manifestations of friction are of a personal nature and can only be a problem for one generation at most.

NOVEMBER 2. Vienna. Ribbentrop was at the station. A new atmosphere. The crowd greeted me with warmth and friendliness. I remember the frigid welcome reserved for me by Schuschnigg's Vienna two years ago. Something has changed—life has come back to the city and the resentment once felt against us has given way to gratitude for our having made possible this happy result.

Conversation with Göring at my hotel. He was in mufti, wearing a flashy grey suit. A tie of the old-fashioned kind, passed through a ring with a ruby. More large rubies on his fingers. In his buttonhole a great Nazi eagle with diamonds. A slight suggestion of Al Capone.

He denounced the Hungarians. He says they are in league with the western democracies. This is going too far—I protested and he did not insist. He hinted at the possibility of a union between Yugoslavia and Bulgaria and attacked King Boris sharply. The question does not interest us. Göring thought that it would on account of Queen Giovanna.[2]

First conversation with Ribbentrop. He is trying to wangle things as much as he can in favour of Czechoslovakia. He does not want to give up all the three towns. Particularly Munkacs, as he declares that, if Hungary has all three, Roumania will have no possibility of life. I insisted, and with some vigour once I was convinced that he means

---

[1] Emanuele Filiberto of Savoy-Genoa, a cousin of the King of Italy.
[2] Queen Giovanna, wife of King Boris of Bulgaria, was a daughter of the King of Italy.

to plead the cause of Prague. He is inadequately, most inadequately, prepared for the discussions. He is not documented at all and even his staff officers are ill informed about the questions. This gives me plenty of scope.

NOVEMBER 3. Belvedere. First official conference. The Slovaks defended their cause well. The Hungarians less well: Kanya really badly, stupidly bitter and argumentative, and unconvincing and un-inspired in his reasoning—Count Teleki[1] better, calm and with more documentation. Since this morning's first conversation Ribbentrop has changed his attitude—he has come nearer to our point of view, and in conducting the discussion he sticks to a procedure substantially favour-able to the Hungarians.

Lunch and conversation with the various delegates. Afterwards Ribbentrop and I, with a small staff, went into conclave in the Golden Chamber. I took control of the discussion and, except for a few disputed points, I was able to trace the line of the new frontier with a red pencil. Ribbentrop's unpreparedness enabled me to assign to Hungary pieces of territory which might easily have given rise to much controversial discussion.

The documents were prepared and the delegates of the two parties came in. Chvalkovsky turned pale when he saw the map, and said to me *sotto voce*: 'I shall have to resign to-morrow. No government could survive such a blow.' Kanya remained impassive but whispered his satisfaction to Magistrati. Many of the Hungarians present were moved —Villani wept.

Evening with the Italian colony in Vienna—they are among the most enthusiastic of our nationals abroad.

Thursday—a shoot on the Bürgermeister's[2] estate. He is an old Nazi who endured fifteen months of prison under the old régime and saw his fourteen-year-old daughter arrested and shut up with prostitutes for several days, because she had lit a nationalist fire. This explains why the Reich Government has to be hard with Schuschnigg and company.

NOVEMBER 4. Return to Rome. I was welcomed at the airport by many hierarchs and by the Hungarian legation.

The Duce telephoned in the afternoon and, under the impression that he was speaking to Anfuso, and believing that I was to arrive by train in the evening, he gave orders to prepare a demonstration for me. Hearing that I had already arrived by air, he asked to see me at the Palazzo Venezia. He is very satisfied and said so to me several times over.

[1] Count Pal Teleki, a former Prime Minister. Prime Minister again from February 1939 until he committed suicide in April 1941.
[2] Hermann Neubacher.

The Duce talked about the growing difficulties presented by the 'dyarchy' of Fascism and the monarchy. It seems that during the ceremony at the National Altar yesterday there was trouble between him and the King, as the crowd shouted for the Duce and the royal march was not played at the moment of the elevation of the host. The King remarked on this. The Duce replied that it must be due to a momentary forgetfulness. The King retorted dryly that for the last eight centuries honours had always been rendered to the sovereigns of the House of Savoy.

The Duce's comments on the situation are sharp and he makes it clear that, if an opportunity to liquidate this state of affairs presents itself, he will not let it slip.

NOVEMBER 5. Received a delegation of Brazilian journalists. Received Blondel on a farewell visit—he is getting ready to leave when the new French Ambassador arrives. Blondel is a classic example of the official of middling rank. He is without talent, initiative, or courage. But he is scrupulous and correct. His merit has been of a negative order: in these two years he has done nothing to aggravate the situation. And it would have been very easy. To do more than this was beyond his capacity. Now we shall see François-Poncet. He does not come under good auspices. 'I shall do everything,' said the Duce yesterday, 'to help him to break his head. I don't like the man.'

The Party has had orders from the Duce to intensify the anti-Semitic campaign and the campaign for Tunisia and Nice.

NOVEMBER 6. Dead calm on the international front—storm on the ecclesiastical horizon.

To-morrow the Council of Ministers will approve the racial law. It includes an article prohibiting mixed marriages except on the point of death or for the legitimization of offspring. The Pope would like the dispensation to be extended also to converts to Catholicism. The Duce has rejected this request, which would make the law confessional instead of racial. The Pope wrote him a letter in his own hand, which was left unanswered. He then turned indignantly to the King and addressed a letter to him, in which he accused the Duce of wanting to destroy the Concordat. I have given Mussolini a copy of this letter, which I received from Pignatti. The King, though he has been in possession of it since last night, has not yet passed it on. I can't say the Duce was very shaken by it. He repeated that the papal thesis is unacceptable, and spoke sharply about the 'denunciation', which the Pope had thought fit to lodge with the King. Naturally the law, which is very severe upon the Jews, will be passed to-morrow according to programme.

Telegraphed to Berlin that no Franco-German agreement should be made until the results of Chamberlain's forthcoming visit to Paris are known.

NOVEMBER 7. Council of Ministers. Nothing particular. The Duce was annoyed at the trumpeting made by Balbo over the sending of colonists to Libya.

In future these colonists will leave in small detachments. All the more as there is a risk of their persuading themselves that they are official personages sent by the régime to cut a fine figure. This is what happened at Littoria, where the peasants at one moment refused to work because they thought their role was to be purely representative.

Perth announced to me the British decision to implement the Pact on November 16. He will present his credentials to me and not to the sovereign, as this is in accordance with etiquette and practice.

Ribbentrop and I have agreed that we should not accept the invitation to send our two Ministers to be present at the Hungarian occupation of Kassa. It would simply serve to irritate the Czechs and to rob the arbitration of its character of impartiality.

François-Poncet has arrived. From the Ministry there went to meet him only the officials strictly concerned with such duties. But Anfuso tells me that there were a lot of people in the station and also outside and that there was some applause, possibly on the part of Italians. I reported this to the Duce on the telephone and he was obviously annoyed.

NOVEMBER 8. It seems to me that there is not much hope of a *rapprochement* with France. The Duce, in my usual interview with him, traced the lines which our future policy will have to follow. 'Objectives: Jibuti, at least to the extent of a *condominium* and neutralization; Tunisia, with a more or less similar régime; Corsica, Italian and never gallicized, to be ruled directly; the frontier to be pushed back to the River Var. I am not interested in Savoy, which is neither historically nor geographically Italian. This is the general pattern of our claims. I do not specify one or five or ten years. The time will be settled by events. But we must never lose sight of this goal.' It is under these auspices that François-Poncet begins his mission.

I saw the Comte de Chambrun again.

Guariglia,[1] on his departure for Paris, received instructions to 'wait and see'.[2] He is a shrewd official, who will tie up the ass where his master tells him to. But it will go against the grain, because he is a democrat and therefore at heart a Francophile.

A little old man, whom I have seen precisely once in the last two years, announced to me that his country has recognized the Empire.

[1] Raffaello Guariglia, Italian Ambassador in Paris, 1938–43. Foreign Minister in the Badoglio Government, 1943.
[2] In English in the original.

It was with some difficulty that I identified him as the Minister of South Africa.[1]

NOVEMBER 9. Council of Ministers.

First conversation with François-Poncet. He tried to be *dégagé*. Picking up the threads of our fleeting contact in Munich, he opened the conversation in the tone of an old friend, dignified and sure of himself—though he is far from being so in fact. He started with more or less desultory talk, mostly about himself and his political antecedents. Then he came to the point and said that his presence in Rome signifies that France has profited by the lesson of Munich and intends to march with a realistic spirit. No suggestion of competing with the Rome-Berlin Axis, but a hope that it may be possible to bring it nearer to the Franco-British system, so that consultation of the four powers may be established as a regular practice. I replied with a list of the proofs we have given of our goodwill. But between us and France there is an obstacle: Spain. Our position is still that laid down by the Duce in his Genoa speech. François-Poncet agreed. He explained the difficulties which the solution of this problem presents to his Government and declared that he will do his best to facilitate an agreement on the subject. When he left, he looked very tired and seemed thoughtful. It is not easy to find one's way about in Rome.

The Lithuanian Minister wants us to use our good offices for a settlement with Germany and Poland.

NOVEMBER 10. Council of Ministers. The law for the defence of the race was passed. Starace wanted to go so far as the unconditional expulsion of all Jews from the Party, but the Duce opposed this. Otherwise, apart from minute alterations, the law was approved in the form proposed by the Minister of the Interior.

In the afternoon I had a meeting at the Palazzo Chigi of all the Consuls in southern France, Corsica, Algeria, etc. The Duce intends to have a campaign to recover the Italians living in France. There are now about a million of them. The September crisis amply demonstrated the dramatic seriousness of this problem. The French General Staff was prepared to enlist eight battalions of our nationals and hurl them against us—with what effect on morale can easily be imagined. Another source of anxiety would have been the fate reserved for the better elements—for some death, for others persecution by internment in concentration camps or forced labour. As Italian policy may oblige us to meet a crisis with France again, we do not want a similar situation to recur. All those who are willing to return will be given the maximum assistance, in the form of employment, subsidies, in some cases pensions. The Consuls expressed themselves unanimously in favour of this policy—

[1] Albert Heymans.

they passed through very tragic hours in September, when the fate of the Italians in France was so extremely precarious. But we must make sure of work for the repatriates. I have fixed a second and longer meeting for Saturday.

NOVEMBER 11. The Hungarian Minister brought me a statue of Hercules as a present from Kanya. He also invited me to visit Budapest in January or February. Then, almost incidentally, he hinted at the possibility of disorders in Ruthenia, such as to necessitate its union with Hungary. I strongly advised him against this. There would be opposition from Germany, and we ourselves might possibly be compelled to recall the Hungarians to strict observance of the arbitration. Hitler has been heard to say that henceforth he regards the Ruthenian question as 'his question'. *E questo fia suggel. . . .*[1] I am sadly disillusioned about the Hungarians—first from a military point of view and now from that of correctness they show themselves to be anything but what we had expected.

I had a talk with a Jew who was at school with me. I remember him as a vain and impudent boy, with the arrogance of wealth: he is now a sad, crushed man. Individual cases are distressing, but it is disastrous to consider a great social and historical phenomenon from the point of view of personal suffering. Nevertheless I telephoned to Buffarini to call his attention to the case of the Jew with an Aryan wife. I think that this gesture of detachment from the Jewish nation and religion should be rewarded with special treatment. If the family nucleus is to be protected, the father must not be placed in a position of inferiority with respect to his children.

NOVEMBER 12. I found the Duce more worked up than ever about the Jews. He approves unconditionally the reprisals carried out by the Nazis.[2] He says that in their position he would have gone even further. He is also furious with the Belgian Ambassador, who has written a report, of which S.I.M. has obtained a copy, saying that the Italians do not want to fight. The Duce has himself sent him four copies of a little book describing our war and also an anonymous note couched in these terms: 'There is reason to believe that you say the Italian people do not like war. They have, however, fought four victorious wars in a quarter of a century.'

He proposes to enact a measure which will make Jews born in Italy in future stateless.

He received Berti while I was there, on a farewell visit. He praised him highly and promoted him on the spot to be General in Command

---

[1] 'And let this be a seal to undeceive all men' (Dante's *Inferno*, Canto XIX, line 21).
[2] Vom Rath, Third Secretary at the German Embassy in Paris, was shot by a Polish Jew on November 7 and died two days later. The murder was the pretext for a savage outburst of anti-Semitism in Germany.

of an Army. In the afternoon he telephoned to tell me that he had cancelled the promotion, because he had learnt that Berti is a bachelor. 'A general must be the first to realize that without men you cannot have divisions.'

Egypt has recognized the Empire—a recognition of great importance.

NOVEMBER 13. Nothing particularly important. The Duce is critical of the German decision to impose a fine of a thousand million marks. He agrees about reprisals of a personal nature but considers the valuation of vom Rath's life at seven thousand million lire to be excessive. Or rather, absurd. He is worried about new threats against the Catholics. He says that any violence against the clergy and the churches makes the Axis unpopular and that, if an open crisis should develop and Catholicism meet with the same fate as the Jews, the Axis might fail to stand the strain. And he is right.

NOVEMBER 14. The Duce has for some time past been non-committal about the Albanian scheme, but this morning, taking his cue from a cruise Zog is making, he once more urged me to act. The date is to remain fixed for the spring.

He was very anti-bourgeois. He said that on January 3 he will publish a strong speech against the Italian bourgeoisie, with the title 'Face and Soul of the Italian Bourgeoisie'. He will also announce his third wave in the *Popolo d'Italia*. This is because the bourgeoisie is against the Axis and fails to realize that, if he had followed a different policy last March, he would have been defeated by Germany. Franco would have been beaten in Spain, and France and England might have taken the Empire from us.

The Duce told me to write a letter to Grandi preannouncing our claims for Tunis, Jibuti, and the revision of the Suez tariffs. I wrote accordingly and informed Starace. Apart from his unique loyalty, it is important that he should know all this so that he can do his work of preparing the masses.

Meeting to set up the permanent committee for the repatriation of Italians abroad. There were present, besides Starace, many Ministers and the Presidents of the Federations. There was a general appreciation of the problem, and we have made our dispositions for the battle very well. We shall win. I found an opportunity to raise in a suitable way the question of irredentism in Tunis.

NOVEMBER 15. Settled with Buffarini our reply to the note of protest—to tell the truth, a very mild protest—sent by the Holy See after the enactment of the recent racial measures, which have struck a blow at the Concordat in the sphere of marriage.

Through Buti I made the final arrangements with the Ambassador of Great Britain for the implementation of the April Pact.

Nothing else worthy of note.

NOVEMBER 16. To-day was dedicated to peace with England. Lord Perth came at 11 in the morning to present to me his credentials addressed to the King Emperor. He was moved and, in order not to get confused, he had written down the few words he had to speak. Poor old man! He really has been through some emotions at the Palazzo Chigi! Twice during his mission to Rome we have been on the brink of war. And now we are leaving behind a crisis which has been very acute and has dragged on for more than three years. I must acknowledge that Perth has worked well—intelligently and honestly. Even the events of September 28 certainly felt the influence of the good relations Perth has established with me. And yet the first day he saw me he wrote to his Government—we have the document—describing the repugnance which he felt, and forced himself to overcome, when he shook hands with me, because I had directed the anti-British press campaign during Abyssinia.

In the afternoon there was a brief ceremony of signing for the implementation of the Pact. Then I went to the Palazzo Venezia to report to the Duce. He was very satisfied with what has happened and praised me for my conduct of the affair. 'All this is very important,' he said, 'but it does not alter our policy. In Europe the Axis remains fundamental. In the Mediterranean we will collaborate with the English as long as we can. France remains outside—our claims upon her have now been defined.'

Perth also broached the subject of an official visit of Chamberlain and Halifax to Rome in the second week in January. The Duce was at first reluctant. But I emphasized the psychological value of this visit and he ended by giving his consent.

NOVEMBER 17. The campaign for the repatriation of Italians abroad has been launched in great style. The Duce has approved the measures I have already taken and my programme of work. I think we have here a fine Fascist battle, which will yield very satisfactory results.

I received the syndical leaders who went with our workers to Germany. In the preface to the book published by the Federation I have already expressed a most favourable opinion of the utility of these mass visits, which serve to open the minds of our workers and of the Germans themselves. Hitherto, for many reasons, the two peoples have been in a strange psychological relation to each other. The Germans have loved us without respecting us. We have respected them without loving them. Through a more precise knowledge, leading to a fusion of these two sentiments, we shall be able in the end to create a true Axis atmosphere. And it will be easier to do this through the working masses than through the more egotistic, more pacifist bourgeoisie, which is more deeply attached to the countries, like France and Great Britain, which represent the crystallization and the defence of systems rejected and overthrown by Fascism and Nazism.

Vittorio Mussolini[1] was to have gone to London, but the visit has been cancelled because his host could find nothing better to do than to write a violently anti-German letter to the *Daily Telegraph*. I have informed Berlin of the incident and of the reason why the visit will not take place.

NOVEMBER 18. Villani returned to the charge about Ruthenia. He says that the expected movement is taking place in the country, that the Ruthenians cannot live torn away from Hungary as they are, and that Germany appears to be indifferent to this fresh development of the situation. This is untrue. I know that the Führer has expressed his refusal. I told Villani quite clearly that I disapprove of this policy and that, if Germany asks us to join her in addressing to Hungary an invitation to respect the terms of the arbitration, we shall march in step with Berlin. I am particularly anxious that the Germans should not believe that we are playing a double game and that it is at our instigation that the Hungarians are throwing oil on the flames. I also invited Villani to consider that Hungary's position with regard to Geneva is now untenable. They will have to leave the League, from which they never have received and never will receive anything. A step of this kind will strengthen Imredy's position, domestically as well, as the parties of the right seem to be more and more active and restless.

The Princess of Piedmont gave me an account of her visit to France and England. Nothing very important. She was very anxious to justify herself for having gone to a concert given by Toscanini in Lucerne in the summer. She was persuaded to go by some friends in Milan and she had not appreciated the political significance of her action.

NOVEMBER 19. Villani made a further communication about the situation in Ruthenia and told me the important news that Budapest has informed Berlin of the situation which has arisen. We shall await reactions.

I started work on the speech I am to make in the Chamber on November 30.

NOVEMBER 20. While I was hunting at La Mandria near Turin, Anfuso telephoned about the departure of 100 aeroplanes for Hungary. The Duce, it seems, in a conversation with the Hungarian Military Attaché, promised him these arms and also authorized the commencement of operations in Ruthenia. This was because Szabo assured him

---

[1] Vittorio Mussolini, the Duce's eldest son, a journalist. His host was to have been Lord Hardwicke.

that the Germans are not against it. This is a lie. In the afternoon
Berlin informed us that, questioned by the Magyars, they remonstrated
sharply and ordered them to respect the Vienna arbitration. I agree
with the Germans. These Hungarians are behaving badly, like a
Balkanized people, which is what they really are.

Meanwhile the Duce has got himself into a serious mess. His honesty
has been exploited. The promises and pledges he made were based on
the premise of German consent. German consent is wholly lacking.
The pledges, then, have no validity. Fortunately the threatening
weather has prevented the aeroplanes from leaving the ground and
reaching Hungary. If I arrive in time, I shall get the decision to send
them cancelled. It would be difficult to persuade the Germans of our
good faith, if at the same time we were sending the Magyars the means
to carry out their aggression.

The Duce has telegraphed orders to Berlin to get in touch with the
Reich Government, inform them of the truth, and agree with them
upon identical action.

I returned to Rome in the evening.

NOVEMBER 21. The German decision is to send a note to Budapest
to recall them to respect of the Vienna arbitration, and they have sent
us a draft of the note. We are in agreement. I communicated its contents
to Villani and Szabo, who are unhappy about the incident. They had
acted in perfect good faith, believing that the Hungarian Government
really had obtained German consent.

The Hungarian action will not take place. Particularly as our aeroplanes have not left and will not leave for some time. Vinci[1] telegraphs
that Kanya, when he received him to accept delivery of the note, was
crestfallen and, though polite, icy. It is Kanya who is responsible for
the incident, just as, through the personal enmities he has aroused, he
is responsible for the anti-Magyar attitude adopted by many Germans.

I spoke to Ribbentrop on the telephone. He is fully aware of what
has happened and has no doubts about our attitude.

NOVEMBER 22. Nothing particularly outstanding, except the meeting of the Committee for the repatriation of Italians abroad.

NOVEMBER 23. Signed the cultural agreement with Germany. It
is an understanding which goes further than the usual cultural agreement, whose value is in general nil. This one really opens the doors of
Germany to Italian culture to an unprecedented extent. For this
reason we have given a great deal of publicity to the event in the press.

My speech for the Chamber is finished. The date remains fixed for
November 30.

As anticipated, Imredy has resigned following his defeat in the

[1] Count Luigi Orazio Vinci-Gigliucci, Italian Minister in Budapest.

Chamber. It is too early to forecast his successor, but there is talk of another Imredy Government, further to the right. It is interesting to note that Colonel Szabo has revealed himself to be hostile to the present Government. In our conversations on Monday, while Villani deprecated the possible fall of the Imredy Government, Szabo did not seem in the least disturbed at the possibility of a Hungarist Government. In his opinion it is the only way to get a policy completely loyal to the Axis and, within the Axis, to Rome. He does not admit that the extremists of the right are, as is usually said, in bondage to Germany.

NOVEMBER 24. The Chargé d'Affaires of Czechoslovakia handed me a note declaring that the questions pending with Germany and Poland are now definitely liquidated. It is not yet the formal *démarche*, but it is the prelude to a request for a guarantee of the frontiers in accordance with the Munich agreement. I do not think we could refuse such a request, if it comes, all'the more as Germany would make no difficulty about consenting.

I informed Cristich of what has happened in the last few days between us, Germany and Hungary. He was very grateful for the information and for the policy we have followed. Had the incursion into Ruthenia taken place, it would have had the result of weakening the position of Stoyadinovich at a moment when he in fact requires support in view of the forthcoming elections. Cristich confirmed that Stoyadinovich, strong in the majority he hopes to obtain, will tend to emphasize more and more the authoritarian character of his Government. During the conversation we mentioned relations between Belgrade and Athens and the question of Salonika. I encouraged him to make a move towards the Aegean, Yugoslavia's natural outlet to the sea, at the earliest opportunity. The chief purpose of this is to facilitate our action in Albania, which is maturing according to plan.

NOVEMBER 25. Conferred with Mosconi[1] and the lawyer Gambino[2] about Albania. They confirmed that the conviction, by no means new, that Italy will very soon seize control of the country, is steadily gaining ground. There are some sections of public opinion which go so far as to express a hope of this intervention. The position of the King gets weaker and weaker. In court circles there has been an increase of anti-Italian feeling.

Gambara was with the Duce. He announced a forthcoming offensive on Barcelona, to begin on approximately December 9. Gambara gave an admirable account of the morale of our troops. He believes that the forces composing the Corps of Volunteers, which amount, including

---

[1] Antonio Mosconi, Chairman of the National Bank of Albania. Former Minister of Finance.

[2] A. Gambino, Director of the National Bank of Albania.

Spaniards, to about 60,000 men, will be able to play a leading role in the forthcoming operations. He asked for—and we agreed to give him—three groups of artillery, 100s and 149s, and also a certain number of men to make up for departures and losses.

In the afternoon I saw Villani, who confirmed that Hungary has suspended all action in Ruthenia. He again talked about Hungary joining the Anti-Comintern Pact. By all means, but first she must withdraw from Geneva. Villani believes that this will be easier if Kanya is replaced by Csaky.

Villani told me that François-Poncet had said to him that one day Hungary will find a Gauleiter in Horthy's place and that she should beware of Italy, which has already abandoned one country. Villani, so he says, made a vigorous rejoinder.

NOVEMBER 26. The Duce has approved almost without alteration the speech I am to make to the Chamber on Wednesday.

Von Mackensen discussed with me the Hungarian proposal to join the Anti-Comintern Pact. In Berlin too they think that this step should be preceded by a withdrawal from Geneva.

The Ambassador also made a statement to me about the present bad relations between Germany and Brazil and tried to draw a parallel between the withdrawal of Lojacono and the forced withdrawal of their Ambassador. What it comes to is that they want us not to send Sola. While declaring that I was ready to examine any proposals and arguments of Ribbentrop's, I pointed out that against us no measures have been taken which would justify such a reprisal. I also emphasized the enormous extent of our economic and political interests in Brazil, not to mention the friendly attitude of Brazil towards us at the time of sanctions.

NOVEMBER 27. Nothing worthy of note.

NOVEMBER 28. I found the Duce in a state of indignation against the King. Three times in the course of their conversation this morning the King said to him that he feels an 'infinite pity for the Jews'. He cited cases of persecution, among them that of General Pugliese, an old man of eighty, loaded with medals and wounds, who has been deprived of his housekeeper. The Duce said that there are 20,000 spineless people in Italy who are moved by the fate of the Jews. The King replied that he is one of them. He also attacked Germany, apropos of the creation of the 4th Alpine Division. The Duce used very violent expressions about the monarchy. More and more he meditates a change of system. But perhaps the moment has not yet come. There would be reactions. At Pesaro yesterday the garrison commander reacted strongly when the *Federale* ordered a salute to the Duce and not one to the King.

Meeting about citizenship for the Arabs. A sharp altercation between

Balbo and Starace, because Balbo made remarks which sounded offensive about the Party's policy.

Perth came to see me at home to draw up a communiqué about Chamberlain's visit to Rome. The news was to have been kept secret, but there has been talk in London and this morning the papers were full of it. I have informed von Mackensen of the visit and of its origin.

Jacomoni gave me a little map showing the dispositions of the bands in Albania.

NOVEMBER 29. The Duce received François-Poncet. The Chief's state of mind, already hostile enough, was aggravated by the heavy cold which has been tormenting him for the last two days. It was a chilly welcome. François-Poncet tried to open the discussion immediately by saying that his Government has sent him here to continue the atmosphere of Munich. The Duce, who even pretended not to remember whether at the time of Munich François-Poncet had or had not been appointed Ambassador in Rome, replied that relations between France and Italy are poisoned by the Spanish affair and that on this subject he is now more uncompromising than ever. He diverted the conversation to the internal situation of France, but Poncet, speaking slowly and with an effort to impress, struggled to return to the field of foreign politics by clutching at the theme of a Four Power Pact. Again he was unsuccessful. The Duce said that the plan failed through the fault of the French Left and that he certainly has no intention of proposing a similar plan. Then, with an absent-minded air, he added: 'Il faut d'abord mettre de l'ordre dans la maison', and rose from his chair. François-Poncet did not add another word. And he left looking much less sure of himself than when he came in.

I talked to Mackensen about the announcement in the *News Chronicle* of the project for a Tripartite Pact. It seems that the leakage took place in Japanese quarters.

Acquarone, the new Minister to the Royal Household, came to see me and said that he wants to get a little fresh air into the atmosphere. 'But I must go slowly in questions of form,' he added; 'for if I remove the forms, a complete vacuum will be revealed inside.'

NOVEMBER 30. I delivered my speech in the Chamber. It went very well. When at the end I spoke of the 'natural aspirations of the Italian people', there burst out a veritable storm of acclamations and shouts of 'Tunis, Corsica, Nice, Savoy'. Nothing had been arranged. Spontaneously the deputies gave voice to their aspirations, which are those of the whole people.

The Duce was pleased. I drove back with him to the Palazzo Venezia. 'A great speech,' he said, 'and a great day for the régime. That is the way to pose a problem and to set a people in motion.'

At the Grand Council he spoke himself at the beginning of the session, more or less in the following words: 'I announce to you the immediate goals of Fascist dynamism. As we have avenged Adowa, so we will avenge Valona.[1] Albania will become Italian. I cannot yet—and I do not wish to—tell you how or when. But it will happen. Then, for the requirements of our security in this Mediterranean which still confines us, we need Tunisia and Corsica. The frontier must be moved to the Var. I do not aim at Savoy, because it is outside the circle of the Alps. But I have my eye on the Ticino, as Switzerland has lost her cohesive force and is destined one day, like many little countries, to be disrupted. All this is a programme. I cannot lay down fixed times. I merely indicate the lines on which we shall march. Anyone revealing what I have said, in whole or in part, will have to answer to a charge of treason.'

DECEMBER 1. Sparano read me a letter from the Brazilian Foreign Minister describing the domineering behaviour of the German Ambassador. He asks for our solidarity. I do not know what we can do, except work as mediators to clear up the incident. But I fear the crisis may be deep-seated. German propaganda measures among their large colonies abroad are of a kind to cause serious and justifiable anxiety to the Rio Government.

Villani, in tears, as he usually has been in the last few weeks when the subject is mentioned, thanked me for what I said yesterday about his country.

I had a long discussion with Jacomoni about the situation in Albania and the projected operation, which is now beginning to take concrete shape. The preparations are going well. The Zog régime reveals itself more and more wobbly and ripe for collapse.

DECEMBER 2. Reactions to my speech are growing sharper everywhere—in France they have become hysterical.

In Italy, meanwhile, its success is great. I have received hundreds of letters and telegrams of congratulation. The Italians now understand that the Axis has objectives which are not solely German—we too have our claims and we have no intention of renouncing them, even if we could.

The Duce, who is very pleased, as he always is when he smells powder, defined our line of action: to set aside the Mussolini-Laval agreement of 1935[2] and synchronize our demands with the German colonial claims. Our demands are Jibuti, Tunis, and a share in the Suez Canal.

[1] Adowa, in Abyssinia, was the scene of an Italian defeat in 1896. Valona, in Albania, was the scene of an Italian defeat in 1920.
[2] Mussolini and Laval signed an agreement in Rome on January 7, 1935, defining the interests of their two countries in Africa.

Conversation with François-Poncet in the evening. He affected to
be very indifferent, but he was worried and anxious to give his *démarche*
a more friendly character than that of a protest. He was captious in
the conversation, of which I have made a Minute. Seizing hold of an
isolated phrase of mine, he tried to get a definite statement that the
Government was not advancing claims. I was very reserved. After his
official *démarche* he made a few observations, emphasizing particularly
that France is not a country fallen so low that she can be asked permanently to give up 'a pound of flesh'. As he was leaving, he asked
whether he could go on unpacking his trunks. 'It would be delightful
to live in peace in Rome,' he added. 'That will depend on you,' I
replied coldly, and after a pause, with a smile, 'and also on us.' He
was as white as a sheet when he left the room.

DECEMBER 3. The European orchestra continues full blast. It
leaves us absolutely indifferent—in fact we are keeping the controversy
alive deliberately. The Duce is very pleased at what has happened.
He believes that all this is very useful for our Albanian plans—it
distracts local attention, it permits us to make suitable preparations
without creating an alarm, and, lastly, it will induce the French to take
our presence in Tirana well, so long as it means that the pressure upon
them is relaxed.

I saw Perth twice. The first time he announced the date of Chamberlain's visit to Rome. Fixed for January 11. The second time he made
a *démarche* about the Tunisian question. My reply was more or less
what I had said to François-Poncet. He recalled me to the observance
of our agreement with England for the Mediterranean. I replied that
I will reject any such protest, until my speech can be shown to have
contained anything which may be judged inconsistent with our
engagements.

As for the Mussolini-Laval Pact, Perth himself agrees that it can no
longer be regarded as in force.

I received Jacomoni. He brought with him ——, the man who is
preparing to strike the blow against the King in Albania. Naturally,
he is an old friend of the King's, but he feels he has been neglected by
him and is discontented.

DECEMBER 4. Nothing particularly important in Rome. But there
are rather serious reports of anti-Italian incidents deliberately created
in Corsica and at Tunis. These clashes help our game very well,
because they produce a violent reaction in even the least sensitive
sections of Italian public opinion.

DECEMBER 5. In view of Ribbentrop's forthcoming visit to Paris,
the Duce and I decided not to dramatize the incidents and to call a
temporary halt to the anti-French campaign in the press. I arranged

for Ribbentrop himself to be informed of this and he expressed his
satisfaction. He had himself summoned Attolico on the eve of his
departure, and made light of the significance and the aims of his visit
to Paris.

With Jacomoni and Giro I fixed certain important points of the
Albanian operation. The work of organization is proceeding well, and
I think that everything ought to develop according to plan. The disappearance of the King will serve to remove any centre of resistance
and the movement will have the whole country in flames in a few
hours. I am wondering now whether we should not advance the
operation, as the machinery is all wound up and delay may produce
unpredictable snags.

Long conversation with Starace. I gave him my frank opinion of
some of his gestures and actions. In the first place the projected anti-
bourgeois exhibition. It is ridiculous to annoy people for no reason,
as he does—you can't torment them just because they go in for five
o'clock tea or evening dress. It is my belief that, especially when you
have a more narrow rigidity in politics, you should leave a larger
margin of personal liberty. Certain of Starace's measures are creating
large pockets of discontent and disaffection.

DECEMBER 6. The Duce examined and approved the plan of
action for Albania. The only reservation he formulated precisely was
on the subject of Yugoslavia. France, England, and Greece do not
worry him at all. He is, however, following the attitude of Yugoslavia
with attention—it is not so much the possibility of a definite counter-
stroke, which would appear to be difficult, that worries him, as that of
weakening her friendship with us to the advantage of Germany. It will
perhaps be as well to talk to Stoyadinovich and study the question of
compensation, possibly at the expense of Greece, i.e. Salonika.

Horthy has sent me an invitation to a hunting party, which I have
accepted. I start on December 19. It is worth while taking a look at
close quarters at the internal situation of Hungary, which is far from
brilliant. The feudal régime still continues under the present Government, and only a sharp turn of the helm to the right can put Hungary
back on the proper course. Szabo yesterday sang the praises of Szalasi
and Hungarism.

Muti is back from Spain. Things are getting into quite good shape
there and the forthcoming attack in Catalonia may assume a decisive
character. I myself am rather sceptical—that phrase has been used too
often to be believed any longer. In any case the Corps of Volunteers,
under the command of Gambara, is in fine form, perhaps better than
ever before, and relations with the Air Force have been cleared up
satisfactorily.

DECEMBER 7. Took Muti to see the Duce. The news is good—even the Bernasconi[1]-Gambara feud has been healed and our troops will engage the enemy under admirable conditions.
Nothing else worthy of note.

DECEMBER 8. Anti-French demonstrations in Italy and anti-Italian demonstrations in France are multiplying. There is no harm in this, as they serve to make the Axis popular with Italian youth. At the moment they are student demonstrations, but then irredentism has always begun in the schoolroom.

DECEMBER 9. The Duce wants a little sand put in the wheels of the anti-French campaign, as, 'if it continued at this rate, we should have to make the cannon speak, and the time for that has not yet come'. But he declared himself pleased with the results of this test of the Italian public's attitude to France.

Perth and I are preparing the programme of Chamberlain's visit. Unofficially, he told me that he disapproves of the French attitude. He has advised Poncet not to dramatize things.

Barella opened his heart to me on the subject of Starace. He too has joined the company of those who bitterly attack the Party Secretary. There is now a veritable popular rising against him. I have made it my rule to disinterest myself in internal politics, but I am wondering now whether I ought not to talk to the Duce. Starace has many merits, but he has made the two most serious mistakes which you can make when you have to deal with the Italian people. He has created an atmosphere of persecution and he has caused annoyance by a thousand little things of a personal nature. Now the Italians like their rulers to rule with heart. They may forgive you if you do them harm, but not if you pester them.

DECEMBER 10. Nothing worthy of note.
Dinner in honour of Perth at the Villa Madama.

DECEMBER 11. Nothing worthy of note.

DECEMBER 14.[2] I reported my conversation with Pignatti to the Duce. He burst out violently against the Pope, whose death he hopes for in the near future. He threatened to 'touch the sensitive nerve' and bring back to life the Ghibelline Italy which has never died. He said that in Romagna the churches were locked and bolted when Fascism began and that if people go to them now it is only because they know that the Duce desires it. He ended, however, by affirming the importance of not provoking a crisis with the Vatican at the present moment, and he authorized me to deny the report about divorce and sterilization.

---

[1] General Mario Bernasconi, commander of the Italian air force in Spain.
[2] The leaf for December 12 and 13 is missing from the diary.

Ceremony of the final sitting of the Chamber. Orano[1] made a long and ineffective speech, while Papa scored a great success with a few simple, spirited words, true to his own nature.

Cristich repeated to me a conversation he has had with Poncet, which confirms what I was told yesterday by the Minister of Uruguay. Poncet, who when he came here expected a very different sort of success, has now been soured. He counted on his personality to remove obstacles and revive pro-French trends. Instead he has found himself isolated, and he realizes now that there is no possibility of manœuvring behind the scenes, since in Rome foreign policy is handled only by the man responsible for it. As the Uruguayan Minister gave me the written text of his conversation with Poncet, and Poncet used some sharp language about the Germans, I shall give the German Embassy a copy. It will serve to weaken the sympathy which Poncet enjoys in certain German circles.

DECEMBER 15. I accompanied General Oshima, Japanese Ambassador in Berlin, to the Duce. His visit has the recommendation of Ribbentrop, as Oshima, like him, is zealous for the transformation of the Anti-Comintern Pact into a Pact of Triple Alliance. Physically Oshima is a perfect specimen of the Samurai, as they appear in old Japanese paintings and porcelain. Small and thickset. An extremely proud carriage. A hard and interesting face. When he began to speak, I realized why Ribbentrop is so fond of him. They are the same type: enthusiasts who see things in simple terms—I am tempted to say wishful, thinkers. He attacked Russia and said that Japan intends to dismember her into so many small states that all thought of revenge will be vain and ridiculous. He also said that Japan wants to eliminate British interests entirely from China and from the Pacific in general. He shed a lurid light on the position of the English in India. The Duce repeated the usual arguments about the necessity of postponing for a certain time the transformation of the Pact and indicated the period in which he is likely to make his decision, viz. between the middle of January and the middle of February.

Giuriati, our Consul-General in Calcutta, reports that on September 27 the Viceroy of India[2] told him that in the event of war he would be quite unable to maintain British rule in India.

Gave Mackensen the memorandum of the Uruguayan Minister's conversation with Poncet.

DECEMBER 16. Lord Perth, with tears in his eyes, asked for our *agrément* for Percy Loraine. In the bottom of his heart he still hopes, though he does not admit it, that during Chamberlain's forthcoming visit to Rome we may persuade the British Government to go back on

---

[1] Paolo Orano, Fascist historian.   [2] Lord Linlithgow.

its decision. I am sorry he is going. He is a man who by a slow and painful process has come to understand and even to love Fascism. He has a genuine friendship for me, as I have for him.

His presence here would still have been useful. Anglo-Italian friendship is too tender a plant to be exposed to shocks. And I do not know whether this Percy Loraine is the most suitable sort of man. Not long ago he said some disagreeable things about Italy and the Duce arranged for some anonymous letters to be sent to him, containing carefully chosen insults and equally carefully chosen newspaper cuttings with photographs of our armed forces. The auspices are not good. To think that Perth had become so friendly to us as to telegraph to his Government—I have the deciphered text—on the day of my speech to the Chamber, that the Deputies' shouts for Tunis and Corsica did not reach the diplomatic gallery!

Perth recommends that while we are waiting for Chamberlain's visit the campaign against France should be abated a little, in order not to create greater difficulties of a domestic nature for the Prime Minister. I gave him assurances.

Received von Mackensen and Strautz[1] and gave them a report on the interview which took place between the Duce and General Oshima at the Palazzo Venezia.

DECEMBER 17. Nothing particularly striking, except that the Duce approved, and I therefore sent, a note to the French Ambassador affirming, with documentation, that the Mussolini-Laval agreement of January 1935 is juridically, politically, and historically superseded. I gave the note a character of perfect serenity, and I concluded with a veiled hint at the possibility of a resumption of negotiations. We must not, just yet, pull the cord too tight. Above all, we must not present the French with an opportunity to blow Chamberlain's visit sky high.

Mussolini has gone to Carbonia, the new coal-producing area in Sardinia. He is very satisfied with the results of the struggle for autarky. He said to me to-day that it was the foreigners who convinced us that our country is so desperately poor that it is quite useless to search in it for resources. The same foreigners who persuaded us in the past that we were not a race, but an unwarlike conglomeration of men and women born to serve and delight the peoples of the north. A classic example of this conception is to be found in the report sent to the Directory by General Berthier after he had held command in Italy.

DECEMBER 18. I set off for Hungary. At Trieste and Postumia the crowds greeted us with fervid demonstrations and shouts of

---

[1] The name is illegible in the original diary, but the reference appears to be to F. von Strautz, Counsellor at the German Embassy in Rome.

'Tunis, Corsica, Jibuti'. These are spontaneous demonstrations on the part of the masses, who feel rising within them a profound rancour which accords with the traditions and the instincts of the Italian people.

DECEMBER 19–20. My reception in Hungary, all the way from the frontier to Budapest, was that reserved for a returning son, not for a foreigner to whom it is desired to pay respect. I was rather moved. It was cold, very cold, but the people were in the streets just the same. Numb with cold and red in the face under the lash of the icy wind, they continued to shout and applaud.

In the Government too I found a new atmosphere. I spoke frankly of what the new Magyar policy will have to be: open, steady, and unequivocal adherence to the Axis. They all agree, though there is an atmosphere of open hostility towards Germany. They are afraid of Germany. Csaky does not conceal his anxiety, nor does Imredy. This explains the intransigence shown towards Szalasi's Hungarist Party, which is, nevertheless, gaining ground among the young. I assured the Hungarians that we will never permit Germany to act towards Hungary as she acted over Austria. In the case of Austria there were very different reasons, which made the German policy logical and therefore acceptable. This assurance of mine did much to calm the Hungarian leaders. They ended by arriving at a concrete policy on the following basis: adherence to the Anti-Comintern Pact after Csaky's visit to Berlin; departure from Geneva in May, after provoking a crisis with the League of Nations by presenting a hopelessly unacceptable memorandum about their minorities; *rapprochement* with Yugoslavia. For the last-mentioned purpose they asked me if I would take the opportunity of my next meeting with Stoyadinovich to lay the foundations of an agreement. This is very satisfactory. Nothing must be done which might take on an anti-German flavour, but from every point of view it is good that a close bloc should be formed between Italy, Yugoslavia, and Hungary.

Towards Roumania Hungarian sentiment is very hostile. Csaky gave me a hint of this, but he was immediately interrupted by Imredy, who had foreseen my objections. The Regent, however, spoke more openly to me of a possible attack on Roumania and added that the Duce had indicated to him in Rome his approval of an action of this kind. I threw cold water on the idea and gave the Regent to understand that such a decision would require to be re-examined in the light of the subsequent developments of the situation.

DECEMBER 21. The internal situation is not altogether clear. The anti-Semitic laws and those for agrarian reform will be launched shortly, and the Government expects large results from them. We shall see.

But there is no doubt that a new ferment is at work among the young, and that the whole feudal structure of Hungary is beginning to be felt as an intolerable burden by them. The Hungarist Party is spreading. Round Szalasi there is growing up an atmosphere of martyrdom which is useful to him. I myself do not believe in the Government's accusation that he wants to sell Hungary to Germany. Hubai, who is leader of the Party while Szalasi is in prison, sent me a very warmly worded telegram. In order not to be the author of a document which the Government might view with disfavour, I made no direct reply, but I let him know through Vinci how pleased I had been to receive the greetings of the nationalist Magyar youth. Who knows what the future has in store?

DECEMBER 22. Return journey.

DECEMBER 23. I reported to the Duce, who was very pleased with the results of the visit. We made a general survey plus programme and settled a few points to be discussed when Chamberlain is here. The Duce also confirmed that it is now his intention to adhere to the triangular pact of assistance, as proposed by Ribbentrop.

The attack in Catalonia has had notable success. Gambara's telegrams are enthusiastic and even Muti's scanty dispatches confirm the success.

DECEMBER 24. I gave the German Chargé d'Affaires and the Ambassador of Great Britain copies of the note addressed by me to François-Poncet. Perth read part of the note and expressed the opinion that it was very temperate—the end seemed to him particularly good. We talked about the pledge France had given us to support our action for the conquest of Abyssinia. Perth said that Laval had sought him out and told him that this pledge related only to economic questions. That is not true. I told Perth that the French were fully informed of our plans for territorial conquest. I also recounted to him a conversation I had with Flandin in Paris in May 1935, in which he gave me some advice about the best method of starting the war. He suggested stirring up a revolt of the Ras against the Negus, which would have given us a pretext to intervene. These statements of mine made a great impression on Perth.

Good news from Spain. The advance continues, in spite of the counter-attacks of the Reds.

DECEMBER 25. Nothing new. More disturbing reports from Yugo-slavia about the position of Stoyadinovich. But although the results of the elections give cause to reflect, I myself am not alarmed for the present Government. I have great confidence in Stoyadinovich. He is a pilot with a steady pulse and he has weathered much heavier storms than this.

DECEMBER 26. France has sent a note in reply to ours. It is a bland contradiction of our statements and is naturally not without certain inaccuracies. I do not think it requires a counter-reply.

Good news from Spain of the Italian units, which are making rapid progress towards their objectives. The Spaniards are not doing so well —once more they show themselves to be slow and irresolute in the offensive.

The Nuncio spoke to me about the position of Catholic Action and launched out into a sharp personal attack on Starace, whom he described as 'a dangerous pagan' and a disgraceful example of immorality in his private life as well. The Nuncio hinted at the possibility of a visit from the Duce to the Pope on the occasion of the tenth anniversary of the Concordat, but I replied that the idea did not seem to me feasible. At most I might go to the Vatican myself bearing a message from the Duce. But even that will require consideration.

DECEMBER 27. Nothing new.

DECEMBER 28. I have intervened in Spain with Franco, and have also got the Germans to intervene, to make him decide to move his troops. There is a possibility of winning a decisive victory, but once again the Spaniards look like letting it slip through their fingers.

DECEMBER 29. Nothing very important. Conversation with our Naval Attaché in Japan, Commander Ghè, who described the enthusiasm of the Japs for Italy and their resentment against Germany. Ghè is a very good friend of Japan, but he says that we should not rely on her too much. After the conquest of China she will need capital and she will need rest, and she won't want to sacrifice her own interests for any foreign country.

DECEMBER 30. Communicated to Lord Perth our *agrément* for his successor.

Monelli, back from Corsica, confirmed what I already knew, i.e. that Corsican irredentism does not exist and that the whole Party of Petru Rocca amounts to about ten persons. The other side, however, is not exactly fervid either—the directors of the Corsican newspapers which are most violent against us told Monelli that, if we give them a little tourist publicity, they will break off the anti-Italian campaign.

Long conversation with Alberto Giannini,[1] who has come back from a long sojourn abroad. I had not seen him since he emigrated, about fourteen years ago. He has got fat and no longer has that rebellious vivacity of mind which characterized him in the old days. He talked about the world of *émigrés*—a wretched little world, without hope or will, split by personal animosities and compelled to move in the orbit

[1] Alberto Giannini, a journalist.

prescribed by the masters of the house, that is, the French Government. A little world of moral and material misery destined to disappear in the near future without leaving a trace behind.

DECEMBER 31. The new Japanese Ambassador visited me to present his credentials. For a career diplomat and a Japanese one at that, he is pretty outspoken and energetic. He talked about the Tripartite Pact, and immediately revealed himself as a partisan of the strengthening of the system. He does not disguise, however, that there is still a strong party in Japan in favour of a *rapprochement* with Great Britain and America.

From Spain Gambara and Viola report a conversation with Franco, in the course of which the Generalissimo seems to have been persuaded to unite his efforts to ours in order to get more concrete results from the offensive in Catalonia. We shall see what happens in the next few days —just now precious time has been wasted.

Bastianini painted a very sombre picture of the internal situation, and he too fulminated against the usual culprit, Starace. There is some truth in it—we are not living in a bed of roses. But Starace is not wholly to blame and one must remember that Bastianini, at forty, is already a discontented, soured old man, who can only talk of what used to be done 'in his day'.

INDEX

Acquarone, P., Minister to the Royal Household, 200

Agostini, A., head of the Forest Militia, 134

Ajello, Umberto, *Federale* of Leghorn, 125, 140

Ajeta, Marchese, B. L. d', one of Ciano's secretaries, 43

Albania, King of (*see* Zog I, King of Albania)

Albania, Queen of, 106

Aldrovandi-Marescotti, Count Luigi, Italian diplomat, 28, 29, 32, 33

Alexander I, King of Yugoslavia, 42

Alessi, Rino, editor of *Il Piccolo*, 140

Alfieri, Dino, Minister of Propaganda, 5, 14, 15, 36, 121, 154, 155, 157, 184

Allard, Paul, writer, 34

Amau, F., Japanese Ambassador to Italy, 210

Ambassador:

American, to Italy (*see* Phillips, W.)

Argentine, to Italy (*see* Cantilo, J. M.)

Belgian, to Italy (*see* Deuterghem, A. de K. de)

Brazilian, to Italy (*see* Guerra-Duval, A.)

British, to Italy (*see* Perth, Lord)

Chinese, to Italy (*see* Tsu Tao Lin)

French, to Italy (*see* François-Poncet, A.)

German, to Brazil (*see* Ritter, K.)

German, to France (*see* Welczek, J.)

German, to Italy (*see* Hassel, U. von, and Mackensen, H. G. von)

Japanese, to Italy (*see* Hotta, M. A., and Amau, F.)

Polish, to Italy (*see* Wysocki, A., and Wienawa-Dglugoszowski, Gen. B.)

Spanish, to Germany (*see* Magaz Y. Pers, A.)

Spanish, to Italy (*see* Conde, P. G.)

Turkish, to Italy (*see* Bajdur, H. R.)

of the U.S.S.R., to Italy (*see* Stein, B.)

Amery, L. S., English M.P., 101, 104

Anfuso, Filippo, Ciano's *chef de cabinet*, 5, 19, 22, 31, 37, 39, 41, 46, 49, 62, 113, 128, 155, 189, 191, 196

Ansaldo, Giovanni, editor of *Il Telegrafo*, 30, 95, 188

Antonescu, Victor, Roumanian ex-Foreign Minister, 98

Aosta, Duke of (Amedeo of Savoy), 17, 40, 45, 121, 130, 144, 186

Appelius, Marius, journalist, 11

Aranha, O., Brazilian Foreign Minister, 201

Aras, T. R., Turkish Foreign Minister, 66

Arisue, S., Japanese Naval Attaché in Italy, 38, 59, 123, 185

Arpinati, Leandro, former Under-Secretary for the Interior, 90, 128

Arrighi, member of the *Parti Populaire Française*, 8

Astray, Gen. Milan, Commander of the Spanish Foreign Legion, 122

Attaché:

Austrian military, in Italy (*see* Lipitsky, E.)

French military, in Italy (*see* Parisot, H.)

Hungarian military, in Italy (*see* Szabo, L.)

Italian military, in Czechoslovakia (*see* Valfrè di Bonzo, C.)

Italian military, in Germany (*see* Marras, Gen. E.)

Italian military, in Greece (*see* Mondini, L.)

Japanese military, in Italy (*see* Hiraide, H.)

Japanese naval, in Italy (*see* Arisue, S.)

Attolico, Bernardo, Italian Ambassador to Germany, 23, 36, 72, 77, 78, 90, 123, 131, 145, 147, 149, 150, 151, 154, 155, 156, 157, 158, 160, 162, 165, 203

Auriti, Giacinto, Italian Ambassador to Japan, 49

Avila, L. L. J. d', Portuguese Minister to Italy, 84, 173

Aymard, Camille, a French journalist, 103

Aymonino, Gen. Aldo, Adjutant to the Prince of Piedmont, 69

Azcárate y Florez, P. de, Spanish Republican delegate at Geneva, 18

Badoglio, Marshal P., Chief of the General Staff, 4, 35, 68, 81

Baistrocchi, Gen. F., former Under-Secretary for War, 70, 71

211